Program Generators with XML and Java

ISBN 0-13-025878-4

90000

9 780130 258786

The Charles F. Goldfarb Series on Open Information Management

"Open Information Management" (OIM) means managing information so that it is open to processing by any program, not just the program that created it. That extends even to application programs not conceived of at the time the information was created.

OIM is based on the principle of data independence: data should be stored in computers in non-proprietary, genuinely standardized representations. And that applies even when the data is the content of a document. Its representation should distinguish the innate information from the proprietary codes of document processing programs and the artifacts of particular presentation styles.

Business data bases—which rigorously separate the real data from the input forms and output reports—achieved data independence decades ago. But documents, unlike business data, have historically been created in the context of a particular output presentation style. So for document data, independence was largely unachievable until recently.

That is doubly unfortunate. It is unfortunate because documents are a far more significant repository of humanity's information. And documents can contain significantly richer information structures than data bases.

It is also unfortunate because the need for OIM of documents is greater now than ever. The demands of "repurposing" require that information be deliverable in multiple formats: paper-based, online, multimedia, hypermedia. And information must now be delivered through multiple channels: traditional bookstores and libraries, the World Wide Web, corporate intranets and extranets. In the latter modes, what starts as data base data may become a document for interchange, but then may need to be reused by the recipient as data.

Fortunately, in the past twenty years a technology has emerged that extends to documents the data base's capacity for data independence. And it does so without the data base's restrictions on structural freedom. That technology is the "Standard Generalized Markup Language" (SGML), an official International Standard (ISO 8879) that has been adopted by the world's largest producers of documents and by the World Wide Web.

With SGML, organizations in government, aerospace, airlines, automotive, electronics, computers, and publishing (to name a few) have freed their documents from hostage relationships to processing software. SGML coexists with graphics, multimedia and other data standards needed for OIM and acts as the framework that relates objects in the other formats to one another and to SGML documents.

The World Wide Web's HTML and XML are both based on SGML. HTML is a particular, though very general, application of SGML, like those for the above industries. There is a limited set of markup tags that can be used with HTML. XML, in contrast, is a simplified subset of SGML facilities that, like full SGML, can be used with any set of tags. You can literally create your own markup language with XML.

As the enabling standard for OIM of documents and structured data, the XML/SGML family of standards necessarily plays a leading role in this series. We provide tutorials on SGML, XML, and other key standards and the techniques for applying them. Our books vary in technical intensity from programming techniques for software developers to the business justification of OIM for enterprise executives. We share the practical experience of organizations and individuals who have applied the techniques of OIM in environments ranging from immense industrial publishing projects to websites of all sizes.

Our authors are expert practitioners in their subject matter, not writers hired to cover a "hot" topic. They bring insight and understanding that can only come from real-world experience. Moreover, they practice what they preach about standardization. Their books share a common standards-based vocabulary. In this way, knowledge gained from one book in the series is directly applicable when reading another, or the standards themselves. This is just one of the ways in which we strive for the utmost technical accuracy and consistency with the OIM standards.

And we also strive for a sense of excitement and fun. After all, the challenge of OIM—preserving information from the ravages of technology while exploiting its benefits—is one of the great intellectual adventures of our age. I'm sure you'll find this series to be a knowledgable and reliable guide on that adventure.

About the Series Editor

Dr. Charles F. Goldfarb is the father of markup languages, a term that he coined in 1970. He invented the SGML language in 1974 and later led the team that developed it into the International Standard on which both HTML and XML are based. He serves as editor of the Standard (ISO 8879) and as a strategic consultant to developers of SGML and XML applications and products. He is based in Saratoga, CA. You can find him on the Web at www.xmlbooks.com.

About the Series Logo

The rebus is an ancient literary tradition, dating from 16th century Picardy, and is especially appropriate to a series involving fine distinctions between things and the words that describe them. For the logo, Andrew Goldfarb incorporated a rebus of the series name within a stylized SGML/XML comment declaration.

The Charles F. Goldfarb Series on Open Information Management

Program Generators with XML and Java

■ J. Craig Cleaveland

PH
PTR

Prentice Hall PTR, Upper Saddle River, NJ 07458
www.phptr.com

Library of Congress Cataloging-in-Publication Data

Cleaveland, J. Craig
   Program generators with Java and XML / y J. Craig Cleaveland.
     p. cm.
   Includes index.
   ISBN 0-13-025878-4
    1. Java (Computer program languages) 2. XML (Document markup language) 3.
  Generators (Computer programs) I. Title.

   QA76.73.J38 C54 2001
   005.7'2--dc21

                                        00-048361

Editorial/Production Supervision: Laura Burgess
Acquisitions Editor: Mark L. Taub
Editorial Assistant: Sarah Hand
Marketing Manager: Kate Hargett
Manufacturing Manager: Maura Zaldivar
Cover Design: Anthony Gemmellaro
Cover Design Direction: Jerry Votta
Series Design: Gail Cocker-Bogusz

© 2001 Prentice Hall PTR
Prentice-Hall, Inc.
Upper Saddle River, NJ 07458

ISBN 0-13-025878-4

Prentice-Hall International (UK) Limited, *London*
Prentice-Hall of Australia Pty. Limited, *Sydney*
Prentice-Hall Canada Inc., *Toronto*
Prentice-Hall Hispanoamericana, S.A., *Mexico*
Prentice-Hall of India Private Limited, *New Delhi*
Prentice-Hall of Japan, Inc., *Tokyo*
Simon & Schuster Asia Pte. Ltd.
Editora Prentice-Hall do Brasil, Ltda., *Rio de Janeiro*

To my family:
Tina,
Tim, and
Bruce

– With love and appreciation.

Contents

Chapter 6

Run-Time Variabilities **134**

Chapter 7

Compile-Time Variabilities **160**

Chapter 8

The Styles of Generated Programs 178

Chapter 13

Composition of Components   350

Foreword

All of the media excitement about XML thus far has been about what XML can do for data:

- You can prepare Web content just once and reformat it dynamically for multiple delivery systems, from desktop browsers to mobile phones.

- Legacy data from disparate systems can be interchanged, shared, and processed by converting it to XML.

- XML can be a universal syntax for message wrappers, enabling safe messaging among incompatible environments with arbitrary payloads.

But skilled programmers aren't letting the action stop there. After all, they reason, when a program isn't executing, it too is data. So why can't the benefits of XML be applied to the creation and maintenance of programs?

Computer scientists have long used tools such as YACC and LEX for *program generation*—the automated creation of programs from precise descriptions of syntax and desired behavior. More recently, the field of *domain engineering* has extended this concept to analyzing sets of related programs, and generating and modifying them over time.

Craig Cleaveland is a leading practitioner of domain engineering. In his 13 years as an award-winning Bell Labs scientist he developed scores of application generators and other tools. And in his current consulting work and as CTO of Internet Games Corporation, he's had a wealth of experience in putting program generators to work.

Now Craig has discovered some breakthrough techniques for using XML and Java to simplify program generation. These techniques—which he teaches you in this book—make program generation a practical tool for the nonspecialist developer, whether you are building Web sites or integrating enterprise applications.

You can quickly join the ranks of the programming pros who let programs write their programs for them. Craig shows you how in *Program Generators with XML and Java*.

Charles F. Goldfarb
Saratoga, CA
November, 2000

Preface

I 've dreamed about writing this book for many years, but it did not turn out as I imagined. XML and Java are recent technologies that did not appear in my dreams. I've been working with program generators and domain engineering for nearly 20 years using primarily C and hand-crafted plain text languages. XML and Java provide a new context for these older technologies and they fit together. It was a joy to retrace the steps I had taken many years ago, and see how much easier and more elegant the trek is using XML and Java.

I toyed with the idea of titling the book, "Program Generators for Fun and Profit." Writing a program generator is a lot of fun because instead of just writing a program, you write a program that writes programs. You think about how smart you can make your program generator. Some program generators are called "wizards!" Program generators are also very profitable. They are a critical piece of many software engineering development environments, particularly in the areas of user interfaces, databases, middleware, and language parsers and lexers.

Once you've written a couple of program generators, you begin to wonder: Is there a better approach to figuring out what a program generator should do? The answer is yes, but it's been kept a secret. The better approach is called *domain engineering,* which is a systematic approach that identifies the important elements and requirements in a domain. This information is essential for efficiently building a program generator that meets customer needs.

Many computer scientists, including myself, are fascinated with self-referential structures.[1] One such structure is a *program generator generator.* A program generator generator is a program generator that generates program generators. It is a program that writes programs that write programs. Chapter 12 recapitulates some of the work I did at Bell Labs in this area, but this time in a simpler and more elegant style using XML and Java. It is simple enough that anyone can create his or her own program generator generator in a matter of days.

---

[1]Structures that refer to themselves (e.g., this sentence).

Acknowledgments

The Internet never ceases to amaze me. Using email and Web pages I contacted several publishers and quickly narrowed the choice to two. Mark Taub and Charles Goldfarb convinced me to go with them in the Prentice Hall XML series. The deal was signed within a few weeks of my decision to write this book, rather than taking months, as I had expected. Thanks to Mark, Charles, and the rest of the Prentice Hall team for all their efforts.

Thanks go to the many reviewers who examined one or more chapters and in some cases the entire book. George Newsome, who reviewed everything, was particularly good at reminding me of benefits I neglected to mention. George is also one of those rare people who makes you think about alternatives and different points of view. Although it is sometimes unsettling to see things through different eyes, I have found that it is worth the effort. Thank you, George.

Near the end of writing, I became aware of Krzysztof Czarnecki and Ulrich Eisenecker's book on generative methods. I was amazed at the breadth and scope of their book. It is destined to become the definitive book on domain engineering theory for years to come. Krzysztof also gave me extensive comments and lots of encouragement.

Tina Cleaveland was the first to see each chapter and her comments made it easier for subsequent reviewers. Special thanks to her for keeping most of my goofs from the other reviewers!

Special thanks to many other reviewers including John Ellson, Peter Halsam, Allegra May, Bill McKeeman, Ruth Munroe, John Sanders, Bob Tatem, Leo Treggiari, Bob Uzgalis, and David Weiss. Finally, thanks must also go to the many colleagues and supporters of the technology while I was at Bell Labs, too numerous to name completely, but including Tom Wetmore, Dan Jacobs, Bill MacDonald, Chandra Kintala, Steve Lally, Jan Fertig, Iris Sindelar, Jack Gehling, Jose Garcia, and Linda Lodzinski.

J. Craig Cleaveland
Windham, New Hampshire
July 20, 2000

Introduction:
The Dictionary
Problem

- What's a program generator?
- The structure of a program generator
- Example program generators
- Why use program generators?

J ack and Jill have a problem. They are writing a software program for playing Scrabble and they need a dictionary to look up words. The most natural way to do this is to read in a file of words when the program first starts up. Depending on the size of the dictionary, this file could become quite lengthy, perhaps 50,000 words. Jack's job is to gather the words into a file named words.txt, with one word per line. He starts out with just seven words, planning to add the other 49,993 words tomorrow or the next day (Example 1–1).

Example 1–1: words.txt File

```
hill
fetch
pail
water
up
down
crown
```

Meanwhile, Jill starts coding the Java dictionary object. She uses a very straightforward approach. When the `Dictionary0` object is created, it will read in the words from the file words.txt and store them in the Vector called "words." A Vector is a variable-length list of items (Example 1–2).

Example 1–2: Dictionary0.java

```java
import java.io.*;
import java.util.*;

class Dictionary0 {
    Vector words = new Vector();

    Dictionary0() {
        loadWords();
    }

    void loadWords() {
        try {
            BufferedReader f = new BufferedReader(
                new FileReader("words.txt"));
            String word = null;
            while ((word = f.readLine())!=null) {
                words.addElement(word);
            }
        } catch (Exception e) {
            System.err.println("Unable to read from words.txt");
            // continue with empty dictionary
        }
    }

    public boolean isWord(String w) {
        for (int j=0; j<words.size(); ++j) {
            String w2 = (String) words.elementAt(j);
            if (w.equals(w2)) {
                return true;
            }
        }
        return false;
    }
}
```

Jill only needs the method isWord to determine whether a word is in the dictionary, which is good enough for her Scrabble game. But she is starting to think that this dictionary object might also be useful in other game programs she would like to write some day. Jill is also thinking that Vector might not be the best way to store the words, and a linear search might not be the best thing to do now, but as a good engineer she knows that she must first get it right, and later she can make it fast. And indeed, she tests the program and everything runs smoothly and fast!

The next day, Jack finishes his job of adding the other 49,993 words to the dictionary, and Jill discovers a major problem when she runs the program. As expected, the linear search is just a bit too slow, but since words are not looked up very often in Scrabble, it isn't too bad. The real problem is that it takes too long to start up the program, because reading in a file with 50,000 words is just too costly.

Jill sighs, but then remembers that the Scrabble game will be distributed as an applet on the Web, and later it will be installed on a Java hand-held game machine, and in neither case will she be able to easily read in the words from a file anyway. So, Jill writes a much simpler and faster program where the words are stored in an initialized array[1] instead of read from a file (Example 1–3).

Example 1–3: Dictionary1.java

```java
class Dictionary1 {

    String[] words = {
            "hill",
            "fetch",
            "pail",
            "water",
            "up",
            "down",
            "crown"
    };

    boolean isWord(String w) {
        for (int j=0; j<words.length; ++j) {
```

---

[1] Some Java implementations may have difficulty initializing arrays with a large number of elements.

```
                if (w.equals(words[j])) {
                        return true;
                }
        }
        return false;
    }
}
```

The dictionary is part of this program, and the words do not need to be read in when the program starts. Again, she runs and tests her new program and is satisfied with the results.

Like any good software engineer, Jill ponders the difference between her two programs (Figure 1–1):

1. **Performance**: The two programs differ in speed. In `Dictionary0` the words must be read from a file and stored in a data structure. This computation is performed every time the program is executed. In `Dictionary1` this work is done at compile time. The resulting executable is larger and therefore may take more time to load, but in general it is much faster than the first approach (and it will be lightning fast for the Java hand-held game machine). Also, compiler optimizations may provide another performance boost. The `words` array could be declared `final` and the compiler could use this information to create faster and shorter code.[2]

2. **Simplicity:** Simplicity is in the eye of the beholder. At first glance it would appear that `Dictionary1` is simpler, because we don't need the initialization code or the `loadWords` method. What will Jack think?

---

[2] Faster and shorter code would result, for example, by removing unnecessary out-of-bounds checking on some array indexes, such as constants.

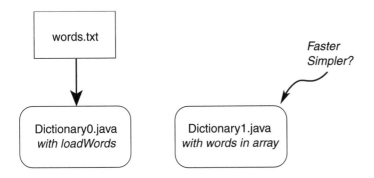

Figure 1–1   Dictionary0 and Dictionary1

When Jack gets wind of Jill's changes, he is upset. He has just spent the whole day typing in 49,993 words into the words.txt file. What will Jack do? He certainly won't want to type them in again with quotes and commas. Besides, he likes his simple file a lot better than one cluttered with quotes and commas. Then he gets an idea: just write a program to read the words in the file words.txt, slap on some quotes and a comma, and output the array data for the Dictionary1 program (Figures 1-2 and 1-3). He can reuse the loadWords method from Dictionary0 and just execute the lines:

```
for (int j=0; j<words.size(); ++j) {
    System.out.println("    \""+words.elementAt(j)+"\",");
}
```

Jack likes this because he can continue using words.txt, and the translation program will create the file that Jill can use for her program. Jill also thinks it's a cool idea, but she doesn't look forward to cutting and pasting the words into her program. So she suggests that, instead of generating a 50,000-line file, why not just generate the whole program, all 50,014 lines? It's only 14 lines longer. And there you have it—the birth of a *program generator* (Example 1–4).

Example 1–4: Dictionary1Generator.java

```java
import java.io.*;
import java.util.*;

class Dictionary1Generator {
    static Vector words = new Vector();

    static void loadWords() {
        try {
            BufferedReader f =
                new BufferedReader(new FileReader("words.txt"));
            String word = null;
            while ((word = f.readLine())!=null) {
                words.addElement(word);
            }
        } catch (Exception e) {
            System.err.println("Unable to read words from words.txt");
            // continue with empty dictionary
        }
    }

    static public void main(String[] args) {
        loadWords();

        // Generate Dictionary1 program
        System.out.println("class Dictionary1 {\n");
        System.out.println("    String words = {");
        for (int j=0; j<words.size(); ++j) {
            System.out.println("        \""+words.elementAt(j)+"\",");
        }
        System.out.println("    };");
        System.out.println("\n");
        System.out.println("    public boolean isWord(String w) {");
        System.out.println("      for (int j=0; j<words.length; ++j) {");
        System.out.println("          if (w.equals(words[j])) {");
        System.out.println("              return true;");
        System.out.println("          }");
        System.out.println("      }");
        System.out.println("      return false;");
        System.out.println("    }");
        System.out.println("}");
    }
}
```

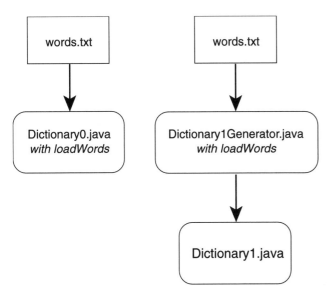

Figure 1–2 The Dictionary1Generator creates Dictionary1.java.

To fully appreciate the differences between these two approaches, we need the concept of *binding time*. This is the time at which certain information is determined or bound to a program. Consider the binding time of the dictionary words. In the first case, the words are read at run time. The binding occurs at the time they are read and stored in the Vector. In the second case, they are read in *before* compile time. This might not seem like a big deal, but it means you must recompile the program if you want to make a change in the words. Program generators introduce a *third* binding time in addition to the two traditional ones (Figure 1–4).

- **Generation time**: The time at which the program is generated after reading a specification of the program (in this case, the specification is simply the list of words).

- **Compile time**: The time at which the generated program is compiled.

- **Run time**: The time at which the generated program is executed.

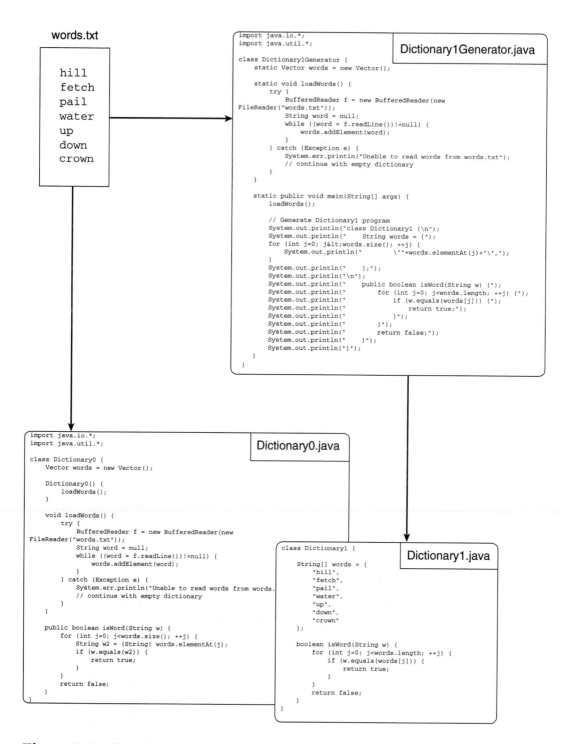

words.txt

```
hill
fetch
pail
water
up
down
crown
```

Dictionary1Generator.java

```java
import java.io.*;
import java.util.*;

class Dictionary1Generator {
    static Vector words = new Vector();

    static void loadWords() {
        try {
            BufferedReader f = new BufferedReader(new
FileReader("words.txt"));
            String word = null;
            while ((word = f.readLine())!=null) {
                words.addElement(word);
            }
        } catch (Exception e) {
            System.err.println("Unable to read words from words.txt");
            // continue with empty dictionary
        }
    }

    static public void main(String[] args) {
        loadWords();

        // Generate Dictionary1 program
        System.out.println("class Dictionary1 {\n");
        System.out.println("    String words = {");
        for (int j=0; j&lt;words.size(); ++j) {
            System.out.println("        \""+words.elementAt(j)+"\",");
        }
        System.out.println("    };");
        System.out.println("\n");
        System.out.println("    public boolean isWord(String w) {");
        System.out.println("        for (int j=0; j<words.length; ++j) {");
        System.out.println("            if (w.equals(words[j])) {");
        System.out.println("                return true;");
        System.out.println("            }");
        System.out.println("        }");
        System.out.println("        return false;");
        System.out.println("    }");
        System.out.println("}");
    }
}
```

Dictionary0.java

```java
import java.io.*;
import java.util.*;

class Dictionary0 {
    Vector words = new Vector();

    Dictionary0() {
        loadWords();
    }

    void loadWords() {
        try {
            BufferedReader f = new BufferedReader(new
FileReader("words.txt"));
            String word = null;
            while ((word = f.readLine())!=null) {
                words.addElement(word);
            }
        } catch (Exception e) {
            System.err.println("Unable to read words from words.
            // continue with empty dictionary
        }
    }

    public boolean isWord(String w) {
        for (int j=0; j<words.size(); ++j) {
            String w2 = (String) words.elementAt(j);
            if (w.equals(w2)) {
                return true;
            }
        }
        return false;
    }
}
```

Dictionary1.java

```java
class Dictionary1 {
    String[] words = {
        "hill",
        "fetch",
        "pail",
        "water",
        "up",
        "down",
        "crown"
    };

    boolean isWord(String w) {
        for (int j=0; j<words.length; ++j) {
            if (w.equals(words[j])) {
                return true;
            }
        }
        return false;
    }
}
```

Figure 1–3 Flow diagram with file contents

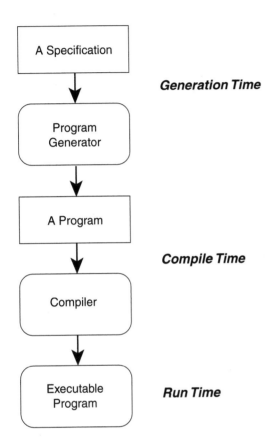

Figure 1–4   Binding times

Jill again ponders the differences among her various programs. As before, she observes the interesting way in which some run-time computation is transferred to other times. In particular, the loadWords method has been literally moved out of the run time (in Dictionary0) to generation time (in Dictionary1Generator). This is good, because it means the run time is faster and more optimized for the task.

Both Jack and Jill are happy with the results. Jack can continue adding to words.txt. A new Dictionary1.java program can be regenerated whenever they want. Jill is pleased as well, because she really didn't want Jack touching her program. Besides, having two people modifying the same text file at the same time is asking for trouble.

Jill now concentrates on the somewhat slow linear search. She decides it would be easiest to retain the array and do a binary search on a sorted list of words. So she tells Jack to alphabetize the words. After frowning for a few seconds, Jack mumbles agreement. That makes Jill think a little harder. Perhaps it would be better to let the program generator sort the words. In fact, it would be a lot better, because she isn't sure that words.txt will always be properly sorted. After it has been sorted, how will she know that alphabetical order will be maintained? Just one little slip-up, and her binary search wouldn't work any longer. It would be a lot safer (less error prone) if the program generator sorted the words. Then she would *know* with more confidence that the words were sorted correctly. Thus, she adds a sortWords method to sort the words after reading them in and before generating the program.

Later that day, she notices that the word "pail" appears twice in the file words.txt. Although this doesn't alter the behavior of the program, it does make the dictionary larger than it needs to be. Jack starts to explain the systematic way he is typing in words which sometimes unfortunately and accidentally leads to duplicate words. Jill doesn't understand, and she decides it is better to simply add one more tweak to her program generator by detecting and removing duplicate words (which is easily done while sorting).

The program generator now has three distinct parts: getting the data, analyzing/transforming it, and generating the program. And this is also the typical structure of other program generators as well. Figure 1–5 illustrates this structure.

Example 1–5 shows the outline of the generated program, often called a template. The parts in italics describe how to create the variable parts of the generated program. The remaining ordinary text is simply copied to the output.

Dictionary1 Generator		Typical Program Generator
The dictionary problem is simply a list of words read by the loadWords method.	**Getting the data**	Typically, the input is structurally more complex (but unlikely to be as large as the word dictionary). It may use a formal specification language, a diagram, database tables, spreadsheets, or user dialogs (as you might typically find in a wizard). And finally, this book will promote XML as a standard way of representing information.
Jill added duplicate word removal. No transformations were needed.	**Analyzing and transforming the data**	The information is validated by checking for completeness or inconsistencies. Jill also sorted the words. In general the information may be transformed into other data structures or forms more appropriate for program generation.
This is typically the most straightforward part of the program. Jill just used print statements.	**Generating the program**	Although print statements are straightforward, such programs can be difficult to read. Later in this book we'll introduce a template approach. An example template for Dictionary1 might look like Example 1–5.

Figure 1–5   Structural comparison between Dictionary1 Generator and typical program generators

Example 1–5: Template for Dictionary1 Generator

```
class Dictionary1 {

    String[] words = {
    for each word in words.txt loop
        "word",
    end-loop
    };

    boolean isWord(String w) {
        for (int j=0; j<words.length; ++j) {
            if (w.equals(words[j])) {
                return true;
            }
        }
        return false;
    }
}
```

1.1 | Onward and Upward

Jack and Jill are so comfortable using their program generator that they expand it to solve more and more problems.

1. **Multiple dictionaries**: They need lots of different dictionaries for variations in the game, including one for English, one for French, one for place names, and others for poets, priests, and politicians. Some games require multiple dictionaries in the same program, so some provision is made for creating and managing multiple dictionary objects.

2. **Different sets of methods**: As Jack and Jill expand their word-game repertory, they find they need other dictionary methods. For Scrabble they needed only the isWord method, but for other games they need a way of enumerating the words, and words that partially match words in the list. They add options to the program generator so that only the methods that are needed will be generated. This keeps their class files lean and mean.

3. **Extended dictionaries**: As Jack and Jill's business expands, they add more information to the dictionary so that a wider variety of games can be created. For each word, they add antonyms, synonyms, homonyms, rhymes, and all manner of other relations. Their dictionary is no longer just a list of words. And the generated data structures are now becoming a lot more complex than just an array of Strings.

4. **Performance differences**: Jill discovers that, depending on the context, different data structures and searching algorithms are needed. In some cases memory is critical; in others speed is critical. For speed-critical applications she

uses hash tables and doesn't care as much about space. For memory-critical applications (such as downloaded applets on low-bandwidth lines or memory-challenged Java hand-held game machines) she employs Huffman[3] encoding to minimize the space needed to store the dictionary (at the expense of a slower dictionary lookup).

With the addition of these variations, the simple program generator grows and evolves into a large, sophisticated piece of software. These variations should also suggest other issues and complexities that need to be addressed when building real-world program generators.

One of the principal issues is simply understanding the set of variations the program generator should support, and how they may change over time. Chapter 2 describes domain engineering, a systematic process for understanding application domains and building tools for supporting software development in the application domain. Domain engineering entails two steps:

1. **Domain Analysis**: The first step determines what a domain is, and the variations that must be supported.

2. **Domain Implementation**: The second step constructs the environment and tools required to support the swift creation of programs within the domain. This step may result in the construction of program generators.

1.2 | Other Program Generators

Jack and Jill weren't the first people to conceive of a program generator. Program generators have been used for many years in certain application domains, including, for example:

---

[3]In 1952, D. Huffman devised an algorithm to create a variable-length encoding of symbols based on their frequency to minimize the number of bits necessary to represent strings of symbols.

1. **Parsers:** A parser reads a sequence of tokens and creates a data structure representing the structure of the information called a parse tree. Creating parsers by hand (writing code manually) is tedious and error prone. Parser generators, such as the classic UNIX utility yacc (bison), read a formal description of the language (expressed in some grammar) along with actions to be taken for each grammar rule, and they output a parser program (Figure 1–6).

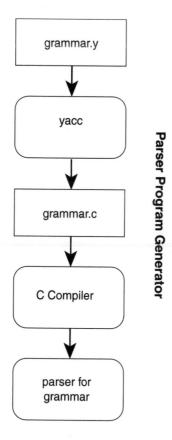

Figure 1–6   Flow diagram for the yacc parser generator

2. **Finite State Machines**: Many programs are based on
   finite state machines. Such programs are best described
   or documented as a table and/or diagram displaying the
   various states, events, and state transitions. Given
   sufficient information about the finite state machine, a
   program generator can validate and generate a program
   implementing it. The classic UNIX utility, "lex," is a
   finite-state-machine program generator and is often used
   with yacc to parse the tokens of a language.

3. **User Interfaces**: Increasingly important components of
   many programs are user interfaces. They vary from
   simple buttons (either physical or virtual) to complex
   graphical interfaces involving many different windows
   and controls. Writing this code by hand is notoriously
   difficult, expensive, and error prone. Most such code
   today is automatically generated from GUI builders and
   visual programming tools.

4. **Databases**: Application generators have a long and
   productive history in the database area. Given a
   description of the database tables, relations, business
   logic, and report templates, a customized database
   program can be generated (sometimes interpreted).

5. **Web Page Generation**: Java Server Pages (JSP) are a
   means for creating dynamic content on the Web. A Java
   Server Page is a template of a Web page with interspersed
   Java code that creates the page's variable parts.

There are many other specialized areas where gains in efficiency and
productivity are possible, but there are no commercially available systems for a variety of reasons, including a smaller niche market or an
immature domain that lacks standardized approaches.

If you can't buy the tools you need, then you'll have to build your own, just like Jack and Jill. And isn't this why you're reading this book? This book will show you how to plan, design, and build program generators in a systematic manner. You will also be able to evaluate different approaches and take various shortcuts to reduce the amount of work needed for building such tools.

1.3 | Why Use Program Generators?

Let's review the motivations for using (and creating) program generators. In general, the number one reason is increased productivity. Some of the reasons below are evident in the simple dictionary example, but others won't become evident until we look at more complex examples.

1.3.1 *Specification Level versus Code Level*

The file words.txt represents what is usually called the *specification*. The specification expresses the *what*. In the dictionary example, the *what* is simply the list of words. In the more general case, the *what* expresses what application software to generate. The words.txt file (representing the specification) and the Dictionary1Generator.java code will be easier to maintain than Dictionary1.java. In general, specifications are much easier to read, write, edit, debug, and understand than the code that implements the specification. For example, the implementation code may contain detailed knowledge about programming techniques, algorithms, or data representation that we don't need in order to understand the specification. For example, if the dictionary program used hash table techniques to implement the word list, the specification would still contain only words and have no references to hash tables. The difference between the specification and generated code will largely determine the increased productivity obtained by using program generators.

1.3.2 *Separation of Concerns*

All too often software is constructed with different concerns all jumbled together. This makes it difficult for different people to sort out and work on the part that they are responsible for without interfering with other people's parts. Jack is responsible for the word list, and Jill is responsible for the data representation and algorithms. Jack and Jill were able to separate their respective responsibilities into two separate files and work independently of each other. In typical software projects, different responsibilities are mixed together in very confusing ways, making it difficult for more than one person to work on a task simultaneously and independently. Domain engineering and program generators provide a way for separating concerns.

1.3.3 *Multiple Products*

In the dictionary problem, only Dictionary1.java was generated. There isn't much else to generate for the dictionary problem, but in more complex yet typical situations many other files may also be generated, including, for example:

- other code files that implement various parts of the problem

- documentation about the software

- user documentation

- test scripts

- other software tools related to the specification
- diagrams or pictures
- simulation tools

1.3.4   *Multiple Variants*

The dictionary solution can handle any number of dictionaries, each producing a specific variant of the original program. Program generators provide an effective way of handling multiple variants of a program. The collection of variants is called a program family. Program generators represent program families, not just single system-specific programs.

1.3.5   *Consistency of Information*

One of the most difficult and expensive software maintenance issues is the consistent-update problem. All too often, fixing a bug or updating software introduces other errors, because a "piece" of information was not updated consistently across the whole product. In a software-generation approach, one simply updates the specification and regenerates the software.

1.3.6   *Correctness of Generated Products*

Many program generators create thousands of lines of code that are far more reliable than if they were hand crafted. Imagine solving the dictionary problem by handing the words.txt file to some coders and asking them to write out by hand the Dictionary1.java file. What confidence would you have that it was done correctly? How would you make sure it was done correctly? If changes were made to words.txt, how confident would you be that the same changes were made to Dictionary1.java? How would you confirm that words.txt and Dictionary1.java were consistent after some changes were made? Imagine the increased difficulties if we also asked Jack to sort the list. Most program generators are far more complex than the dictionary problem, and the correctness issue becomes more critical. Verifying the correctness of a program generator is more difficult than just verifying the correctness of a generated program.

1.3.7 *Improved Performance of Customized Software*

In some cases, program generators can construct optimized code. If there is sufficient information to analyze how the program will be used, this can be used to create very specific customizations for optimal performance. There are many trade-offs between time, space, and other resources. Depending on the context, one resource may be more important than others, and program generators can use this information to create very specific optimized programs. For example, Jill chose between hash tables and Huffman encoding to optimize speed or memory use.

1.4 | Organization of the Book

Jack and Jill stumbled into program generators and learned by painful experience. You can skip some of those painful experiences, and you can skip around the various chapters of this book (Figure 1–7). Chapters 2, 3, and 4 provide glimpses into Domain Engineering concepts that provide the systematic development framework for program generators.

Chapter 5 is an introduction to XML. Chapters 6 and 7 show alternative techniques to program generation. Chapters 8 through 12 focus on program generators, Chapter 8 showing "what to generate" and Chapters 9 to 12 "how to generate." Finally, Chapter 13 is devoted to the relationship between program generators and component-oriented programming.

The story of Jack and Jill continues in Chapter 3. A more substantial example is created called the Play domain. The Play domain language in XML is created in Chapter 5 and then extensively used in Chapters 6 through 12. Visit `http://craigc.com` for copies of the examples or the latest information about program generators.

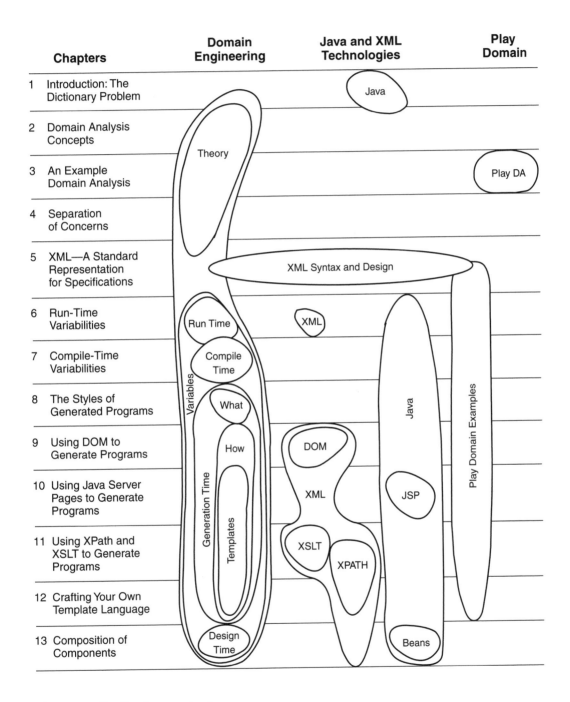

Figure 1–7 Book organization

Domain Analysis Concepts

- Decisions—the atoms of domain engineering
- Roles in domain and application engineering
- Binding times
- Variabilities and commonalities
- Domain analysis methods

 **D**omain Engineering is a process for efficiently creating members of a family of applications (programs or software components). Domain engineering is divided into two processes:[1]

- **Domain Analysis** is a process for determining the terminology, boundaries, commonalities, and variabilities of a domain—the subject of this chapter.

- **Domain Implementation** is the creation of processes and tools for efficiently generating a customized application in the domain, which may include program generators—the subject of this book.

---

[1]Domain engineering is sometimes divided into three processes: domain analysis, design, and implementation. In this book, we use the term *domain implementation* to cover both design and implementation.

Since this book deals primarily with program generators, we treat domain analysis more from a pragmatic viewpoint and therefore focus on the concepts, rather than specific domain analysis techniques. A domain analysis sometimes leads to the development of a program generator. We will limit technical jargon and concepts to what is needed for constructing program generators. Books and references at the end of this chapter will provide other sources of information on domain engineering.

2.1 | Domains

Domains and domain engineering often involve two complementary viewpoints: problem oriented and solution oriented. The problem-oriented viewpoint considers domains from the perspective of a systems engineer or designer who views the construction of systems as a means for solving problems. From this viewpoint, a domain is a set of related problems.

The solution-oriented viewpoint considers domains from the perspective of an engineer who constructs software systems. From this viewpoint, a domain is considered a set of related software application programs. Both viewpoints are needed to achieve a well-balanced domain analysis.

In the dictionary example of Chapter 1, a problem-oriented viewpoint includes the range of games that the dictionary supports and the features and capabilities a dictionary should provide. Jack and Jill primarily adopted a solution-oriented viewpoint by working in the solution space. It is sometimes difficult to separate these viewpoints. What is important is not to be blinded by just one viewpoint. This sometimes happens when individuals have worked for a long time on only one side of the aisle (marketing or programming).

2.2 | Decisions—the Atoms of Domain Engineering

Decisions are the fundamental units of domain engineering. A *decision* includes the following elements:

1. a range of options

2. a decision maker who selects an option

3. the selected option

4. when the option is selected

Any development process is a series of decisions. Decisions are made during requirements, software architecture, interface development, software design (algorithms, data structures, data representation), software coding and testing, and application use. According to Fred Brooks,[2] the hard thing about software is making the decisions, not coding them. The hard thing about domain engineering is figuring out *what* the important decisions are, *who* should make them, and *when* they should be made. There are lots of relatively unimportant decisions, such as formatting code conventions. Then there are significant decisions, such as the functionality of the application or an implementation decision to favor space over time when selecting data representations.

As an example of a decision, consider the background color of an application's user interface. The range of options might be snow white, pale yellow, and sky blue. A programmer might choose snow white for all applications at compile time. Alternatively, the decision maker could be an end user that selects pale yellow at run time.

---

[2] F.P. Brooks, "No Silver Bullet," *Computer*, Vol. 20, No. 4, April 1987.

In Chapter 1, the decision is what set of words to use for the dictionary. As we saw, the programmer can decide at generation time the set of words. Alternatively, the decision can be made at the time the program is started by the user.

2.3 | Variations—the Heart of Domain Engineering

Application engineering is the process of creating a single application. Domain engineering is the process of creating a family of applications. The chief distinction between the two is the concept of variation. Although good software engineers will construct a single application with variations in mind and design the application so that it can be easily modified, the domain engineer takes this concept to the extreme. Domain engineers consider how single applications may change over time, but they also look at a whole range of applications in the domain to determine differences among those applications. We call these differences *variabilities*. Variabilities are important because they are the main ingredients in building program generators.

Understanding variations also implies a need to understand what does not vary across a family. We call such things *commonalities*. The principal effort during domain analysis is the identification and organization of all the commonalities and variabilities of a domain.

2.4 | Roles—Who Makes Decisions

In the context of domain engineering, a *role* is a way of defining who should be making which decisions. The domain engineering process involves a variety of roles. Each role operates during part of the process and is concerned with making some set of decisions. For example, an application engineer may be concerned with making decisions about how to represent colors, while an application user may be concerned with which colors to use. The three primary roles are:

Domain Engineer—defines and builds processes and tools such as program generators

Application Engineer—creates applications using tools such as program generators

Application User—uses the application

Additional roles may be required. For example, creating an application may require roles for usability experts, graphics artists, performance engineers, and many others. Using an application may require roles for administrators, teachers, and students.

2.5 | Binding Times— When Decisions Are Made

The time at which a decision is made is called the binding time. In software development, compile time and run time are the two classic binding times. A decision made at compile time means it cannot be altered at run time. The three most prominent times and some of the minor binding times are illustrated in Figure 2–1.

Consider the background color decision. This decision could be made at any of the three major binding times. Domain analysis will determine when and who might make the decision. Some possibilities are:

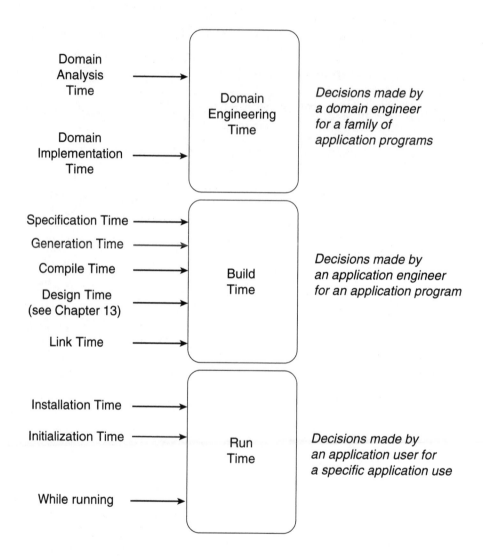

Figure 2–1 Binding times

- A domain engineer decides that all application backgrounds in the domain should be snow white.

- An application engineer makes the decision. So, one application engineer may decide to use pale yellow for his application, but other colors may be used for other applications.

- Application users make the decision. Thus, for each application use, a user may select the background color for their particular use.

- The application engineer either selects one fixed color or allows the application user to select the color.[3]

As a second example, consider the set of words in the dictionary example of Chapter 1. Using `Dictionary0`, the words are determined when the program starts execution. At loading time, the words are read into memory from a file. Up to that time, the words can be changed by simply changing the file. Using `Dictionary1`, the words are determined at generation time. That's the time the words are read from a file, and the Dictionary1 program is generated with the words "hard-wired" into the code.

2.6 | Domain Engineering Lifecycle

Like most development activities, domain engineering doesn't happen just once. It evolves over time with appropriate feedback from the application engineering lifecycle. Also, just as each application may have many different users, so domain engineering tools such as program generators may be used to create many different applications. Figure 2–2 shows a simplified example of the parallel but intertwined lifecycles for domain engineering and application engineering.

The domain engineering process is like the application engineering process except that its feedback loop is from a set of application development lifecycles.

---

[3]This is actually two different decisions. One decision is selecting a color. The other decision is when and who selects the color.

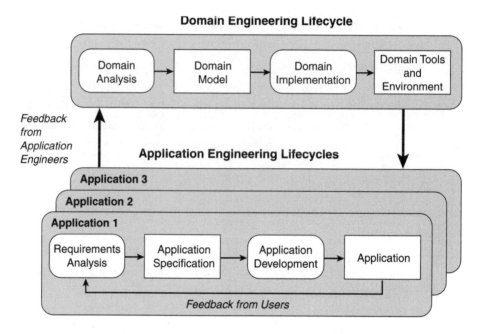

Figure 2–2   Domain engineering and application engineering lifecycles

2.7 | Commonalities

A commonality is a decision or assumption made during domain engineering about what is common across the domain. Commonalities can determine the scope of the domain, software functionality, interfaces to other domains, operating environment, limitations of the software, standards, and implementation details of the common parts of the application software.

Sometimes commonalities are unstated assumptions about the program family. In a company dominated by C++ programmers in a UNIX environment, a domain analysis might not explicitly state that their domain only includes C++ programs operating in a UNIX environment. Other common assumptions that are made include the scope or boundaries of a domain, development processes, testing issues, and customer base.

Additional implicit commonalities arise during domain implementation. Private implementation decisions made during domain implementation are common across all applications in the domain. These decisions are not normally part of the domain analysis, since implementation decisions are normally not made at that time. Nor should they be part of it, since they would unnecessarily constrain the construction and evolution of the domain implementation process.

Commonalities and standards have much in common. A standard is a common way of doing something. Many standards efforts are primarily a domain analysis. Conversely, many domain analysis efforts piggyback on standards to help create a larger set of commonalities that will be accepted by a large group of people.

Commonalities are significant because they are the determining factor in software productivity. Commonalities tell you what is common or shared across a family of applications. This shared part is implemented once and reused for each application in the family (Figure 2–3). Thus, commonalities represent the potential savings or productivity increase. Viewed in another light, commonalities represent the "domain knowledge" that is being employed. This domain knowledge is analyzed and packaged as tools, components, and frameworks and reused each time an application is created or modified.

While increasing productivity is a benefit of using commonalities, the negative aspect is that each new commonality may constrain or shrink the size of the family. Consider the domain of card games. If you add the commonality of a 52-card deck, you shrink the family from all possible card games to just those using a deck of 52 cards. In exchange, however, you can now incorporate and reuse the domain knowledge associated with a deck of 52 cards into the domain implementation.[4] You might then add an additional commonality that further constrains card games to poker and its variations. This further shrinks the family, but in exchange you can use the domain knowledge associated with poker into the domain implementation (Figure 2–4).

---

[4]This is not strictly true, since you could incorporate the 52-card-deck domain knowledge into a more general card domain, but this is more like incorporating a subdomain into a larger domain.

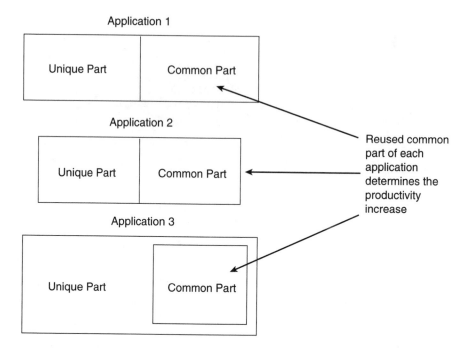

Figure 2–3   Productivity increase is determined by the reused common parts of the software application

2.8 | Variabilities

A variability is a decision that is identified during domain analysis but not made until build time or run time. Build-time variabilities represent what is different across the programs of a program family. The set of build-time variabilities is the most important piece of information required for building a program generator. This set is used to define a specification language and an architecture or framework to support those variabilities.

Run-time variabilities are decisions made at run time. These decisions may be implemented as information from configuration files, databases, user profiles, or data from sensors or may be obtained directly from a user through a user interface. Typically, run-time variabilities are built into the common parts of the application software, since an application

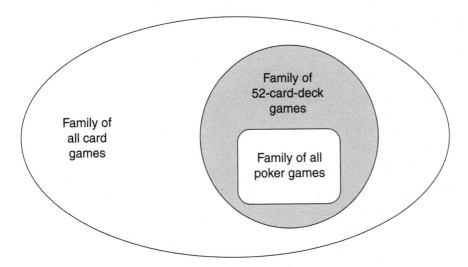

Figure 2–4   Adding commonalities adds domain knowledge but decreases the size of the family

engineer may have little or no control over this variability (Figure 2–5). For example, let's say that the background color is always stored in a configuration file. Then the application software that reads in the configuration file is common code across all applications.

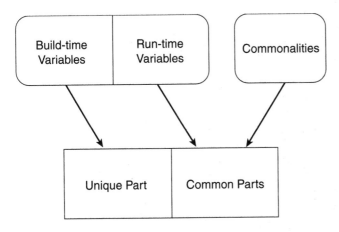

Figure 2–5   How commonalities and variabilities map to the unique and common parts of a software application

2.9 | A Balancing Act

Domain analysis consists largely of exploring the decisions in a domain and determining which decisions should be commonalities and which ones variabilities. This determination is not a scientific process of discovery but one of design and engineering, and it involves trade-offs among many objectives. Making a decision a commonality means standardizing, which promotes increased productivity and efficiency. Making a decision a variability means parameterizing, which promotes increased variation and larger product families. Domain analysis is an attempt to achieve a good balance between these two objectives. A domain analysis that results mostly in commonalities does little more than build a single program. A domain analysis that results mostly in variabilities may achieve little, because software reuse may be limited. The dictionary example of Chapter 1, however, shows a very convincing example of the benefits of program generators independent of any software reuse. The dictionary program generator makes it possible to work in parallel on words and programs, to ensure that the data is well formed even when it's not your job to produce it, to reuse data that's already available (such as existing dictionaries), and to radically change the data structures at low cost. These benefits are sufficient to justify the technique independent of any software reuse benefit.

Over time, commonalities may become variabilities and vice versa. For example, the background color of an application may initially be a commonality. Then, it's noticed that many customers want their own particular color for the background, so during the next cycle the background-color commonality becomes a variability. This is known as *parameterization*. Likewise, a variability may become a commonality; this is *standardization*. The background-color variability may be unused or perhaps unimportant, and a new domain analysis effort may decide that the cost of supporting the variability is too high (Figure 2–6).

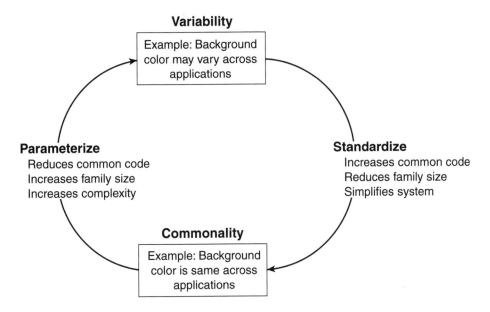

Figure 2–6   Transitioning between commonalities and variabilities

2.10 | Domain Analysis Methods

Unfortunately there is no standard definition of domain analysis, and the field has many different ideas about what it is, and what it may or may not include. In this book, the "minimal" domain analysis must result in a domain model that includes:

- Domain Scope (domain boundaries)
- Domain Terminology
- Domain Commonalities and Variabilities

Family-Oriented Abstraction, Specification, and Translation (FAST) is a domain engineering process developed by David Weiss at Lucent Technologies Bell Labs. The notion of family is derived from the early work of Parnas, who defined a program family as a set of programs in which "it is worthwhile to study programs from the set by first studying the common properties of the set and then determining the special properties of the individual family members."[5] FAST is described in more detail in the next section.

Other domain analysis methods will result in domain models that differ from FAST in varying degrees. Organization Domain Modeling (ODM), chiefly developed by Mark Simos, and Feature Oriented Domain Analysis (FODA), developed at SEI,[6] are mature and documented domain analysis methods. They both result in domain models that include domain scope and terminology. Features are used in both methods to identify commonalities and variabilities. Constraints on features may also be identified. Constraints, sometimes called dependencies, include feature inclusion (feature A requires feature B), mutually exclusive (feature A or B, but not both), and possibly more complex relationships (value ranges of a feature may depend on the values of other features).

A domain analysis such as FAST focuses on what an application engineer must do to create an application rather than focusing on the application software. In some cases, experts in the domain who have little or no programming experience can create substantial programs by working only at the specification level.[7] Specification-level work (reading, writing, analysis, and debugging) is more effective than the equivalent work at a programming level.[8] An emphasis on the process of creating applications is more likely to result in creating program generators. The problem with some domain analysis methods is that the underlying software structure is considered more important than how the application is viewed by the application engineer.

---

[5] D. Parnas. "On the design and development of program families," *IEEE Transactions on Software Engineering*, Vol. SE-2, No. 1, 1976, pp. 1–9.

[6] Software Engineering Institute at Carnegie Mellon University. FODA is now a part of Model-Based Software Engineering, a more comprehensive domain engineering process.

[7] Bruce Blum's Tedium is a good example of this. See Bruce Blum, *TEDIUM and the Software Process*, Cambridge, MA, MIT Press, 1990.

[8] Sometimes a specification-level language is called a fourth-generation language, where the first generation refers to machine code, the second to assembly language code, and the third to programming languages. Each generation is significantly more productive than the previous generation.

2.11 | FAST Domain Model

Thus far, we have presented the minimal required understanding of domain analysis concepts for the purposes of this book. However, a very brief overview of the FAST Domain Analysis method will help you understand how you might benefit from a more serious approach to domain engineering. A method such as FAST will provide a precise process for systematically creating efficient and complete application development environments, including program generators.

The hallmarks of a FAST process are:[9]

- The separation of domain engineering and application engineering into distinct, systematic processes.

- The explicit definition of the family based on commonalities and variabilities for the predicted family members.

- The capability to specify family members by the ways they differ from one another and the capability to analyze such specifications for desired properties.

- Generation of all or most of the code and documentation for all or most family members.

This chapter has focused primarily on just one part of the FAST domain analysis, called the Commonality Analysis. Other parts include:

- Economic Model: an analysis of the costs and benefits of producing an application development environment (as opposed to building the family members one at a time).

- Decision Model: an ordering of the decisions that must be made by the application engineer.

---

[9]D.M. Weiss and C.T.R. Lai, *Software Product-Line Engineering*, pp. 63–64.

■ Family Design: a software design common to all family members (in other domain engineering methods sometimes called a domain architecture, an additional step between domain analysis and domain implementation).

■ Composition Mapping: a mapping of decisions made by the application engineer to the software components needed to implement the decision.

■ Application Modeling Language: a specification language used to describe applications. This is a way to specify the variabilities (as discussed further in Chapters 4 and 5).

■ Tool Set Design: a design of a set of tools that the application engineer would use for creating applications. Tools include specification editors, analyzers, and program generators.

■ Application Engineering Process: an explicit process used by the application engineer for modeling and creating applications.

In this book, we regard some of the above items as part of the domain implementation process rather than domain analysis, since some of these items are intimately connected with implementation issues. For example, choosing between a program generator, an application framework, or some combination is considered a domain implementation decision rather than a domain analysis decision. Consequently, specification language design and software structure are left to the domain implementation process. Regardless of what you put where, all of these items are important steps in a complete systematic domain engineering process.

2.12 | Summary

Domain engineering is a process for creating an application engineering environment that supports the rapid development of software within a family of application programs. Domain engineering is commonly divided into domain analysis and domain implementation. The fundamental units in domain engineering are decisions. During domain analysis, decisions are identified, analyzed, and categorized as commonalities or variabilities. Commonalities are decisions made during domain analysis about what is common across a family of application systems. Variabilities are decisions made during application development (generation-time and compile-time variabilities) or application use (run-time variabilities).

Program generators are tools for creating application programs from specifications. Generation-time variabilities determine the content of the specification language input to a program generator. The commonalities, domain implementation decisions, and compile-time and run-time variabilities largely determine the scope and implementation of the program generator and the generated programs.

Further Reading

G. Arango, "Domain Analysis Methods," in *Software Reusability,* W. Schäfer, R. Prieto-Díaz, and M. Matsumoto (Eds.), Ellis Horwood, New York, 1994, pp. 17–49.

James Coplien, *Multi-Paradigm Design for C++,* Addison-Wesley, 1999.

James Coplien, Daniel Hoffman, and David Weiss, "Commonality and Variability in Software Engineering," *IEEE Software* 15(6), November, 1998.

Krzysztof Czarnecki and Ulrich Eisenecker, *Generative Programming: Methods, Tools, and Applications,* Addison-Wesley, 2000.

Even-Andre Karlsson, *Software Reuse: A Holistic Approach,* Wiley, 1995.

Ruben Prieto-Díaz and Guillermo Arango, *Domain Analysis and Software Systems Modeling,* Los Alamitos, CA, IEEE Computer Society Press, 1991.

M. Simos, D. Creps, C. Klinger, L. Levine, and D. Allemang, Organization Domain Modeling (ODM) Guidebook, Version 2.0. Informal Technical Report for STARS, STARS-VC-A025/001/00, June 14, 1996, available from `http://direct.asset.com/stars`.

Jag Sodhi and Prince Sodhi, *Software Reuse: Domain Analysis and Design Process*, McGraw Hill, 1999.

Will Tracz, *Confessions of a Used Program Salesman: Institutionalizing Software Reuse*, Addison-Wesley, 1995.

David M. Weiss and Chi Tau Robert Lai, *Software Product-Line Engineering: A Family-Based Software Development Process*, Addison-Wesley, 1999.

An Example Domain Analysis

- Domain analysis: theory versus practice
- Domain analysis reports

3

Jack and Jill have a new problem. Building upon the success of their award-winning word-game products (see Chapter 1), they created a large company, diversifying into other software product lines, acquiring smaller companies, and creating wealth for themselves and their stockholders. Now, however, competition is heating up, profit margins are declining, and a crisis looms. They are meeting in Jill's office to discuss how to meet the challenge by cutting the cost of development.

They agree that in the past couple of years there has been little concern about the cost of product development, since every product has sold well. But to retain market share, they've had to cut prices, and now development cost has become an issue. They note that their current software products have a lot in common with each other and that, although there is some software reuse, a substantial amount of work is done over and over for multiple products within organizations as well as across organizations. They work long into the night hatching a plan that will make their company more efficient at developing software.

Maxim   *Increased productivity is the #1 reason for doing domain engineering.*

They select three divisions that they feel have the most in common and the most to gain. These divisions are:

Interactive Fairy Trails Division (IFT)—This division has created a successful line of software products for children. Each is based on a fairy tale or nursery rhyme that allows the inquisitive child to explore a richly detailed world populated with forgettable poetry and pictures.

Online Courseware for Smarties Division (OCS)—This division has created a series of course materials in esoteric technical topics such as Mylar Wrapping, GPS Modules, and OCS style courseware development. The courses are designed to allow the students to go at their own pace and direction. A unique feature of the series is the self-testing sequences that evaluate a student's weaknesses and strengths.

Adventure Plus Plus Division (APP)—This newly acquired division has created two award-winning software products that allow users to follow their hearts as they wander through a world that is part real and part magical, solving puzzles along the way, and most importantly scoring points for finding clues to the big mysteries of life and the universe.

Each division has its own product designers, technologists, and process for building products. The three divisions were recently collocated, and some personnel have been swapped among divisions to increase synergy and begin sharing some common concerns. A proposal has floated up to Jack and Jill to fund a project that would automate a portion of the software development of all three divisions. When Jack and Jill created their word-game program generators (Chapter 1), they just happened to be lucky to get it mostly right. This time they want to make sure a more methodical approach is taken, so they plan on recruiting a professional to guide them through a domain analysis prior to starting any major effort.

Maxim   Domain Engineering without Domain Analysis is like software without a plan.

So what are Jack and Jill discussing today? Is it the technical issues? No. Nor are they discussing the financial situation, product designs, marketing directions, or the weather. They are discussing who should be on the domain analysis team. This is a difficult decision, because people are not just a resource that you throw at a problem. You have to have the right kind of people. And you have to know the politics that comes with any organization.

They are discussing whether Bill should be on the team. He knows a lot about the technology behind IFT, but he's very opinionated and is not likely to be very supportive. Barbara, on the other hand, might not know as much, but getting her buy-in is crucial. Bonnie is the marketing wizard behind APP and has very definite ideas about where it should be heading, but she's involved at the moment in a very sensitive project. Bob is the visionary and lead technical architect for OCS, but he doesn't get along well with other potential team members.

Maxim   Domain Analysis is as much a social process as it is technical.

Jack and Jill know they need to have a fair representation of people from all three organizations, and they know the people should be representative across the various disciplines that make up the products. It is important to get a balance between the technical folks and the product design and marketing folks. The team can't be too large, or too small, can't be dominated by any one individual or be a team of just "yes" people. The team needs the visionary as well as the folks who will make sure the result is grounded in reality. Finally they choose six people, two from each organization.

Maxim   *Diversity of experience, disciplines, technology, and design are essential for a well balanced and useful Domain Analysis.*

The following week Jack and Jill gather the new team, which they have dubbed the Mercury Task Force. Jack explains in economic terms the company's motivations for supporting the effort. He emphasizes that software development should be viewed as a capital investment rather than an expense, and that building tools to automate software development is equivalent to investing in building a factory and assembly lines.

Maxim   *Domain Engineering efforts are capital investments.*

Jill explains the need for an early small success rather than an ambitious long-term effort. She states that the domain analysis phase should take only a week and should focus on the first few phases of a possibly long-term project. The domain analysis should result in a phased approach, where the first phase is small enough that a two-person team can complete a demonstration project within one month. Jill clearly expects something quickly and is persuasive that an incremental phased approach can deliver something credible in just a couple of months' time.

Jack and Jill introduce the team's members (Figure 3–1).

- **Pedro** from APP is the author of the initial proposal for building an application generator. He has a strong technical background and has created similar tools for APP.

- **Olive** from OCS is the chief architect of the OCS systems and is well-versed in Web techniques. Her latest initiative was the architecture of a Java Server Pages based system for OCS.

- **Simon**, also from OCS, is a developer of two of the courses in OCS and has been writing specifications for two more courses. He has proposed several new ways of testing students including a new "challenge" approach that pits their wits against a hypothetical protagonist. He also has extensive knowledge of the courseware market.

- **Peter** from APP was the assistant designer for the award-winning "Around the World in 80 Hours" adventure.

- **Francis** from IFT is a principal fairy-tale designer involved in more than 12 IFT productions. She has received numerous awards for her innovative design approaches.

- **Fred**, also from IFT, is a skilled programmer.

- **Tyler** is a consultant hired to guide the team's domain analysis efforts.

The team quickly schedules five days for the domain analysis, spread over a three-week period. They agree that the first day will be devoted to Pedro's proposal and a presentation by each of the three organizations.

3.1 | Day One

After some early morning chitchat and after the last straggler (who shall remain nameless) enters the room, the team quickly gets down to business. They reintroduce themselves. Tyler, the domain analysis moderator, outlines his role, emphasizing that he simply guides and can't and won't make decisions. The group must make the decisions.

Mercury Task Force
Cast of Characters
Jack and Jill, Managers

Interactive Fairy Tales
Francis, fairy-tale designer
Fred, skilled programmer

Adventure Plus Plus
Pedro, technical toolsmith
Peter, adventure designer

Online Courseware for Smarties
Olive, system architect
Simon, course developer

Tyler, domain analyst

Figure 3–1 Domain analysis team members

The group's response quickly degenerates into an overlong discussion about how the group should make decisions. They finally agree that a consensus approach will be taken, where consensus doesn't necessarily mean unanimity, but rather those who are in disagreement agree to be silent and move onward.

Tyler tries to continue his description of his role. He explains the domain analysis process and the hoped-for results—namely, a domain description, a set of terms, the variabilities and commonalities, and the ranges and binding times of the variabilities. Tyler notes that there are many well-defined domain analysis methods that could be used, but that he will use an informal FAST-style commonality analysis. Techniques from different domain analysis methods will be used when appropriate. Other than that, he intends mostly to listen and suggest directions or discussion topics. Tyler reminds everyone that he is the only person in the room who is NOT a domain expert. All the knowledge, experience, and intuition about the domain will come from the six domain experts, not the moderator. Fred reflects that he likes that job description and wonders what it would take to become a domain analysis moderator himself.

> **Maxim**   *The domain analyis moderator is typically not one of the domain experts.*

Next, Pedro outlines his proposal. He notes that the three organizations basically do the same thing. Each product is a collection of abstract places that include things of various kinds and links to other abstract places. Olive interrupts and states that he's describing a hypertext system, like the World Wide Web. Pedro demurs. Fred notes that it doesn't have to be the Web, it could be something like Macintosh's HyperCard. Pedro continues to explain that in all three organizations, each project starts from scratch and rebuilds an infrastructure for supporting hypertext capabilities. Olive again interjects that in OCS, they simply reuse the Web each time rather than rebuild from scratch. Pedro concludes by claiming that a program generator could be used to build much of the hypertext infrastructure and that the domain analysis is needed to figure out how to do this.

Tyler is not sure how to respond, since Pedro has put the cart before the horse. Tyler gently explains that a program generator may be the ultimate result of a domain engineering effort, but it probably isn't a good idea to enter a domain analysis with a preconceived idea that a program generator is the only possible outcome. He explains that domain analysis simply describes the context, the domain, the boundaries, and the variabilities and does not necessarily describe an implementation plan. In fact, there may be faster and smarter ways to accomplish the same objectives without resorting to a program generator.

> **Maxim**   Domain Analysis is a time for understanding the problem, not the solution.

Francis begins her presentation of how things are done in IFT. Each fairy tale or nursery rhyme is reimagined as a world of interconnected places. The child roams the world discovering a part of the story at each place. Various gimmicks and animations flesh out each place. From each place, the child chooses where to go next. Francis says that this ability to choose the next setting is what makes ITF unique in the industry. Most storybooks are just a linear sequence of scenes. Tyler notes that Francis, as a designer rather than a technologist, has described IFT in terms of products, customers, and markets rather than the supporting technology.

Fred gives a brief technical history of a few IFT products. In most cases, each product is a separate and independent development effort. Fred is aware that a lot of software is rewritten for each product rather than reusing software from previous products. Francis notes that each product is different, having new innovations that usually require new software. The latest IFT product has over 100 scenes and was built with some home-grown tools that aided IFT designers to compose scenes from various piece parts. The bottleneck in producing new IFT products seems to be getting the designer's thoughts and ideas down into code and graphics.

Olive is next and states bluntly that, unlike IFT and APP, OCS is an online set of Web pages. Each course is developed as a set of Web pages. CGI-bin scripts are used to gather student responses to questions, and tests for evaluation purposes (sometimes self-evaluation, sometimes under teacher supervision). Olive says the course is designed to accommodate a variety of students and their situations. Self-pacing comes with the territory, but self-interest may also lead students in a particular direction. Other students may already know some of the subject matter. The course is designed to allow many different ways of viewing and traversing the material. The Web with its built-in hypertext capabilities is an ideal way to represent these kinds of interconnections. Olive closes by saying she doesn't see how an automation tool or a program generator could possibly be of any use to OCS, since the Web provides everything they need.

Tyler asks if Simon has anything to add. Somewhat reluctantly Simon mentions that some people have asked if they could get a standalone version of the courses. They have complained that if they download the pages to their laptop, they can view most of the course material, but the questions and tests don't work. Olive injects that the CGI-bin scripts only work online, and that a standalone version would require duplicating the server-side services on arbitrary plat-forms—an obvious impossibility. Even if you limit it to one or two kinds of machines, she asserts, the effort to duplicate the server side software is just not worth the effort.

Next, Pedro and Peter jointly describe the two products of APP. Pedro says that the products share many features and, although they share some common software, it could have been a lot more. Pedro hopes that the next two products, currently in the planning phase, can have a larger common software base. He notes that the schedule pressure limits opportunities to think about sharing and the larger picture.

It's now late afternoon. After a long, exhausting series of presen-tations, sometimes getting into too much technical detail, the par-ticipants are tired. They also feel somewhat dejected and confused about what they are doing and where they are going. Simon won-ders if they are accomplishing anything. Tyler tries to encourage them by saying these reactions are normal this early in the domain analysis.

Maxim *The early portion of a domain analysis is often frustrat-ing and confusing and appears to be a waste of time.*

3.2 | Day Two

The next day, the Mercury Task Force (a.k.a. the Domain Analysis Team) meets again. Pedro obviously has something on his chest and leads off by saying that even if OCS isn't interested in increasing productivity, the effort is still worth it for both IFT and APP. Tyler interrupts and asks if they could rephrase Pedro's statement. The issue isn't whether OCS is interested in increasing productivity—what organization isn't? The issue is whether there are common needs and solutions across two or three organizations. Tyler also emphasizes that the effort is often well worthwhile if even a single organization, or perhaps even a single project, used the results of a domain engineering effort. Tyler therefore suggests that they continue the domain analysis without prejudging what organizations or projects will ultimately benefit.

Tyler suggests that the day be spent trying to define the domain of interest and some common terminology. He notes that on the previous day various people used the terms *place, page, scene, stage, view,* and *site* and he wonders about the similarities and differences. A rather long discussion ensues on exactly what these terms mean. It is discovered, for example, that IFT uses (at least for some projects) the term "site" to mean a place where a number of different scenes might take place. APP uses "site" to mean strictly one place, which can be reached from different places at different times. OCS, meanwhile, simply uses "page" to mean one physical Web page, but often gathers related material (a set of pages) together to form a "unit" or "site."

Maxim   The Tower of Babel failed for lack of a common language.

Everyone agrees that they need to adopt a standard terminology to avoid getting confused in their conversations. Tyler explains a bit about the philosophy of naming and defining terms and relates it to object-oriented methods, in particular the art of designing object-oriented systems, by trying to identify objects, their responsibilities, contracts, and operations. After a break and another hour of discussion they agree on the following terms:

> **Scene**: A view or page where something takes place, a unique place in a script, course, adventure, book, play, story, or subject. A scene is composed of a background and any number of props. (They couldn't decide whether the background was just another prop.)

> **Prop**: An element of a scene. Props include "hot areas" that can be clicked, such as buttons which may result in an animation, taking the person to a new scene, or changing some attribute of the prop. Props may also be simple images or formatted text.

> **Link**: Scenes can be linked together by using props. A prop such as a button when clicked can take a person from one scene to another.

> **Trail**: The sequence of scenes that a user traverses in going from one scene to another.

 Maxim   When I use a word it means just what I choose it to mean—neither more nor less.

Even though some team members reluctantly agree on using terms such as "scene" and "prop," they aren't willing to agree on what to call the whole product. Suggestions include "Play," "Book," "Story," "Adventure," "Trails" (the set of trails that users may take), "Plot," and "Subject." They agree on the temporary term "Play" only because it feels as if they were just playing around.

In the afternoon, the team considers the domain of interest. Pedro is sure it is the infrastructure for supporting hypertext systems. Simon and Francis see this as just a small piece of the domain, which they assert is really the composition of scenes. This, they feel, is the essential critical piece in their projects, the linking being just a tiny piece of the whole. Francis goes on at length about the need for composing many elements, visual, textual, and audio, as well as timed events and animation, into a single coherent scene. Peter supports this with example problems in APP, particularly how scenes change over time depending on what previously happened. Peter tells some interesting war stories that demonstrate the confusion and rework caused by misunderstandings between designers and software developers about what constitutes a scene. Meanwhile, Pedro is squirming in this seat. He keeps thinking that this is way too ambitious and there is no way it can be done in one or two months.

Maxim   *Don't assume you're talking about the same domain.*

Simon suggests that if they could take into account the user profile, such a system would be ideal for OCS. He explains that the user profile keeps track of the user's trail, the test results, and analysis of the student's level. Peter points out that the user profile is nothing more than a prop. But Simon and Pedro disagree and say it can't be a prop since it isn't in any scene. Olive asks why it can't be an "invisible" prop. Francis wonders if Olive is trying to cause trouble. Simon says that even if it is invisible, it still can't be a prop, since it spans more than one scene. Francis injects that she has been assuming a prop is independent of a scene and in fact can be in many different scenes. She gives some examples of props in IFT products that were used in multiple scenes. Now Olive pipes in that if you allow invisible props that span many scenes, this could include the user profile. Tyler calls time out for a coffee break—"or an ice cream break if that suits you better."

Maxim   *A Term is trickier than you think, even after it's defined.*

The day ends sooner than anyone had expected, and they have to depart without deciding exactly what a prop is, let alone what domain they are doing. This comes as a surprise to most of the participants, who at the outset had thought they had a clear idea of what domain they were discussing. Now they feel even further behind than they were the first day. Tyler again offers encouragement, saying that they have made wonderful progress today.

Privately, Olive tells Tyler she doesn't see any benefit for OCS and may not be available for the next meeting. Pedro privately tells Tyler that in his opinion he should have just been allowed to build his tool without doing the domain analysis. From past experience Tyler knows that these are typical reactions. He knows that teams will make progress if people will keep trying and listen with open minds. Tyler wishes he could inject a little more humor into the process.

3.3 | Day Three

Because of scheduling conflicts The Mercury Task Force can't meet until the following Monday. Everyone arrives promptly, including Olive. Tyler opens by asking everyone to present his or her view of what the domain is or is not. After going around the table, they realize they are a lot closer to a common understanding than anticipated. Pedro mentions his misgivings about making the domain too big and ambitious to be practical. Tyler suggests the big domain is a framework in which you can work. If there are subsets of the domain worth doing by themselves, consider the whole domain as an eventual goal and the initial subsets as initial phases. Pedro and the others like that idea, but then Pedro mentions he is really bothered by the idea of user profile as a prop. He says it doesn't make sense to him and is really making a mockery of the concept of a prop. This generates significant discussion on what is and what isn't a prop. Tyler tries to clarify by reiterating that one can think of the prop concept as its own subdomain, which doesn't need to be fleshed out fully right away. This leads to a discussion of "escapes." Tyler says you can think of a prop as either a complete enumerated list of possible things—say, buttons, images, formatted text, and animations—or as anything that could be provided by the underlying implementation language. In the one case a user profile would not be a prop, and in the other it could be, even if invisible.

After this discussion, people begin thinking of a prop as something independent of a scene. If so, then a prop could certainly be in more than one scene. And so, props, rather than scenes, become the morning's major topic. Characteristics of props can be specified, such as the color and label of buttons. Props can have events associated with them; for example, pushing a button prop creates an *action* event. And these events can be associated with *scripts* that specify what happens when an event occurs, including changing the traits of props and moving to a new scene. And thus a new model emerges, one where props and scenes are independent entities. A prop can exist in multiple scenes and has its own properties and behavior independent of a scene. It is suggested that some properties and behaviors may be influenced by what scene they are currently in. Out of this discussion a new series of terms emerge, including:

> **Trait:** a characteristic or property of a prop.
>
> **Event:** an occurrence such as a user action (clicking on a button) or program action (timer expiration).
>
> **Script:** actions executed when an event occurs, such as changing the traits of a prop or moving to a new scene.

 Maxim   Domains and their boundaries evolve and change over time.

After lunch, the domain analysis team is feeling a bit better about the direction taken. They spend more time pinning down definitions for the new terms, as well as pinning down domain boundaries. There is some confusion about whether the domain is about props or scenes or both. However, the whole conversation shifts direction when Peter initiates a series of questions about the goals of the analysis. He wants to know if the point is simply to create some common understanding, perhaps leading to standards, or to create some useful tools for development. He questions the idea that brainstorming on a fantasy development environment and tools will really lead to something useful in the short term on current projects with real deadlines. To make his point clear, Peter asks if there is any value to their domain analysis work. "Here we are, more than halfway through the allotted time for doing the domain analysis, and what have we accomplished?" Peter notes that they are not even sure what domain they are analyzing. Tyler asks the following series of questions:

1. How many of you have a new appreciation of the work in the other organizations? *They all did.*

2. How many of you view your own work in a new light? *They all did with some qualifications.*

3. How many of you see new ways of doing your own work? *Some did; some didn't.*

4. Do you think the three organizations have more or less in common with each other than you did prior to the domain analysis? *Most thought more; some about the same.*

5. If the domain analysis eventually leads nowhere, do you think the domain analysis was of any value? *Half said yes; half were not sure.*

Maxim *Exchange of ideas and knowledge is one of the key intangible benefits of domain analysis.*

Tyler gives his assessment. He feels that terrific progress has been made, and he expects to have a first draft of a domain analysis by the end of the fifth day. He recommends that for the rest of the afternoon each person write out what they feel should be the domain or domains. In particular he asks people to divide things into categories for Phase 1 and Phase 2. Phase 1 will be used to create the results that Jill wants in two months, and Phase 2 will be used for subsequent work. He also asks Pedro and Francis to work on the terminology and try to pin down meanings further.

3.4 | Day Four

The domain analysis team shares their work on Phase 1 versus Phase 2 details by email. Pedro and Francis also work on a list of terms and share this in advance with the group. This gives them a jump-start on the fourth day. Based on the success of these small-group efforts, the domain analysis team does more work outside of team meetings.

Maxim   Don't try to do everything in a group, particularly details, but be sure to review everything.

The most contentious unresolved term is what to call the domain. They decided a while ago to temporarily call it the "Play" domain. The OCS folks think it is just not right for their products, and they insist it should be called "Book." To proceed with more productive work, Tyler finally says that the issue has to be tabled and that the temporary term will have to do for now. All the other terms are accepted. See the domain analysis report at the end of this chapter for the final set of terms.

Maxim   Sometimes you can't find just the right word for a term.

The team now focuses on the assumptions about the operating environment of the Play domain. The most serious division is between OCS, where the Web is used, and ITF and APP, where a standard PC is assumed. Olive and Simon feel that their products are too different to give the domain reasonable commonalities. They agree that perhaps future standalone course products might fit in. Pedro also points out that creating a set of Web pages that mimics a product's scenes would provide useful testing and might lead to an alternative approach for creating on-line course products, but Olive and Simon are skeptical.

 Maxim   *A domain can't be all things to all people.*

Once this issue is understood, they agree on the operating environment of a typical Play domain. They select the Java™ programming language ("the Java language") as the implementation language, since it removes many platform dependencies. Fred says it is reasonable to restrict implementations so that the products can also run as applets over the Web in addition to running on a standalone computer.

The team spends a very productive morning sorting through variabilities. For each one, the team discusses the need for the variability, the differences between Phase 1 and Phase 2, the binding time, and the range of possible values. Most variabilities are made generation-time decisions. For example, the initial label of a button is a generation-time decision. A script might change the label of the button at run time, but both the script and the new label are still generation-time decisions. Pedro asks if the new label is always known at generation time or if there are cases in which the label has to be computed at run time. This issue opens a Pandora's box: "escapes."

The rest of the fourth day is spent on the issue of "escapes." An *escape* provides access to the underlying implementation language from the specification language. Consider the button label feature.

The label of the button might be a constant character string determined at generation time. Alternatively, it might be variable and computed at run time. If it is variable, it might be limited to a few possibilities that can be enumerated during domain analysis. In the extreme case, the possibilities might be unlimited and unrestricted. In such a case, the domain analysis team is presented with a difficult dilemma. The easiest way to express unlimited and unrestricted possibilities is to use a programming language. Rather than inventing such a language, one normally just uses the implementation programming language as part of the specification language. The use of the implementation language in the specification language is called an *escape* since one is escaping to the implementation language.

An escape can appear in various forms. It might be a direct use of the programming language in some places of the specification language. It might also be indirect, such as references to particular hand-coded objects and methods. Either way these are escapes.

Escapes are powerful ways of providing great flexibility. However, they seriously degrade the advantages of the specification by making it more difficult to analyze or understand. They also make the specification language dependent on the underlying implementation language. If escapes are used too often, then the specification language really isn't much better than just writing a program to begin with. One of the most serious questions for any domain-specific language is to what extent, if any, to use escapes. Escapes are double-edged swords—powerful if used properly, but also a potential disaster waiting to happen. Unfortunately, there is no free lunch.

 Maxim   *Escapes are double-edged swords.*

Tyler feels uncomfortable as the team discusses the issue of escapes. He feels that this is an implementation issue, but he also understands that what they are really discussing is whether certain features should have limited or unlimited variations, so he lets them continue. The team lists the places where escapes might be used:

- Trait values—without escapes, the value of a trait would probably be limited to string constants. With escapes, the value of a trait could be computed at run-time based on the state of the system.

- Prop initialization—without escapes, one would simply initialize traits and event scripts. With escapes, one could perform some sophisticated initialization (perhaps based on some persistent data).

- New scene initialization—without escapes, one would simply add props. With escapes, scenes could be customized upon each entry.

- Events—without escapes, one could only change the traits of props. With escapes, one could perform many other and unforeseen actions, such as changing the state of the system.

The discussion on escapes, including their advantages and disadvantages, continues into the early evening. Often one person argues both sides of the issue without realizing it. Simon argues that escapes are necessary so that they can fully implement user profiles. Later he argues against escapes, otherwise the system can never be used for generating Web-based solutions using CGI-bin scripts rather than the Java language.

Fred, who has been quiet during most of the domain analysis, provides one of the truly inspired moments of the day when he says in exasperation, "A prop should be an escape all by itself." This eventually leads to the realization that a prop can be implemented as a JavaBean.[1] This would allow any JavaBean to be easily incorporated into any scene. The expressive power of prop JavaBeans gets everyone excited as they suddenly realize it would eliminate almost all the work that might otherwise have gone into developing a prop subdomain.

---

[1]A Java bean is a Java class that follows some conventions and rules. See Chapter 13 for more information about Java beans.

This leads to an extended design session making sure that, if desired, one can specify props as just Beans.

 Maxim   *A subdomain may be best left for another day.*

During this session, Fred asks why they aren't simply using standard object-oriented techniques for the entire Play domain. This gets everyone considering exactly what benefits they are getting from the Play domain. Seizing the moment, Fred pushes further, stating that the entire system can be built by creating a new JavaBean that implements a scene. This will avoid all of the domain analysis nonsense, as well as the specification languages and program generators. Tyler, feeling a bit defensive once again, gently reminds Fred and the team that the domain analysis phase should not presume the implementation. Fred asks Tyler what he thinks about object-oriented techniques. So, Tyler feels obliged to make the following points:

- To do an object-oriented implementation would require an analysis equivalent to domain analysis, generating basically the same kind of information, perhaps in a different form. The domain analysis is not necessarily wasted, even if the final implementation is an object-oriented design and not a program generator.

- Domain engineering techniques don't compete with object-oriented techniques. Objects are the major way of doing abstractions in software, which is the essential attribute for separating concerns. A classic method for achieving separation of concerns is object subclassing (see Chapter 7). In the best cases, both technologies are employed.

- Using an object-oriented approach to the exclusion of domain engineering is not likely to achieve the critical separation of concerns between what you want to build and how you are building it. If you can't separately identify the "what," then you will continue to be locked into the code and dependent on it.

Maxim   Domain engineering complements object-oriented techniques. Neither is a substitute for the other.

Tyler allows the discussion to drift into many domain implementation issues and acknowledges that progress doesn't always follow the presumed ideal process. Often you wander all over the map before you can make good decisions. After exploring different alternatives, including a specification-language approach and an object-oriented design, one can decide which path, or which combination, is appropriate. It may turn out that a pure object-oriented approach is best, but you won't know until you have sufficient information to make an informed decision. Tyler also notes that the domain analysis team must have members who have extensive and expert software experience in the domain to understand the implementation issues in order to avoid excessive exploration at the implementation level. If this experience doesn't exist, then the domain is too immature for domain engineering.

Maxim   Sometimes you have to wander all over the map to find the best route. You need a guide who has covered the territory.

3.5 | Day Five

The fifth day starts with a suggestion from Olive. She thinks that no escapes or other assumptions about the underlying implementation language should be made for Phase 1. This will allow a variety of Phase 1 experiments, such as generating code for the Web and other languages. Then in Phase 2, escapes and Java language dependencies can be made. The domain analysis team likes this approach, mostly because it makes it much easier to decide what should go in which phase. To keep things really simple, they also decide Phase 1 will support only prop buttons with a single trait, the button's label. In addition, a single button event will be used (clicking on the button). The team works very hard to keep Phase 2 a simple evolution from Phase 1, where a minimum of variabilities and commonalities will have to be changed.

The team spends most of the day working out the commonalities and variabilities. Although the team does not achieve completion on the fifth day, it only takes a few more days of work by Pedro and Francis. The domain analysis report is presented next.

3.6 | The Domain Analysis Report

The Play domain analysis report is divided into three sections, one for each phase. The first phase, representing a prototype for testing feasibility, is described with a set of terms, and tables for commonalities and variabilities. Phase 2 is a more serious project with capabilities sufficient for creating small applications. The description of Phase 2 provides just the table of variabilities, focusing on the changes from Phase 1. The Phase 3 section lists some possibilities for work beyond Phase 2.

3.6.1 *Play Domain Phase 1*

The Play domain represents the common underlying structure of many of the products of IFT, OCS, and APP. This structure includes scenes and props and their traits, events, scripts, and actions (Table 3-1). Users will view one scene at a time and will move from one scene to another based on their actions or other events.

- **Play:** a series of interconnected scenes.

- **Scene**: a window on a computer display. A scene has a background (color or image) and any number of props.

- **Prop**: an element of one or more scenes. In Phase 1, only button props with label traits are supported. In Phase 2, props may also include formatted text, images, animations, or arbitrary JavaBeans with any number of traits, including JavaBean properties. A prop may also have events and scripts. In Phase 1, only the action event (clicking on a button) is supported. In Phase 2, any JavaBean event can be a prop event.

- **Trait**: a property or characteristic of a prop. Traits include labels, colors, images, audio, text, animations, and location.

- **Event**: something that happens as a result of a user action or other autonomous agent, such as a timer. The single most important event in this domain is the user clicking on a prop such as a button or "hot area" of a scene. Other types of events may be defined by the application, such as moving the mouse over a prop. When events occur, a script associated with the relevant prop or scene will be executed.

- **Script**: a sequence of actions that are executed when an event occurs. Actions include moving to a new scene, changing the value of a trait of a prop, or escaping to the underlying implementation language. Escapes are supported only in Phase 2.

3.6.2 *Play Domain Commonalities*

Table 3–1: Play Domain Commonalities

ID	Description
C1	Every Prop is a button (Phase 1 only).
C2	Each button has a single trait: Label (Phase 1 only).
C3	Each button has a single event: Action, which occurs when the button is clicked by the user (Phase 1 only).
C4	Java is the language of escapes (actions, events, types of Props for Phase 2).
C5	Java's Abstract Window Toolkit (AWT) is the display mechanism.
C6	A Play is a set of scenes.
C7	A Scene may have any number of Props.
C8	A Prop has an existence independent of a scene and may be involved in multiple scenes.
C9	There's just one window displaying one scene at a time.

In Table 3–2 the binding column, B, uses the following codes:

G: Generation time

H: Generation time provides a default value that may be overridden at run time

Table 3–2: Play Domain Phase 1 Variabilities

ID	Description	B	Range	Default
BT	A Play has a *title*.	G	String	No Title
BN	A Play has a *name*.	G	Identifier	None

(continued)

Table 3–2: Play Domain Phase 1 Variabilities *(Continued)*

ID	Description	B	Range	Default
BS	A Play has one or more **scenes**.	G	Nonempty set of Scenes	None
BP	A Play has any number of **props**.	G	Set of Props	None
BI	A Play has a **start scene**.	G	Identifier (of a Scene name)	None
BW	A Play window has a **width**.	H	An integer	500
BH	A Play window has a **height**.	H	An integer	250
SN	A Scene has a **name**.	G	Identifier	None
SB	A Scene has a **background color**.	G	#rrggbb value	#dddddd
SP	A Scene has any number of **props**.	G	Set of Prop names	None
PN	A Prop has a **name**.	G	Identifier	None
PE	A Prop may specify a **script** for Action events (when the Prop is "clicked") and optionally what scene is next.	G	Script consisting of an optional next scene name and a set of Traits (TP and TV)	None
PV	A Prop may specify the **initial label** (trait).	G	String	None
TP	Each label (trait) is associated with a **prop**.	G	Identifier (a Prop name)	None
TV	Each label (trait) has a **value**.	G	String	Empty String

3.6.3   *Play Domain Phase 2*

The important changes from Phase 1 to Phase 2 are generalizing props, traits, events, and scripts. A Phase 1 prop is limited to a label. In Phase 2, a prop can be any JavaBean Component. The JavaBean will determine the set of traits (JavaBean properties) and set of events. Scripts are extended to include escapes to Java code. Phase 2 introduces a number of dependencies between variabilities. For example, the choice of prop type (PC) determines the ranges of TN and EN. (See Table 3–3.)

Table 3–3: Play Domain Phase 2 Variabilities*

ID	Description	B	Range	Default
BT	A Play has a *title*.	G	String	No Title
BN	A Play has a *name*.	G	Identifier	None
BS	A Play has one or more *scenes*.	G	Nonempty set of Scenes	None
BP	A Play has any number of *props*.	G	Set of Props	None
BI	A Play has a *start scene*.	G	Identifier (of a Scene name)	None
BW	A Play has a *width*.	H	An integer	500
BH	A Play has a *height*.	H	An integer	250
SN	A Scene has a *name*.	G	Identifier (of a Scene name)	None
SB	A Scene has a *background color*.	G	#rrggbb value	#dddddd
SP	A Scene has any number of *props*.	G	Set of Prop names	None

(continued)

*Variabilities that are new or changed in Phase 2 are marked with an asterisk.

Table 3–3: Play Domain Phase 2 Variabilities* *(Continued)*

ID	Description	B	Range	Default
SE*	Upon entry into a new Scene, a Prop may specify additional **scripts** to execute for each possible event.	G	Set of Events	None
PN	A Prop has a **name**.	G	Identifier	None
PC*	A Prop is implemented by some **JavaBean**. The choice of JavaBean determines the set of possible properties (traits) and possible events.	G	Name of a JavaBean Component	Button
PT*	A Prop has any number of **traits**.	G	Set of Traits	None
PV*	A Prop may specify **initial trait values**.	G	Set of Traits	None
PE*	A Prop may specify a **script** for each possible event.	G	Set of Events	None
TN*	Each trait has a **name**. The possible names are determined by the properties of the underlying JavaBean.	A	Identifier (property name of a JavaBean)	Label
TP	Each trait is associated with a **prop**.	G	Identifier (a Prop name)	None
TV*	Each trait has a **value**.	G	Depending on TT as follows: String: String Color: #rrggbb Code: Java expression	None

(continued)

*Variabilities that are new or changed in Phase 2 are marked with an asterisk.

Table 3–3: Play Domain Phase 2 Variabilities* *(Continued)*

ID	Description	B	Range	Default
TT*	Each trait has a *type* that specifies what kind of value is being assigned to the trait.	G	String, Color, Code, …	String
EN*	Each Event has a *name*.	G	Identifier (under-lying JavaBean determines the possible event names, as well as entering and exiting scenes)	Action
ES*	A Script is a *list of actions* to take for an event. Actions are either changes to traits (a Trait) or escapes to Java code. In addition, scripts may specify a move to a new scene.	G	Sequence of Code escapes and Traits and an optional Scene name	None
EM*	Each Event has a *method name* that is used to invoke the Event's action.	G	Identifier (determined by the Event Type)	Action Performed

3.6.4   *Play Domain Phase 3*

The domain analysis team didn't spend much time on what is in Phase 3, but they did some brainstorming about what kinds of things might go into it. These included:

- Background images for each scene (rather than just colors).

- Transition magic between scenes (different ways of moving between scenes such as special effects).

---

*Variabilities that are new or changed in Phase 2 are marked with an asterisk.

■ Scene layout: support different Java layout methods including absolute positioning. This would allow other tools to be used by artists or designers to lay out a scene using WYSIWYG tools, and then to convert the tools' output to a specification file that includes the positioning data for each prop.

3.7 | Summary

Chapter 3 describes an imaginary domain analysis based on real experiences. Domain analysis is as much a social process as a technical one. Many of the social issues are easier to describe and appreciate in the context of a real or imaginary domain analysis. Important observations during the domain analysis are highlighted. The domain analysis participants other than Tyler are first-timers. Those who have been through it once tend to be less argumentative. For further information on domain analysis, see the references at the end of Chapter 2.

The Play domain analysis is used throughout the book as an example of program-generation techniques. In Chapter 5, XML is used to describe the generation-time variabilities, and a simple example is demonstrated. In the remaining chapters, the Play domain is used to demonstrate different program generation techniques.

Separation of
Concerns

▐ The "What" and the "How"

▐ Abstractions

▐ Techniques for separating concerns

4

Chapter 2 showed that decisions are the fundamental concept that drives the domain analysis process. This chapter shows that "separation of concerns" is the fundamental concept underlying domain implementation. Whether the domain implementation is a program generator, an application framework or a library of reusable components, the significant conceptual tool is "separation of concerns." In this book, the term "concern" is synonymous with "decision," and although the phrase "separation of decisions" is accurate, it is neither historical nor a good sound bite.

Domain analysis results in what's called the domain model. The domain model includes the set of decisions, which are categorized by binding times or roles and are called commonalities and variabilities. Domain analysis results in a set of decisions that are distributed to various times, places, or roles (Figure 4–1).

Domain implementation picks up where domain analysis leaves off, which is determining how to structure the system so that the decisions are properly distributed according to the analysis. The domain

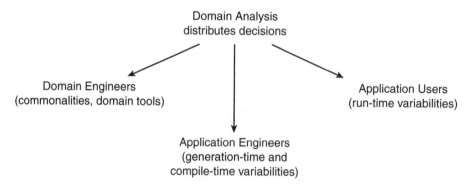

Figure 4–1   Domain analysis distributes decisions

engineer designs a system that distributes the decisions into separate system elements. This separation allows application engineers to independently create each system element. This is what is meant by separation of concerns.

It might seem that separating concerns should be a straightforward process, simply isolating each independent set of decisions into a separate element or component of the system. Separate files or directories could contain separate sets of decisions. People responsible for each set can then work on the files or directories independently (Figure 4–2).

If only things were this simple. Software is notoriously difficult, because the decisions are typically all mixed and tangled with incredible complexity. These complex structures are difficult to change: a little change in one place may affect many other places and decisions. For similar reasons, it is difficult for a group of people to write software because of all the possible interactions and linkages between different parts. Effective separation of concerns will result in a software structure that is both easier to change and easier for a group of people to construct concurrently. To work efficiently, an organization must allow the right people to make decisions at the right time without getting into each other's way. So, what is the *magic* that will allow us to separate concerns? The magic is *abstraction*.

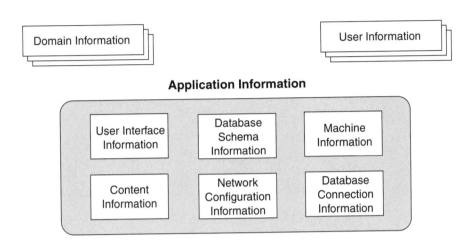

Figure 4–2   Physical separation of concerns

4.1 | Abstractions

Separating concerns involves creating abstractions to support a domain model. Abstraction is the major technique for making software more general, flexible, understandable, and reusable. Abstractions occur in many forms and at many different levels and are the principal preoccupation of software architects and designers. Abstractions are also intimately connected with software reuse. Peter Wegner[1] views abstractions and reusability as two sides of the same coin. Charles Krueger[2] asserts that abstraction is the essential feature in any reuse technique. It shouldn't come as a surprise that abstraction still plays center stage in the domain implementation process. Unfortunately abstraction is a difficult skill and is the major technical obstacle to successful software systems. It becomes doubly difficult when applied to families of software systems in the domain implementation process.

---

[1] Peter Wegner, "Varieties of reusability," reprinted in *Tutorial: Software Reusability*, edited by P. Freeman, IEEE Computer Society Press, 1987.

[2] Charles W. Krueger, "Software Reuse," *ACM Computing Surveys*, Vol. 24, No. 2, June 1992, pp. 131–183.

So, how does abstraction help separate concerns? Abstraction is often portrayed as the ability to separate the important from the unimportant. Unimportant details are suppressed to highlight the important essential features, thus permitting users of the abstraction to focus their attention on the relevant aspects of solving a problem. This portrayal, however, is "user-centric." It misses the essential contribution of abstraction to software design—the separation of concerns between different development roles. The terms "important" and "unimportant" are misleading, because they look at the abstraction from only one viewpoint—that of the user of the abstraction. Another viewpoint is that of the developer of the element or component that implements the abstraction. This developer is concerned with implementation and makes decisions about representation and algorithms. As long as the developer conforms to the abstraction interface, he or she is unconcerned about how it will be used. A software abstraction is more properly viewed, then, not as a separation between important and unimportant details, but as a separation of concerns between the users and implementers of the abstraction (Figure 4–3).

A software abstraction is an interface between two parties. The interface, variously called a contract or application program interface (API), defines the invariant or fixed part of an abstraction, which neither party (acting alone) can change. The abstraction user, or application

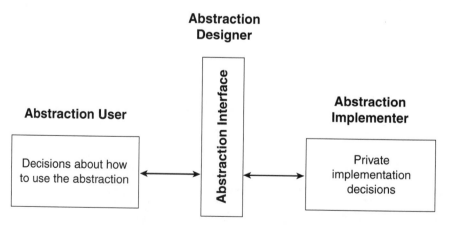

Figure 4–3 Anatomy of a software abstraction (separation of concerns)

engineer, makes decisions (the variabilities provided by the domain analysis) and expresses them in a form appropriate for the interface. The abstraction implementer makes the decisions needed for an implementation of the abstraction. The abstraction separates these two sets of decisions so that they are "hidden" from each other. The implementer can make implementation decisions without affecting the user's decisions and vice versa.

The implementer's decisions being "hidden" means the user does not need to know or care about them. In this sense, "hidden" is a misnomer, since what we're trying to do is not to keep the information secret but rather to make sure that no one depends on it. What hasn't been appreciated in the past is that the two sides are symmetrical. The implementer also does not need to know about the decisions made by the user. Both user and implementer rely solely on the interface and do not make decisions that depend on the private decisions of the other.

There is a third party—the abstraction designer, who defines the abstraction by identifying the interface that both users and implementers will rely upon. He or she determines the separation of concerns that the abstraction will support. The abstraction designer needs to know the variabilities from the domain analysis and make them explicit parameters of the interface. The process of creating an abstraction or interface is thus sometimes called parameterization, because the designer takes something specific (and concrete) and makes it more general by adding a parameter to the interface.

4.1.1 *Separating the "What" from the "How"*

If abstraction is the magic for separating concerns, it still begs the question of exactly what are we separating from what. The short answer is that abstractions separate the "what" from the "how." The "what" is the system we specify and the "how" is how it is implemented.

The set of decisions that we've labeled as variabilities in the domain analysis is sufficient to uniquely identify a member of a family of application programs. That is, the domain defined by a domain analysis is a family of software systems, whose members vary according to the variabilities. Using the variabilities, the application engineer makes a set of decisions. We call this set of decisions a specification because it specifies or selects a family member. We can also call this the "what" because it specifies *what* member of the family we want.

The set of decisions that we've labeled as commonalities along with a host of implementation decisions that are made during domain implementation constitute the "how" of the system. That is, it specifies *how* the system is built.

Thus, separation of concerns is a separation of the "what" from the "how" and equivalently the separation of the domain "variabilities" from the domain "commonalities" (and domain implementation decisions). Such a separation allows the domain engineers to work independently from application engineers (Figure 4–4).

What	Focus	How
Application Engineers	*Who*	Domain Engineers
Concerned with what domain application to build	*Concerns*	Concerned with how to build applications in the domain
Generation-time and compile-time variabilities	*Decisions*	Commonalities and implementation decisions
Specification for program generator or components for an application framework	*Result*	Domain tools (such as program generators and application frameworks)

Figure 4–4   Roles and separation of concerns

Separation of concerns is a technique or method for untangling the set of decisions that go into creating a system. In addition to separating the "what" from the "how," it is also used to separate information along other lines, including content from form (such as XML, see Chapter 5) and to separate development, design, and production roles (for example, separation of work between graphic artists and Web designers).

4.2 | Techniques for Separating Concerns

If we can isolate each set of decisions to separate files, then it becomes much easier to manage the concurrent construction and maintenance of a software system. Each technique discussed in this section results in physical separation, usually on a file-by-file basis.

4.2.1   *Physical Separation*

In the bad old days before the Java language, programmers had to pay particular attention to machine dependencies. This caused sufficient trouble that programmers began putting machine-dependent parts of their program in separate files. Entire books have been written on how to write portable C programs.[3] No matter how careful you are to avoid the many machine-dependent parts of C, you usually end up with machine-dependent code that is physically separated from the rest of the program in one or more separate files, or even in directories. They become quite obvious as the ones to change when the program is ported to a new machine or environment. These files will usually contain such information as the length of numeric types (for

---

[3] Mark R. Horton, *Portable C Software,* Prentice-Hall, 1990.

example, an int is 32 bits), byte ordering, word alignment, graphics, communication, and networking. Sometimes this information can be captured in a header file; at other times procedures and data must also be included (Figure 4–5).

This same technique will also work to separate concerns in a domain engineering context. However there are a couple of major disadvantages to using this technique in isolation.

- **Untangling a jumbled mess is difficult**. Most software is intricately written and trying to isolate and separate certain pieces of information is not always easy. The mystery constants section described later gives a good example of why this is difficult.

- **Program structure may suffer.** Separating and isolating particular parts of the program without regard to other abstraction principles will usually create a more unwieldy software system. Certain organizing principles may be violated. For example, the separation of the machine-dependent parts of a program into separate configuration files usually creates an artificial structure that is typically

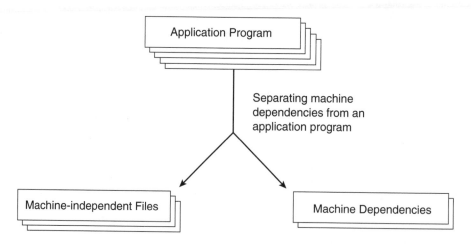

Figure 4–5 Separating machine dependencies from the application

contrary or at cross purposes with the natural software structure of the system. It is as if someone came along and decided to put all arithmetic expressions in one place. This "arbitrary" structure perhaps makes it easier for someone trying to understand and change the formulas of a program, but in general such arbitrary structure degrades the overall software structure.

4.2.2 *Configuration and Resource files*

Installing software on a new system usually requires configuration information such as directory locations for storing application information, locations of system resources, performance parameters, user profiles, and default values for various application values. This information is separated from the rest of the system and stored in what are sometimes called configuration files or resource files. Some configuration files are needed at installation time when the application is compiled or installed. Others are read when the application starts up or dynamically as needed. Chapter 6 will explore this technique in depth.

4.2.3 *Mystery Constants*

A *mystery constant* is any numeric, string, or other constant literal found in a program. It is common to replace mystery constants with named constants in order to improve a program's readability. Named constants also consolidate information fragments and separate that information from the structure of the program. Consider the code fragment shown in Example 4–1 for computing the percentage of perfect test scores.

Example 4–1: Percentage of Perfect Test Scores Using Mystery Constants

```
int[] scores = new int[100];
int perfectScores = 0;
readScores(scores);
for (int j=0; j<=99; ++j) {
        if (scores[j]==100) {
                ++perfectScores;
        }
}
print("percent perfect scores: "+perfectScores);
```

It's easy to dismiss problems with this code segment because it's so simple and easy to understand. However, when you imagine a program significantly larger than this with the same problems, the flaws become major obstacles to software maintenance. We'll focus on just one issue: the number of test scores. From the code segment, we can deduce that there are 100 test scores. This piece of information, which can be formulated as a decision, is scattered and intertwined with the rest of the program. Our objective is to separate this piece of information from the rest of the program. To do this, we introduce a new named constant and use it instead of our mystery constant, "100" (Example 4–2).

Example 4–2: Replace Mystery Constant with Named Constant

```
final int NSCORES = 100;
```

Now instead of using "100" we use the named constant "NSCORES" in the rest of the program. Finding the proper "100"s that need to be replaced by "NSCORES" can be a challenge (Figures 4–6 and 4–7). Here are four categories to consider:

- **Visible "100"s.** This is the simplest and easiest to replace. The "100" is simply replaced with "NSCORES"—for example, the first line of the program.

- **False "100"s.** One can't simply replace all "100"s with "NSCORES." For example, one of the "100"s in the code fragment represents a perfect test score, not the number of scores. This "100" is a different mystery constant which should have its own named constant to represent it.

- **Disguised "100"s.** The literal "99" really represents "100 – 1" where the "100" can be replaced with "NSCORES." The piece of information has been transformed. Such transformations make untangling programs very difficult.

- **Invisible "100"s.** And finally there is a "100" in the program that's simply not visible. The expression "perfectScores" is really a simplification of "perfectScores*100/100" where the first 100 is "NSCORES" and the second 100 is the percentage divisor (and also an "invisible false 100").

After analyzing and altering the program, we get the program shown in Example 4–3.[4]

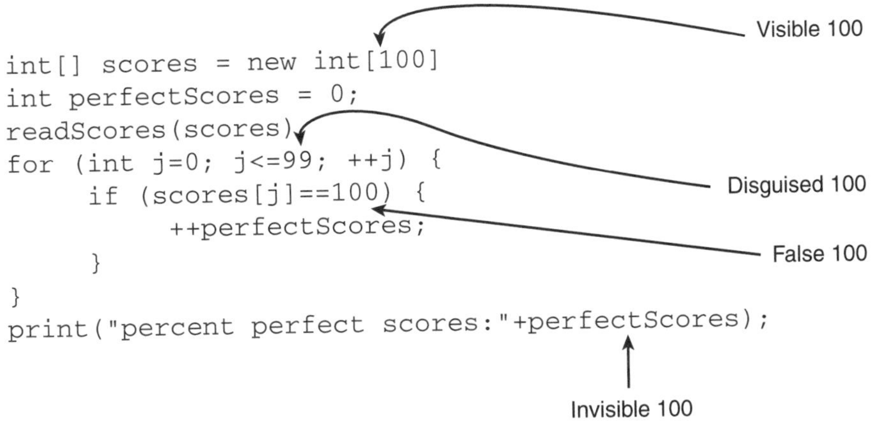

```
                                                      Visible 100
int[] scores = new int[100]
int perfectScores = 0;
readScores(scores);
for (int j=0; j<=99; ++j) {
    if (scores[j]==100) {                             Disguised 100
        ++perfectScores;
    }                                                 False 100
}
print("percent perfect scores:"+perfectScores);

                           Invisible 100
```

Figure 4–6 Analyzing information in the program

---

[4]Note that this program still needs some work. We still have one or two mystery constants!

Example 4–3: Percentage of Perfect Test Scores with NSCORES Named Constant.

```
final int NSCORES = 100;

int[] scores = new int[NSCORES];
readScores(scores);
for (int j=0; j<NSCORES; ++j)  {
        if (scores[j]==100) {
                ++perfectScores;
        }
}
print("percent perfect scores:  "+perfectScores*NSCORES/100);
```

Although simple, this example illustrates the difficulties in separating concerns, even at the lowest levels of code. When scaled up to normal program sizes, these difficulties can become insurmountable.

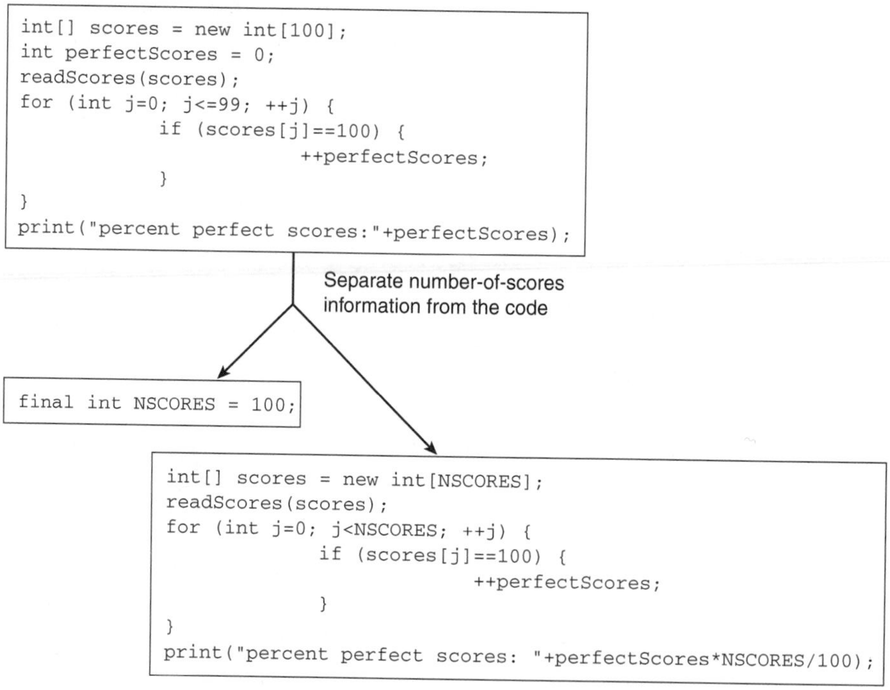

```
int[] scores = new int[100];
int perfectScores = 0;
readScores(scores);
for (int j=0; j<=99; ++j) {
        if (scores[j]==100) {
                ++perfectScores;
        }
}
print("percent perfect scores:"+perfectScores);
```

Separate number-of-scores
information from the code

```
final int NSCORES = 100;
```

```
int[] scores = new int[NSCORES];
readScores(scores);
for (int j=0; j<NSCORES; ++j) {
        if (scores[j]==100) {
                ++perfectScores;
        }
}
print("percent perfect scores: "+perfectScores*NSCORES/100);
```

Figure 4–7   Mystery constant example of separating concerns

4.2.4 *Classic Procedural Abstractions*

Assembly-language subroutines were a major advance in software abstractions in the 1950s. Assembly-language subroutine libraries were created and became the first major widespread software-reuse techniques. FORTRAN took this technique farther and brought about the first widespread use of platform-independent reusable software packages and components. Procedural abstractions led to data abstractions (data and a collection of procedures on that data) and object-oriented abstractions (where procedures are now called methods).

A procedure is a body of code with one (or more) entry points, one (or more) exit points, zero or more parameters, and possibly a return value. A procedure is a perfect example of separation of concerns, separating the "how" and the implementer (body of code) from the "what" and the user (the parameters). Once the interface is established (the syntax and semantics of parameters and return value), then the implementer's decisions about how to implement the procedure and the user's decisions about how to use the procedure are independent of each other.

The more parameters a procedure has, the more "abstract" it becomes. A sort procedure without any parameters sorts a particular instance. A sort procedure with an array parameter can be used to sort any array. A sort procedure with an array parameter and a comparison operator can sort any array in various ways.

A closely related concept is a macro (also first realized in assembly languages). Like procedures, macros have a body, entry and exit points, and parameters. Unlike procedures, macros are expanded at compile time rather than executed at run time. The distinction between macros and procedures is often overdone in some programming languages. For example, the C language forces programmers to decide at coding time whether something should be a macro or a procedure. In other languages, such as C++ methods and Ada, one can independently determine whether a method is expanded at compile time. Java leaves that decision up to an optimization compiler (with some help from the programmer, who provides clues such as using the "final" keyword). Partial parameterization is a technique that allows some subset of a procedure's parameters to be "executed/expanded" at compile time. Such a handy feature would permit the binding times of variabilities to be easily changed.

Consider the Java language method shown in Example 4–4 with a single numeric parameter that returns a fixed-width string of the numeric value, padded on the left with blanks. If the integer can't fit in the string, then the value "######" is returned.

Example 4–4: Convert a Number to a Fixed-Width String

```
String pad(double x) {
    String s = new Double(x).toString();
    if (s.length()>6) {
        return "######";
    }
    return "     ".substring(0, 5-s.length())+s;
}
```

This method may have been the result of a domain analysis in which a variability was the number to be printed and the width of the string was a commonality (6). If we change the width commonality to a variability, in a process that Chapter 2 called parameterization, we may end up with the new method shown in Example 4–5 (where repeat is a method that repeats a string).

Example 4–5: Convert a Number to a Fixed-Width String

```
String pad(double x, int width) {
    String s = new Double(x).toString();
    if (s.length()>width) {
        return repeat("#", width);
    }
    return repeat(" ", width-s.length())+s;
}
```

This example shows how methods become more general and abstract. Let's make it a bit more general (Example 4–6) by adding a formatting style parameter which selects a style (currency, exponential, decimal, ...), a justification parameter (left, right, center), and a padding string (rather than always using blanks).

Example 4–6: Convert a Number to a Fixed Width-String

```
String pad(double x, int width, String style, int justify, String pad) {
        String s = new Double(x).toString();

    if (s.length()>width) {
            return repeat("#", width);
    }
        ... a lot of complex formatting code ...

        return s;
}
```

The method pad now has five parameters and is a lot more complex internally. One of the drawbacks of using only parameters is that such procedures can become very complicated by trying to handle every variation. Software-reuse libraries have at times been criticized for providing bloated code with too many variations. Highly general methods may be too inefficient for applications that don't need the full generality.

There are several techniques to help overcome these difficulties. The only technique explicitly available in the Java language is method overloading (Example 4–7). It lets you provide a variety of methods with the same name, distinguishable only by the set of parameter types. Although this makes it easier to invoke the pad method with just the parameters you need, it doesn't solve the bloated-code problem.

Example 4–7: Method Overloading in the Java Language to Provide a Variety of Pad Methods.

```
String pad(double x, int width) {
    return pad(x, width, "normal", RIGHT, " ");
}

String pad(double x, int width, String style) {
    return pad(x, width, style, RIGHT, " ");
}
```

```
String pad(double x, int width, String style, int justify, String pad) {
    . . .
}
```

The Chart Applet Program Generator (see Section 10.3) shows an example with many variabilities. A traditional implementation would result in an applet with many parameters. The Chart Applet Program Generator creates a program with the parameters embedded where appropriate, thereby freeing up the run-time applet parameters to include only those that are explicitly run time.

4.2.5   *Object-Oriented Abstractions*

Objects separate the use of data from how it is represented and manipulated. Like procedural abstractions, the decisions of the implementer and user are separated and independent of each other.

Consider the classic example of a sorted list. The single most important decision of the implementer is how to represent the list. It could be an array, a vector, a linked list, a hash table, binary tree, or many other things. Strangely enough, the implementer could even choose to represent the list as an unsorted array. In such a case, a method for getting the first element will have to search through the whole list, looking for the first element. The representation decision is a decision private to the sorted list object. Programming languages, such as the Java language, will enforce this privacy by not permitting access to the representation outside of the object. The object is considered a black box. It's opaque. It hides the representation (Figure 4–8).

Thus objects provide an excellent means for separating concerns. Objects can be used to structure systems to support different sets of decisions. Object-oriented techniques are particularly important to use during domain analysis in order to understand and begin this separation as early as possible. Using the same structure in the software as in the domain analysis is powerful and efficient.

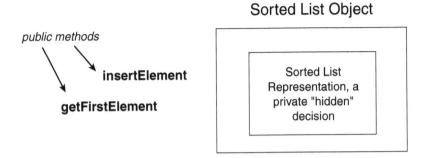

Figure 4-8 Private decisions hidden in objects

In the Play domain analysis in Chapter 3, the major elements of the domain were treated as objects, and, as we will see in future chapters, these objects translate directly to software objects. The relationships and understandings between the domain analysis objects translate directly to equivalent software structures. Thus the variabilities and commonalities can be mapped directly to specific software elements. In particular, the domain analysis went so far as to consider the Prop object as simply being a JavaBean for Phase 2.

More detailed examples are in Chapter 7.

4.2.6 *Inheritance*

Inheritance is an elegant approach to separating concerns. Although it is very closely associated with object-oriented approaches, inheritance is a general technique that can be and is used in other situations. The basic concept is that the common elements of a set of classes can be shared rather than replicated. Classes are hierarchically arranged. A subclass "inherits" the elements of its parent class, called a superclass. The elements of the superclass represent the common parts, and the subclasses represent the variations. Thus superclasses separate the common concerns from the variations of the subclasses. An example is given in Chapter 7.

Consider a simple non-object-oriented inheritance example. A user interface often includes various parameters that determine preferences or past history that we'll call a "user profile." User profiles are often stored as configuration files. Many of these preferences have default values. Different categories of users may have different sets of defaults (students versus teachers, for example). A hierarchy of configuration files might be used to manage these sets of preferences. Each configuration file in the hierarchy inherits preferences from the parent and simply adds the preferences that are specific to its own category (Figure 4–9).

4.2.7 *Application Frameworks*

An application framework is a reusable, partially complete application that an application engineer can use to create customized applications. Unlike a component-based or software-library approach to reuse that could be called a bottom-up approach, application frameworks are top-down approaches, sometimes referred to as inversion of control. An application framework is primarily a reuse of a software architecture or design. The essence of a framework is how to divide a system into components and how the components interact with each other.

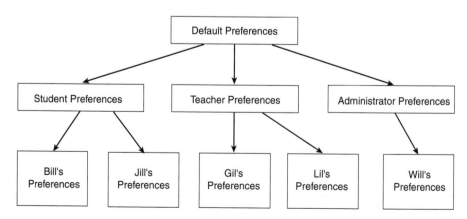

Figure 4–9 Inheritance hierarchy for user interface preferences

There is a strong relationship between application frameworks and domain analysis,[5] and they have even been called two sides of the same coin.[6] The success of an application framework obviously depends on how well suited it is to a variety of applications, and, of course, that will be largely determined by the domain analysis. The core of both application frameworks and domain analysis is the determination of commonalities and variabilities.

There is also a strong relationship between application frameworks and program generators. The construction of a program generator often must include the development of an application framework, although in many cases it is implicit. Essentially the common or invariant code generated by the program generator constitutes the application framework. The quality of the program generator can be improved by first designing an application framework.

Application frameworks are sometimes contrasted with software component-reuse libraries. An application framework is considered a top-down approach to software reuse, whereas composing an application from software components is sometimes referred to as a bottom-up approach. In practice almost all approaches combine the two. Application frameworks, for example, usually include a set of components that can be used as default elements in the framework. Similarly, software component libraries often include the equivalent of application frameworks or portions of them.

GUI environments are often designed as application frameworks. The application programmer simply plugs in specialized objects for a specific application. The event model and how it changed from Java 1.0 to Java 1.1 demonstrates this evolution of a framework. In Java 1.0, UI events were handled directly by methods on the relevant object. For example, a click on a Button object calls the method "action" of the Button object. In Java 1.1, the event model changed by transforming the "action" method to an "action" object, called an `ActionListener`.

---

[5] Arango, 1993 (see Further Reading at the end of the chapter).
[6] Giancarlo Succi, Paolo Predonzani, Andrea Valerio, and Tullio Vernazza, 1999 (in *Building Application Frameworks,* see Further Reading at the end of the chapter).

The Button object has a new method, "addActionListener," that associates the ActionListener object with the button. This change more clearly separates the common aspects of a button (the usual button behavior) from what a button is supposed to do for each application (Figure 4–10).

4.2.8 *Specification-Driven Techniques*

Specification-driven techniques use specification-level information to create or directly execute applications. These include program generators, application generators, fourth-generation languages, little languages, and application-oriented languages, but can also include such varied systems as spreadsheets, GUI builders, and visual programming tools. In each case, a specification (the "what") is input to a tool that parses, analyzes, and either creates programs and other files or directly executes or simulates the desired behavior.

Consider the dictionary program generator of Chapter 1. The list of words is the specification. The program generator reads the specification and outputs a program. The program generator effectively separates the concerns of the list of words from the implementation

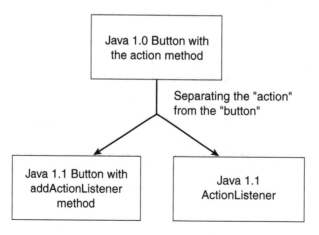

Figure 4–10   Separating the action from the button

representation. The list of words can be represented in many different ways, including:

■ Unsorted linear array

■ Alphabetically sorted array

■ Hash table

■ Huffman encoded strings

All too often, representation decisions are heavily intertwined with the rest of the program. Changing these decisions may involve radical and extensive changes to the software or object, sometimes so extensive that making such changes is not considered practical. If the list of words was hand coded in Dictionary1.java (without using Dictionary1 Generator.java), then changing the data structure is impractical, because it would require rewriting thousands of lines of code (no matter how simple those lines of code are). However, if `Dictionary1-Generator` is used, then the data structure can be changed much more easily, because one merely rewrites the simple 30-line code generator (Figure 4–11). The ability to easily change the representation is crucial when a different context or environment demands optimization for some particular resource such as memory or time.

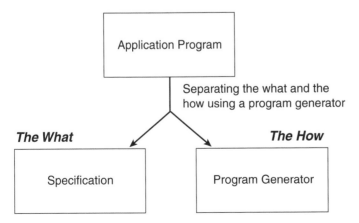

Figure 4–11   Using a program generator to separate concerns

4.2.9 *Expressing Specifications*

Whatever approaches or techniques are used, the domain engineer must also design a way for application engineers to specify "what" application they desire. For some approaches, such as application frameworks, the specification may be customizing and composing a system from piece parts. For program generators, however, this usually means designing a language for expressing a specification of the desired application. Traditionally this has meant designing a textual language from scratch and building a translator that will read and parse that language. There are many alternative approaches. In this book, we advocate the use of XML as a standard representation of the specification, but that doesn't preclude these other approaches. A specially designed textual language, a database query, or graphical descriptions can all be converted to and from XML data. Chapter 12 gives an extended example of using both XML and a specialized textual language.

Consider the Play domain. In the next chapter we will design an XML language for Play. In addition, we could also design a special text language and a tool for converting the text language to or from XML. The Play data could also be stored in a database and converted to and from XML. The Play data in XML format could also be edited with special XML editors. A graphical version could also be used to create a visual-editing environment. A variety of ways to view and use the Play specification allows different sorts of expertise to use the information (Figure 4–12).

4.3 | Summary

The key principle during the domain implementation phase is separation of concerns. Separating the variable parts from the common parts of a software system is essential in order to easily reuse the common

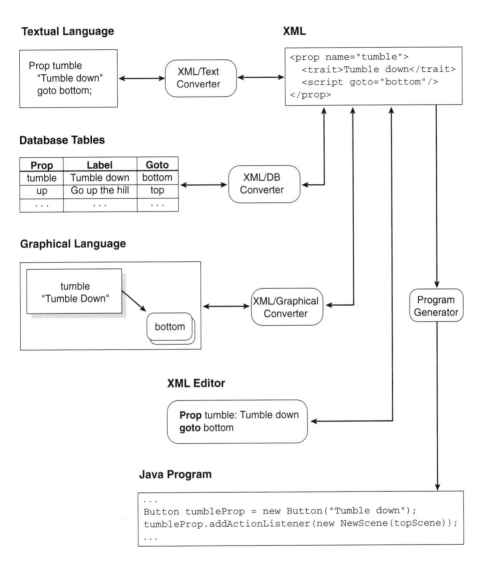

Figure 4–12 Specification languages and XML

parts. Abstraction is the principal method to separate concerns, chiefly by separating the "what" from the "how." Engineers use a variety of techniques to separate concerns, most of which are standard software engineering practices. One technique is program generation. A program generator separates concerns by placing generation-time variabilities in a specification. There are many different ways for expressing specifications from simple textual languages to sophisticated visual languages. XML provides one standard way for expressing specifications.

Further Reading

J. Craig Cleaveland, Janet A. Fertig, and George W. Newsome, "Dividing the Software Pie," *AT&T Technical Journal*, Vol. 75, No. 2, March 1996, pp. 8–19.

J.W. Cooper, *Java Design Patterns: A Tutorial*, Addison-Wesley, 2000.

James O. Coplien and Douglas C. Schmidt, *Pattern Languages of Program Design*, Addison-Wesley, 1995.

Mohammed E. Fayad, Douglas C. Schmidt, and Ralph E. Johnson, *Building Application Frameworks: Object-Oriented Foundations of Framework Design*, Wiley, 1999.

E. Gamma, R. Helm, R. Johnson, and J. Vlissides, *Design Patterns: Elements of Reusable Object-Oriented Software*, Addison-Wesley, 1995.

Charles W. Krueger, "Software Reuse," *ACM Computing Surveys*, Vol. 24, No. 2, June 1992, pp. 131–183.

Peter Wegner, "Varieties of Reusability," reprinted in *Tutorial: Software Reusability*, ed. P. Freeman, IEEE Computer Society Press, 1987.

XML: A Standard Representation for Specifications

- What's XML?
- Designing domain-specific languages
- Using XML for specifications

X ML is a standard representation for information. Unlike HTML, XML can be used to create custom information structures for any domain or application. Although originally developed with the World Wide Web in mind, XML is useful for any application needing to represent structured information. As shown and used in this book, XML is used as the syntax for representing program specifications, from which we generate software programs.

XML is a streamlined subset of Standard Generalized Markup Language (SGML) which grew from the initial work of Goldfarb, Mosher, and Lorie at IBM. Both XML and SGML provide a way to define new *document types* to represent the content of a specific kind of document. One such document type created by Tim Berners-Lee and made publicly available in 1991 is HTML, the language for representing Web pages. Like other markup languages, HTML was intended to separate the abstract content from its rendition as a Web page. HTML elements were used to provide information at an abstract level without providing specific details about its presentation on a Web page. For example, the heading element H1 was used to denote a major heading, but it did not specify details about font size or layout. This allowed different browsers that converted HTML to a specific representation to choose what was appropriate for the situation. A pure text display would use a different approach from a rich graphical display. It could even be converted to a purely audio form. However, the market demand for more control over Web page layout eventually forced HTML to evolve to include not just abstract content but also detailed control over the layout and display of Web pages. This mixing of abstract content and presentation style is, of course, counter to everything we discussed in Chapter 4.

A second major drawback of HTML is that it is a document type with a fixed nonextensible set of element types specific to displaying general Web pages. The combination of the degeneration of HTML to a formatting language and the limited set of element types made HTML unusable for other general purposes. XML is intended to fill this void.

XML has a number of important characteristics that make it a great idea not only for the Web but also for many other application areas, including program generators. These characteristics include:

> **Extensibility**—the X in XML stands for "extensible." XML can be extended to define new information structures to create domain-specific and application-specific languages. XML itself has no predefined element types or meanings. Each XML document type defines its own structures, element types, and meanings.

> **Markup Language**—A markup language allows one to "mark up" a document. The markup provides additional information about the document. Typically, it breaks up the content of the document into parts, called elements, which may be further divided to create a hierarchy. Each element is identified by a tag, which gives some particular meaning to that part of the document. Thus, rather than

being just a sequence of characters, the document now has additional information that identifies the structure and properties of its different bits and pieces.

Separation of content from form—The classic time-honored purpose of a markup language is to separate the abstract content of a document from its presentation style. The abstract content can be rendered in different forms. As already discussed in Chapter 4, we extend this notion to include any kind of separation of concerns.

Standard—XML is a standard. Adopting a standard has the advantage that one can simply use it rather than trying to re-invent something new. Adopting a standard may also minimize the problems inherent in reaching agreement among a diverse set of people or organizations about how to design or create something. And last, but not least, a standard provides the opportunity of creating a marketplace of tools, resources, courses, books, experts, and people familiar with the technology.

5.1 | To XML or Not?

How should one decide whether to use XML? After all, inventing your own domain-specific language can provide most of the advantages mentioned earlier, plus the very important one that the language may be a lot easier to use. After all, who wants to say the following in XML:

```
<expression>
    <number>2</number>
    <operator>+</operator>
    <number>4</number>
</expression>
```

when one could more simply put it this way:

2+4

Domain-specific languages with their own syntax may be a lot more intuitive and easier to read and write than XML. These are the factors to consider when trying to make this kind of decision.

1. Domain-specific languages require building your own parser, tools, editors (text), generators, etc. For example, you may find that it's trivial to create Web pages directly from XML, and difficult enough from a home brew language that you may decide it's not worth the trouble.

2. XML may be hard to read as a text file, but using the right XML editor may limit or even remove this disadvantage.

You may also find that you can have the best of both worlds by building translators between the domain-specific languages and XML (as illustrated at the end of Chapter 4 and Chapter 12).

5.2 | XML Elements

The basic unit of XML is the *element*. XML elements are enclosed in a start-tag and end-tag. The end-tag is identified by a slash character preceding the element-type name (Figure 5–1).

The element-type name identifies what kind of element it is. Each domain or application area will define the set of valid element-type names and their meanings within that domain or application area.

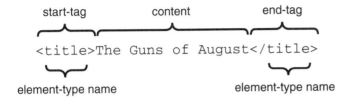

Figure 5–1   An XML element

An element may be empty, in which case it can (but needn't) be represented by an empty element tag—that is, a combined start-tag and end-tag identified by the slash character at the end of the element-type name (Figure 5–2). Empty elements usually exhibit attributes, which will be discussed in the next section.

Each domain-specific language is a set of element types and their meanings. A phone-book language may have the following element types:

1. phonebook—The root element

2. phonebookentry—One entry in the phone book

3. name—The name of a person(s)

4. phone—The phone number

Elements can be nested. Using the element types above, a phonebook is a series of phonebookentry's, each having a name and phone. Example 5–1 shows a simple phone book with this element

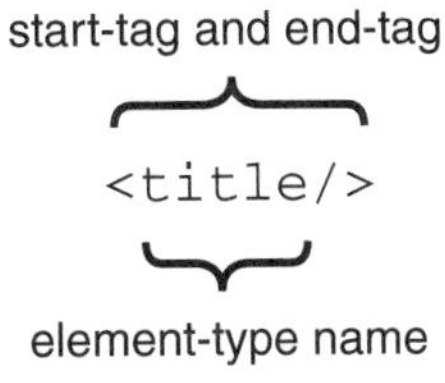

start-tag and end-tag

```
<title/>
```

element-type name

Figure 5–2   An empty element

nesting. The first line is usually present in an XML document, and it provides version information and possibly other information about the document.

Example 5–1: A Phone Book in XML

```
<?xml version="1.0"?>
<phonebook>
  <phonebookentry>
    <name>Jack</name>
    <phone>x133</phone>
  </phonebookentry>
  <phonebookentry>
    <name>Jill</name>
    <phone>x104</phone>
  </phonebookentry>
</phonebook>
```

An XML document expresses information structure. This structure is a hierarchy of elements. The indentation in the XML document in Example 5–1 is merely a convention but visually shows this structure. A diagram of this structure graphically illustrates how the elements are related to each other (Figure 5–3).

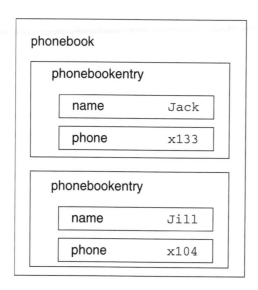

Figure 5–3   Phone-book structure

To maintain well-formed XML and enforce a hierarchical structure, XML markup must follow certain rules. The rules are:

1. **No unclosed elements.** Every element must either have a start-tag and an end-tag, or be an empty element. Tags for empty HTML elements such as `<hr>` would be rewritten as `<hr/>`.

2. **No overlapping elements.** Elements must form a tree structure. The character sequence

   `<b><i>XML</b></i>`

   is not well-formed XML and should be replaced with either

   `<b><i>XML</i></b>`

   or

   `<i><b>XML</b></i>.`

5.3 | XML Attributes

In addition to content, XML elements may also have *attributes*, using the notation shown in Figure 5–4.

Unlike HTML, attribute values are always enclosed in quotes or apostrophes. Attributes are used to provide additional information about an element. In Example 5–2, a date attribute is added to a phonebookentry to indicate when the entry was made, and a title

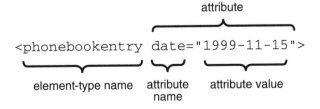

Figure 5–4   An XML attribute

attribute is used in a name element. Attributes are normally used to provide additional information about the element. In domain-specific languages there is considerable leeway about what kind of information should be represented as attributes.

Example 5–2: Example XML with Attributes

```
<?xml version="1.0"?>

<phonebook>
  <phonebookentry date="1999-11-15">
    <name title="Mr.">Jack</name>
    <phone>x133</phone>
  </phonebookentry>
</phonebook>
```

5.4 | XML Predefined Entities

Since XML documents use characters like "<" and ">" for markup, we need to be able to write these characters in the data without getting them mixed up with tags. An XML predefined entity reference (Table 5–1) is an expression for specifying objects that should not be parsed as XML. A well-formed XML document will always use XML entity references for angle brackets, the quote, the apostrophe, and the ampersand characters.

Table 5–1: XML Predefined Entities

Entity Reference	*Character*	*Name of Symbol*
&amp;	&	Ampersand
&lt;	<	Less-than symbol
&gt;	>	Greater-than symbol
&quot;	"	Quotation mark
&apos;	'	Apostrophe

An XML entity reference[1] always begins with the ampersand and ends with a semicolon (Example 5–3).

Example 5–3: Example XML with Predefined Entity References

```
<?xml version="1.0"?>

<phonebook>
  <phonebookentry>
    <name>Jack &amp; Jill</name>
    <phone>x133</phone>
    <note>Ask for &quot;Jack&quot; if x&lt;4</note>
  </phonebookentry>
</phonebook>
```

5.5 | Creating a Domain-Specific XML Structure

The Play Domain Analysis at the end of Chapter 3 provides an example of translating an abstract description to a concrete language using XML. Most of the variabilities translate directly and naturally to XML. In this section we'll take a quick look at how to do this by using only elements and no attributes. In Section 5.7 we'll design a language using both elements and attributes. Both designs are good ones. The choice of whether to use attributes or not is discussed in Section 5.6.

Consider the graphical description of a particular Jack and Jill Play shown in Figure 5–5.

The first step in creating an XML structure is to understand the structure of the data you want to represent. Thanks to the domain analysis at the end of Chapter 3, we can confidently create the structure shown in Figure 5–6.

Once the structure is determined and we've decided to represent all information with XML elements, then the XML specification of the Jack and Jill play naturally follows (Example 5–4).

---

[1] In general, an XML entity is a "piece of text" and you can define your own entities.

bottom
Go up the hill
top
Fetch a pail of water
Fall down, break crown
Key
Scene
Prop

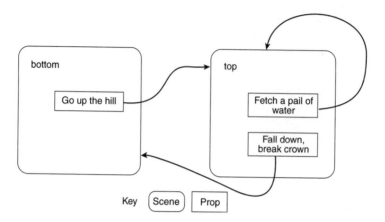

Figure 5–5 A Jack and Jill Play using two Scenes and three Button Props

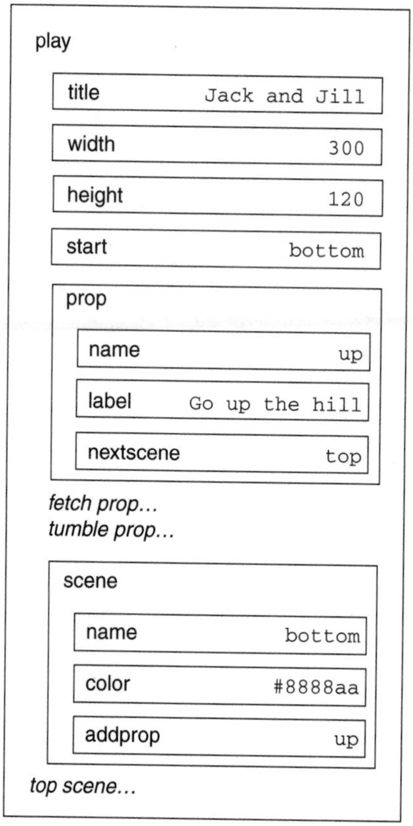

play
title
Jack and Jill
width
300
height
120
start
bottom
prop
name
up
label
Go up the hill
nextscene
top
fetch prop...
tumble prop...
scene
name
bottom
color
#8888aa
addprop
up
top scene...

Figure 5–6 The structure of the Jack and Jill Play specification

Example 5–4: One Possible XML Structure for the Play Domain

```xml
<?xml version="1.0"?>
<play>
  <title>Jack and Jill</title>
  <width>300</width>
  <height>120</height>
  <start>bottom</start>

  <prop>
    <name>up</name>
    <label>Go up the hill</label>
    <nextscene>top</nextscene>
  </prop>

  <prop>
    <name>fetch</name>
    <label>Fetch a pail of water</label>
  </prop>

  <prop>
    <name>fall</name>
    <label>Fall down, break crown</label>
    <nextscene>bottom</nextscene>
  </prop>

  <scene>
    <name>bottom</name>
    <color>#8888aa</color>
    <addprop>up</addprop>
  </scene>

  <scene>
    <name>top</name>
    <addprop>fetch</addprop>
    <addprop>fall</fall>
  </scene>

</play>
```

In the language in this example, each variability is an element and is assigned an element type name (such as color or name). When variabilities include other variabilities (for example, a scene may have any number of props), then elements are nested. The root element is play. The element-type name addprop is used in a scene to emphasize that it refers to a prop elsewhere in the specification. The content of the `addprop` and `nextscene` elements must be the data of `name` elements within `prop` and `scene` elements elsewhere in the specification. These constraints can be checked by tools (see Sections 5.8 and 9.2).

5.6 | Elements or Attributes?

The approach to making every variability an XML element is straightforward, and one wrestles only with the structure. An alternative approach is to use attributes for carrying some of the information. For example, consider how the `start` scene, `width`, and `height` are elements in Example 5–5.

Example 5–5: Using Only Elements to Express a Play

```
<play>
  <title>Jack and Jill</title>
  <width>300</width>
  <height>120</height>
  <start>bottom</start>
</play>
```

Instead of using elements, one could use XML attributes to represent this information (Example 5–6).

Example 5–6: Using Attributes to Express a Play

```
<play title="Jack and Jill" width="300" height="120" start="bottom">
</play>
```

There is no clear-cut method to decide whether a piece of information should be represented by an element or by an attribute. It is reasonable to decide to represent all information as elements. If attributes are used, then here is a list of considerations.

1. Generally, attributes are considered as properties or characteristics of an element. In contrast, elements usually represent parts of objects. Elements can usually be thought of as independent things, whereas attributes might not be able to stand alone as independent objects.

2. Elements usually represent information of primary importance, attributes that of secondary importance.

3. Use attributes when they name an element or refer to other elements. For example, the `name` of the `prop` and `addprop` elements should probably be an attribute. In a DTD (see Section 5.8) you can easily specify these relationships if they are attributes.

Example 5–7: DTD Fragment for Expressing Prop Names and References

```
<!ATTLIST prop name ID #REQUIRED>
<!ATTLIST addprop name IDREF #REQUIRED>
```

In Example 5–7 the first line says that the prop element must have an attribute called `name`, and by the DTD rules this attribute value must uniquely identify this element. The second line says that the `addprop` element also has a `name` attribute, which is a reference to another element in the XML file and is also required. Using this DTD, an XML tool can identify invalid XML files such as those using an `addprop` element that doesn't refer to any `prop`, or files that have multiple `prop` elements with the same name.

4. Use attributes for simple, unstructured information. Use elements when they have parts, structure, or more complex information. Attributes can't have attributes or elements. For example, a `Play` has lots of parts, including any number of props and scenes, so it should be an element. But the width of a Play window is simply a number and is

unlikely to become any more complex than that, so it could easily be represented as an attribute. This also means you need some foresight about information that may evolve to be more complex in the future. If you're not sure, then it is usually safer to use elements that would permit more structure and flexibility in the future.

5. Attributes can occur only once in an element, so use elements for complex information that can occur more than once.[2] For example, a scene can have any number of props, so addprop should be an element rather than an attribute of scene.

6. Finally, don't sweat over deciding between attributes and elements. For small documents like ours, it's not difficult to change your mind at a later time. Let's say you decide in version X that you want to change an attribute to an element or vice versa. Using tools or languages such as XSL, you can write a simple converter program that will transform your old version XML files to new version XML files.[3]

Using these guidelines, we can argue long into the night about each little piece of information and whether it should be an element or an attribute.[4]

5.7 | The Play Domain Using XML

The design of an XML language for the Play domain is based directly on the domain analysis provided at the end of Chapter 3. There are two phases, and we'll consider both in this design. This is

---

[2]However, an attribute can have multiple simple values.

[3]Altering the XML structure is not as feasible when there are enormous quantities of XML data to convert.

[4]For more information see Megginson, *Structuring XML Documents,* Prentice Hall, 1999.

important to ensure a smooth transition from Phase 1 to Phase 2. Certain decisions—for example, how to represent the label attribute—might seem odd if you consider only Phase 1. Phase 1 is a simplified Play containing only one kind of prop (a button), one kind of trait (label of the button), and one kind of event (mouse click on a button), and having no escapes to the underlying implementation language.

The general structure of a Play is very clear from the Play domain analysis. Each play has any number of Props and Scenes. In Phase 1, each Prop has a single Trait and at most one script. Each Scene may include references to any number of the defined Props called `addprop`. The term `addprop` is used because it indicates that we are adding a Prop (defined elsewhere) to a particular scene. Figure 5–7 shows this structure, which we will use to guide our XML design for Phase 1.

Here are the decisions that are made for the Play Domain and the reasoning used.

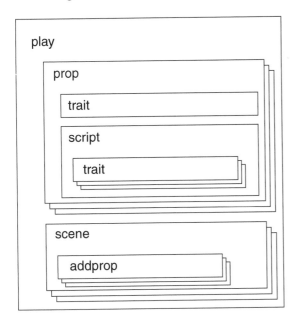

Figure 5–7   Basic structure of a play

Play: obviously an element (many parts)

Scene: obviously an element (many parts)

Prop: obviously an element (multiple traits, scripts)

Trait: should be elements, because we need to identify different pieces such as name and value, but this may evolve to something more complex in the future

Script: obviously an element (multiple actions)

Addprop: an element (in Phase 2 there will be many parts, including scene-specific scripts)

Name (of props and scenes): should be an attribute, since we need to uniquely name props and scenes and refer to them from other places

Play title: should be an element (because someone thought it might become more than just a string in the future, that you may want to give some attributes about the style of the title; an equally good argument could have been advanced to make this an attribute)

Play width and height: attributes (simple information of secondary importance)

Scene color: attribute (simple information of secondary importance; however, one could argue that it should be an element, if we want to merge this with future enhancements regarding backgrounds that would allow more than just a simple color, or a possible escape into code that computes the color of the scene depending on context)

Based on this rationale, the Play domain language in XML can be described with two tables that define the elements and attributes of the Play domain for Phase 1 (Tables 5–2 and 5–3; Figure 5–8). Phase 2 tables are given at the end of this chapter. The Content column of the XML element types (Table 5–2) describes the content of the element, which could just be text, but may also include nested elements. We use a simple language to indicate what kind of nested elements may occur, such as using the phrase "(s)" to indicate multiple elements. Table 5–3 lists the valid attributes for each element.

Table 5–2: XML Element Types for the Play Domain Language (Phase 1)

Element Type	Content	Meaning
play	title prop(s) scene(s)	A play has a title and any number of props and scenes
title	Data	Title of the play
prop	trait script	A Button prop has a trait that sets the label and a script that is executed when the button is clicked
trait	Data	The initial or new label of a Button prop. A trait can appear in either a prop element type (initial value) or a script element type (new value)
scene	addprop(s)	A scene contains any number of props
addprop	Empty	A prop in a scene
script	trait(s)	The action(s) to perform when an event occurs. The traits change the labels of Buttons

Table 5–3: XML Attributes for the Play Domain Language (Phase 1)

Element Type	Attribute Name	Default Value	Meaning
play	name	Required	The name of the play
	width	500	The default width of the play window
	height	250	The default height of the play window
	start	Required	A reference to a scene in the specification
prop	name	Required	The prop's name
trait	prop	The enclosing prop	The name of the prop that the trait belongs to
scene	name	Required	The scene's name
	color	#dddddd	The background color of the scene
addprop	name	Required	A reference to a prop in the specification
script	goto		A reference to a scene in the specification

A standard play example will be used in this and future chapters to demonstrate different program-generation techniques. The standard example, called the Jack and Jill play, has just a couple of scenes and four props. The fall prop is defined as

```
<prop name="fall">
        <trait>Fall down, break crown</trait>
        <script goto="bottom">
          <trait>Break crown</trait>
```

```
        <trait prop="tumble">Tumble after</trait>
      </script>
    </prop>
```

The first trait element means the initial label of the fall button is
"`Fall down, break crown.`" The fall prop also has a script that is
executed when the fall button is clicked. The script says to change the
label of the fall button to "`Break Crown`" and change the label of the
tumble button to "`Tumble after.`" Finally, the script says to leave the
current scene and go to the bottom scene. No scene change occurs if
there are no `goto` attributes.

The bottom scene is defined as

```
<scene name="bottom" color="#8888aa">
  <addprop name="up"/>
  <addprop name="fall"/>
</scene>
```

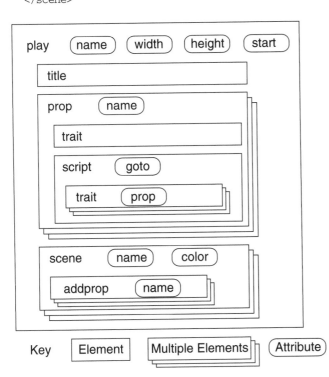

Figure 5–8   Structure of the play domain language (Phase 1)

This means the bottom scene has two props and a bluish background color.

The entire standard Jack and Jill play specification is given in Example 5–8. The second line declares a Play domain DTD that is described in Section 5.8.

Example 5–8: Standard Example Play Specification

```
<?xml version="1.0" standalone="no"?>
<!DOCTYPE play SYSTEM "file:play1.dtd">
<play name="JackAndJill" width="300" height="120" start="bottom">
  <title>Jack and Jill</title>

  <prop name="up">
    <trait>Go up the hill</trait>
    <script goto="top">
      <trait prop="fetch">Fetch a pail of water</trait>
    </script>
  </prop>

  <prop name="fetch">
    <trait>Fetch a pail of water</trait>
    <script><trait>Fetch another pail</trait></script>
  </prop>

  <prop name="fall">
    <trait>Fall down, break crown</trait>
    <script goto="bottom">
      <trait>Break crown</trait>
      <trait prop="tumble">Tumble after</trait>
    </script>
  </prop>

  <prop name="tumble">
    <trait>Tumble down</trait>
    <script goto="bottom"/>
  </prop>

  <scene name="bottom" color="#8888aa">
    <addprop name="up"/>
    <addprop name="fall"/>
  </scene>
```

```
<scene name="top">
   <addprop name="fetch"/>
   <addprop name="fall"/>
   <addprop name="tumble"/>
</scene>
</play>
```

To get a feeling for how this specification works in practice you can use Figure 5–9. It shows all six possible states of the play. Start with the state in the upper left corner. To click on a button, follow the arc departing from the button to the next state.

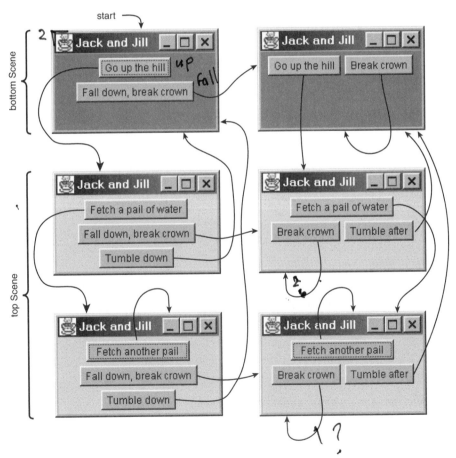

Figure 5–9 The complete set of states of the standard Jack and Jill play

5.8 | DTDs

In the previous section we provided an informal definition of the Play domain language using diagrams and tables (Tables 5–2 and 5–3) that list all the element types and attributes and their constraints. This information is called a *Document Type Definition* (DTD). A DTD can be specified formally using DTD declarations, but they are not required. An XML document is *well-formed* if it simply meets the syntactic constraints of XML. A *valid* XML document, however, is one that also meets the conditions imposed by a formally declared DTD. Many XML tools check for the validity of the XML document if there is such a DTD. Although we provide DTDs for the Play domain for completeness, a complete description of DTDs is beyond the scope of this book.[5]

DTD declarations include definitions for element types, attributes, and other items such as entities that are not used in this book. An element type declaration has the form:

```
<!ELEMENT element-type-name  spec>
```

where *element-type-name* is the name of the element type being defined and *spec* defines the content of the element. Attributes are declared using the form:

```
<!ATTLIST element-type-name  attr-name  type-decl  default>
```

Using these two kinds of declarations, we can create the formal description of the Play domain language shown in Example 5–9. The first line says that a `play` element consists of a `title` element followed by zero or more `prop` elements followed by zero or more `scene` elements. The second line says that the `title` element is character data.[6] The third line says that a `prop` contains any number of `trait` and `script` elements (in any order). Although for Phase 1 a prop is limited to a single trait (label) and script (mouse click), the DTD is more generous in anticipation of Phase 2.

---

[5]See Megginson's *Structuring XML Documents* in this series.

[6]PCDATA means data that has been parsed. For our purposes we only need to know that it represents character data without any nested XML elements.

Example 5-9: DTD for the Play Domain (Phase 1)

```
<!ELEMENT play (title, prop*, scene*)>
<!ELEMENT title (#PCDATA)>
<!ELEMENT prop (trait|script)*>
<!ELEMENT scene (addprop*)>
<!ELEMENT trait (#PCDATA)>
<!ELEMENT script (trait*)>
<!ELEMENT addprop EMPTY>

<!ATTLIST play width CDATA "500">
<!ATTLIST play height CDATA "250">
<!ATTLIST play name ID #REQUIRED>
<!ATTLIST play start IDREF #REQUIRED>

<!ATTLIST prop name ID #REQUIRED>
<!ATTLIST addprop name IDREF #REQUIRED>

<!ATTLIST trait name CDATA "Label">
<!ATTLIST trait prop IDREF #IMPLIED>

<!ATTLIST scene name ID #REQUIRED>
<!ATTLIST scene color CDATA "#dddddd">
<!ATTLIST script goto IDREF #IMPLIED>
```

Alternatives to DTD declarations include the XML Schema Definition Language (XSDL). An XSDL schema definition has a number of areas of potential improvement over DTD declarations. The areas most important to the subject of this book include the following:

- XSDL schema definitions use XML to represent the DTD. Consequently, this information is available for processing by XML tools. In particular, one could generate programs more easily from XSDL schema definitions than from DTD declarations.

- XML Schema datatypes can be used to constrain the character data in an element's content or attribute values.[7] For example, the data can be restricted to numbers, dates, URLs, and user-defined datatypes.

---

[7]Datatypes can also be used with DTD declarations, see *The XML Handbook* in this series.

5.9 | XML Tools

XML is designed to be accessible and usable by ordinary text editors and character-processing tools. However, XML-aware tools can be used to increase productivity. The world of XML and XML tools is rapidly developing and evolving, so for more information you should look to the Web for the current status. For the here and now, here is a brief survey of tool categories and examples.

5.9.1   *XML Viewers*

The easiest way to view the content of an XML file is to use any ordinary text viewer or editor. XML files are plain text files designed to be human readable. If the element-type names were well chosen, it should be easy for most people to directly interpret the structure and meaning of the different elements of the file.

However, using only text editors for viewing XML data is like reading HTML files directly instead of using a Web browser. Instead of using tags to identify the structure, other means can be used to display the data, including the full range of HTML capabilities. The structure of the document can be made more visual and the full range of formatting options such as fonts, colors, and layout can be used to create a powerful presentation of the data. Tables can be used where appropriate, and implicit relations can be made visible. Sorting and other rearrangements of the data can be used to create a page that is easy to navigate. Other data analysis could be used to create useful information about the data that would be difficult and in some cases nearly impossible to determine by looking at the XML file.

The accompanying figure shows a rendering of the data in Example 5–8. Figure 5–10 is a fairly straightforward view of the data without a lot of enhancement. Keep in mind that these Web pages are automatically generated from the original XML files. Thus the presentation is always up to date and is applicable to any XML file in the Play domain.

Where does the conversion from XML to HTML take place? There are two possibilities (Figure 5–11):

> Client-side conversion directly in the Web browser. The browser reads the XML and rules for rendering the XML as HTML. Unfortunately, older browsers do not have this capability.

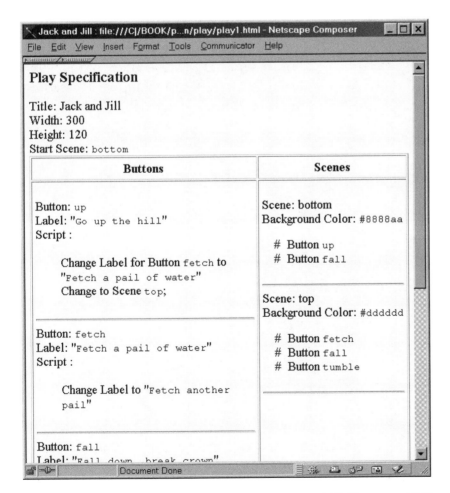

Figure 5–10 A simple rendering of the Jack and Jill Play using XML

Server-side conversion in conjunction with the Web server. When a request is made for a document, the Web server can do the conversion and return the HTML file, thus avoiding any need for XML-aware browsers.

There are many ways to render XML as HTML. One such method is the use of Extensible Stylesheet Language (XSL). XSL includes both transformations and formatting. An XSL file, which itself is an XML file, is used to specify how to translate the bits and pieces of another XML file to HTML (or to an XML language).

Although the most logical and likely way to present XML files is by using XSL-like techniques and HTML, we are by no means limited to these. We can use other rendition techniques (cascading style sheets [CSS]) and other presentation languages (such as Adobe's PDF).

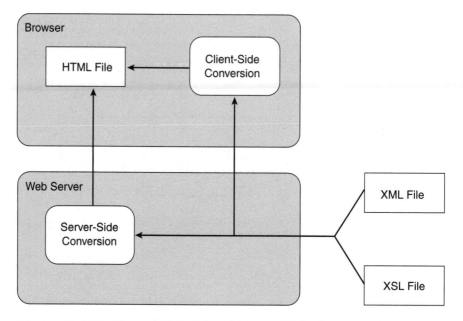

Figure 5–11   Two methods for converting XML files to HTML

5.9.2   *XML Editors*

Editing old or composing new XML files is most simply done using text editors. But just as people use sophisticated tools for composing Web pages, editors that reveal the structure of the data without the tags can be used easily and naturally to add, edit, and remove elements that preserve well-formed and valid XML. Flexible generic XML editors can be customized for each domain-specific language by providing editing rules for each element type. Customization could include such things as automatic indentation, colored elements, editable attributes in popup menus, or property/style sheets that you might find in a standard development environment.

5.9.3   *XML Conversion Tools*

XML data can be transformed to other XML files, plain text files, or other files for input to other tools. Generic transformation tools with an input file that describes the transformation rules can be used to generate output limited only by one's imagination. In this book we focus on generating Java programs. But by no means should you limit your thoughts to just programs. Other possible outputs include:

> **Documentation for developers**: Tools can generate graphs, charts, manual pages, and Web pages focusing on system structures.

> **Documentation for end users**: Tools can generate documentation describing a system including a list of all scenes and props, their interconnections and probably other information as well (see below).

Testing tools: Tools can generate input test files for regression test suites ensuring coverage of all system elements. Test stubs and drivers can also be generated for all relevant system components. White box test scripts can be generated.

Scenarios: Tools can generate a range of scenarios for a variety of purposes (documentation, testing, …). Such scenarios would describe a series of events to navigate through the software. Such events could be user interface actions or other system actions such as timers and external interfaces.

Modeling tools: Tools can generate a complete simulation and modeling environment based on a particular specification. Performance modeling can provide detailed information about the anticipated behavior of the system.

Interfaces: Tools can generate the required interfaces to other systems by creating the configuration files, code, or language files.

For some of these other outputs you will find that additional information is required (Figure 5–12). For example, user documentation will normally need additional descriptive information about the props and scenes. This information can be easily added to an XML file by creating new element types (or attributes). For example, a new element type, called userdoc, can be added to the Play XML. This information could be accessed when creating user documentation and ignored by most other tools.

5.10 | Play Domain Phase 2

Phase 2 of the Play domain significantly extends the range of props, traits, events, and scripts. To fully appreciate these exten-

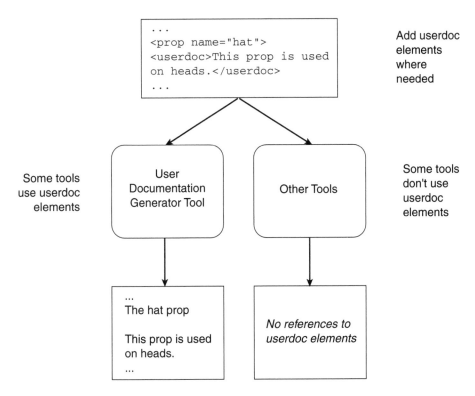

Figure 5–12 Adding new information for new tools

sions, we'll look at some simple examples. The most significant change is that props can now be any JavaBean Component. Example 5–10 defines a TextField prop for entering your name. The `TextField` JavaBean is a Java `Component` that displays a text field where someone can enter text data. The `TextField` Bean has a property, called `text`, which holds the current value of the data in the text field; therefore the prop has a trait by the same name. The `TextField` Bean also generates action events when the Return key is pressed. In Example 5–10, there is a script (using the default action event) that will be executed whenever the Return key is pressed. The script sends the user to a new scene.

Example 5–10: A Phase 2 Prop Example

```
...
<prop name="name" type="TextField">
  <trait name="text">Enter your name here</trait>
  <script goto="WelcomeScene"/>
</prop>

...
```

In Example 5–11, mouse events are used to control the image displayed on a button. A new JavaBean component with a `String` property, `image`, specifies what image to use for the button. Two scripts are defined that change this image when the mouse enters or exits the image button prop.

Example 5–11: A Phase 2 Mouse Events Example

```
...
<prop name="gotoCave" type="ImageButton">
  <trait name="image">CaveEntrance.gif</trait>
  <script event="Mouse" method="mouseEntered">
    <trait name="image">LightedCaveEntrance.gif</trait>
  </script>
  <script event="Mouse" method="mouseExited">
    <trait name="image">CaveEntrance.gif</trait>
  </script>
  <script goto="caveScene"/>
</prop>

...
```

Example 5–11 shows a feature that is commonly used, so it makes sense to provide a new trait that implements this feature directly. We do this in Example 5–12, where a `mouseOverImage` trait is used to specify the image to display when the mouse is over a button prop.

Example 5–12: A Phase 2 Example with mouseOverImage **Trait**

```
...
<prop name="gotoCave" type="ImageButton">
  <trait name="image">CaveEntrance.gif</trait>
  <trait name="mouseOverImage">LightedCaveEntrance.gif</trait>
  <script goto="caveScene"/>
</prop>

...
```

The last Phase 2 example (Example 5–13) shows a scene with a single prop. A special event called `enterScene` is provided in Phase 2 to allow the execution of a script upon entering a scene. In the example, the script has an escape to Java code, which is used to play an audio file. This example also shows how props may override scripts to provide scene-specific scripts. In the example, the `action` event will also alter the `gotoCave` image trait (in addition to going to a new scene).

Example 5–13: A Phase 2 Scene Example

```
...
<scene name="streamScene">
  <addProp name="gotoCave">
    <script event="enterScene">
      <code>Audio.play("riverSounds.au");</code>
    </script>
    <script goto="caveScene">
      <trait prop="gotoCave" name="image">NewCaveEntrance.gif</trait>
    </script>
  </addprop>
</scene>

...
```

The Play domain Phase 1 is used as the basis for examples in Chapters 6 through 12. To fully understand the concepts, extend the examples to one or more features of Phase 2. Source code for all Phase 1 examples is available at `http://craigc.com`. The Play domain Phase 2 XML tables and DTD are given in Tables 5–4 and 5–5 and Example 5–14.

Table 5–4: XML Element Types for the Play Domain Language (Phase 2)

Element Type	Content	Meaning
play	title, prop*, scene*	A play has a title, and any number of props and scenes
title	Data	Title of the play

(continued)

Table 5–4: XML Element Types for the Play Domain Language (Phase 2) *(Continued)*

Element Type	Content	Meaning
prop	(trait| code| script)*	A prop may describe any number of traits, scripts and initialization code (only Button props in Phase 1)
trait	Data	The value of the trait (only the Label trait in Phase 1)
scene	addprop*	A scene contains any number of props
addprop	script*	A prop in a scene with additional scene-specific scripts
script	(trait|code)*	The action(s) to perform when an event occurs (only the Action event in Phase 1)
code	Data	Escape to underlying implementation language (Phase 2 only).

Table 5–5: XML Attributes for the Play Domain Language (Phase 2)

Element Type	Attribute Name	Default Value	Meaning
play	name	Required	The name of the play
	width	500	The default width of the play window
	height	250	The default height of the play window
	start	Required	A reference to a scene in the specification
prop	name	Required	The prop's name
	type	Button	The type of the prop (Phase I only supports the Button)

(continued)

Table 5–5: XML Attributes for the Play Domain Language (Phase 2) *(Continued)*

Element Type	Attribute Name	Default Value	Meaning
trait	name	label	The trait's name
	prop		The name of the prop that the trait belongs to
	type	String	The type of the trait's value, including "code" allowing an escape to a Java expression that computes the value at run-time.
scene	name	Required	The scene's name
	color	#dddddd	The background color of the scene
addprop	name	Required	A reference to a prop in the specification
script tion	goto		A reference to a scene in the specifica-
	event	Action-Event	The name of an event (phase 2)
	method	action-Performed	The method invoked when the event occurs (phase 2)
code	language	Java	The underlying implementation language

The DTD for Phase 2 requires some additional rules and changes, but has nothing conceptually new about it.

Example 5–14: DTD for the Play Domain (Phase 2)

```
<!ELEMENT play (title, prop*, scene*)>
<!ELEMENT title (#PCDATA)>
<!ELEMENT prop (trait|code|script)*>
<!ELEMENT scene (addprop*)>
<!ELEMENT trait (#PCDATA|string|color|code)*>
```

```
<!ELEMENT script (code|trait)*>
<!ELEMENT code (#PCDATA)>
<!ELEMENT addprop (script*)>
<!ELEMENT color (#PCDATA)>
<!ELEMENT string (#PCDATA)>

<!ATTLIST play width CDATA "500">
<!ATTLIST play height CDATA "250">
<!ATTLIST play name ID #REQUIRED>
<!ATTLIST play start IDREF #REQUIRED>

<!ATTLIST prop name ID #REQUIRED>
<!ATTLIST prop type CDATA "Button">

<!ATTLIST addprop name IDREF #REQUIRED>

<!ATTLIST trait name CDATA "Label">
<!ATTLIST trait prop IDREF #IMPLIED>

<!ATTLIST scene name ID #REQUIRED>
<!ATTLIST scene color CDATA "#dddddd">

<!ATTLIST script goto IDREF #IMPLIED>
<!ATTLIST script event CDATA "ActionEvent">
<!ATTLIST script method CDATA "actionPerformed">

<!ATTLIST code language CDATA "Java">
```

5.11 | Summary

XML is a standard language for representing information. Although it is used primarily in the context of Internet applications and communications, it can also be used for expressing the specification input to a program generator. The essence of XML is the separation of abstract content from presentation. In the context of program generators it is used to separate "what" application you want from the software that implements the program.

XML has elements and attributes. In adapting a set of variabilities to XML, one must decide whether and how to use attributes for what pieces of information. There is no clear-cut method for making these decisions, but this chapter provides some general guidelines for making such decisions. The chapter explains and defines an XML document type for the Play domain.

A major advantage of using XML is the range of XML tools that can be applied. These include viewers, editors, and translators.

Further Reading

Bob DuCharme, *XML Annotated Specification*, Prentice Hall, 1999.

Charles F. Goldfarb and Paul Prescod, *The XML Handbook*, Prentice Hall, 2001.

David Megginson, *Structuring XML Documents*, Prentice Hall, 1998.

Run-Time Variabilities

- Java Property files
- Using XML files

Run-time variabilities are decisions made at run time. Therefore, such decisions cannot be determined at either generation time or compile time and must be part of the program. In this chapter we will see how run-time variabilities are implemented using run-time mechanisms. One of the mechanisms will include reading XML files at run time. In Chapter 9 we will also read XML files, but at generation time rather than run time.[1] Run-time variabilities can be represented and controlled in a number of ways, including the following:

- **Resource or configuration files**: Files contain the information and are read in during run time. Typically these files use the prevailing standard configuration file form in their operating environment.

---

[1] This parallels the use of the loadWords method of Chapter 1.

- **Databases**: Queries to databases are another typical way of obtaining information at run time. Databases also provide the most convenient platform for storing changes to run-time information.

- **User Interfaces**: In some cases, run-time decisions are made while interacting with a user. For example, a user might select the font and colors of the user interface.

- **Dynamically Loaded Classes**: In some cases, very general behavior can be determined, created, compiled, and loaded directly into a running Java program.

In this chapter we will explore two forms of configuration files: Java property files and XML.

6.1 | Java Property Files

Most run-time variabilities are fairly simple data types consisting mostly of numbers and strings. In these cases, very simple files containing these values can be read at run time. Such files are often called *resource files* or *configuration files*.

Java property files are nearly ideal candidates for resource files. The Java type `Properties` (in `java.util`) is a class that can be used to represent a set of *properties*. A property has a name and a value, both of which are ordinary `String` values. Methods include adding, changing, or removing properties, and loading and saving properties to a file.

The Properties built-in file format includes comment lines (lines beginning with #) and uses escape-character sequences for new lines, tabs, and other unusual characters. Blank lines are ignored. Each remaining line represents a single property and uses an equal sign to separate the property name from the property value (Figure 6–1).

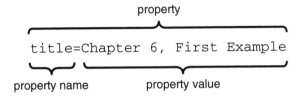

Figure 6–1 Syntax of a property in a property file

As an example, consider the simple configuration file in Example 6–1.

Example 6–1: Simple Configuration File, myconfig.txt

```
# example config file
title=Chapter 6, First Example
label=Here's a sample button ...
foreground=#220000
background=#ffffdd
width=300
height=120
```

An extension of the Property class provides a cleaner and more useful class for our purposes, which we will call `Config` (Example 6–2). The Config class is used to load a configuration file and easily obtain values. The `get` method is preferred over the Properties `getProperty` method because it will always return a value (possibly a default value), thus avoiding excessive code (checking for null values).

Example 6–2: Config.java

```
class Config extends Properties {

    public Config(String fname) {
        loadFile(fname);
    }

    public  String get(String key, String defaultValue) {
        String r = getProperty(key);
        if (r==null || r.equals(""))
            return defaultValue;
        return r;
    }
```

```java
    public String get(String key) {
        String r = getProperty(key);
        if (r==null)
            return "";
        return r;
    }

    public boolean loadFile(String filename) {
        FileInputStream f = null;
        try {
            f = new FileInputStream(filename);
            load(f);
            f.close();
        } catch (Exception e) {
            error("Unable to load file "+filename+" "+e.getMessage());
            return false;
        }
        return true;
    }

    /** Gets all keys with a given prefix and suffix */
    public Vector getKeys(String prefix, String suffix) {
        Vector r = new Vector();
        Enumeration e = propertyNames();
        while (e.hasMoreElements()) {
            String key = (String) e.nextElement();
            if (prefix!=null && !key.startsWith(prefix))
                continue;
            if (suffix!=null && !key.endsWith(suffix))
                continue;
            r.addElement(key);
        }
        return r;
    }

    /** Get value as a list of strings (separated by white space) */
    public String[] getList(String key) {
        return parseList(getProperty(key));
    }

    int getInt(String key, int defaultValue) {
        return parseInt(get(key), defaultValue);
    }

    /** Get integer list */
    int[] getIntList(String key) {
        String[] d = getList(key);
        int[] r = new int[d.length];
```

```
        for (int j=0; j<d.length; ++j) {
            r[j] = parseInt(d[j], 1);
        }
        return r;
    }

    // more
}
```

An example program that uses this configuration file to create a simple graphical window (Figure 6–2) is shown in Example 6–3.

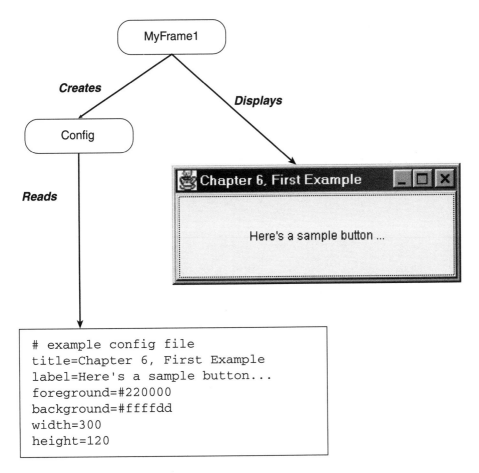

Figure 6–2   Executing MyFrame1

Example 6–3: MyFrame1.java

```java
package com.craigc.progen;
import java.awt.*;

class MyFrame1 extends Frame {

    public MyFrame1(Config c) {
        super(c.get("title", "MyFrame1 Example"));
        Button myButton = new Button(c.get("label", "exit"));
        myButton.setBackground(Color.decode(
            c.get("background", "#000000")));
        myButton.setForeground(Color.decode(
            c.get("foreground", "#ffffff")));
        add(myButton);
        setSize(c.getInt("width", 100), c.getInt("height", 100));
        show();
    }

    public static void main(String args[]) {
        if (args.length>0) {
            Config c = new Config(args[0]);
            new MyFrame1(c);
        } else {
            System.out.println("No config file specified");
        }
    }
}
```

The main method is invoked with the name of the configuration file, which is passed to create an instance of `Config`. Whenever a run-time variability is needed, this configuration file is consulted, using phrases such as:

```java
c.get("title", "MyFrame1 Example")
```

The first parameter is the property name and the second parameter (if any) is the default value if this property is not found in the configuration file. Since the get method always returns a non-null value, almost no additional complexity is added to the code. Many mystery constants are easily replaced with get method calls to convert a program to one that is easily customized with a configuration file. Note that not all mystery constants have been removed. In particular, default values have been introduced and scattered throughout the program.

Configuration files are a simple first step to creating easily customizable programs. Let's now explore some of the next steps to fully featured run-time variables.

6.1.1 *Lists*

After numbers and strings, the next most popular kind of data is lists of numbers or strings. Lists can be represented in several ways in a configuration file. Lists of numbers and identifiers can be represented in a compact single definition as shown in Example 6–4.

Example 6–4: Simple Lists in a Single Definition

```
scores=34 56 78 78 96
names=john paul george ringo
```

Accessing simple lists is easy with another built-in method in the `Config` class, "`getList`", which returns an array of the list values, as in:

```
String[] names = c.getList("names");
```

Lists that are not easily separated by characters (such as blanks) can still be created in configuration files by using multiple definitions. Example 6–5 shows how a list of titles can be represented.

Example 6–5: Lists Using Multiple Definitions

```
title1=The End of History
title2=Life as We Know It
title3=The Beatles: The Life and Times of the Famous Quartet
```

6.1.2 *Hierarchical Data*

Information is typically easiest to organize and manage as a hierarchy. Hierarchical information can be easily represented in a configuration file by using the property names. Each level of the hierarchy is represented by a new set of property names, and each level of the hierarchy is separated from other levels with a period. Example 6–6 shows a configuration file with a hierarchy of information about buttons.

Example 6–6: myconfig2.txt Shows a Set of Buttons

```
# example config file
title=Chapter 6, Second Example
buttons=one two three

one.label=here's the first sample label ...
one.foreground=#002200
one.background=#ddffff

two.label=Button Two
two.foreground=#220000
two.background=#ffffdd

three.label=Third button
three.foreground=#000022
three.background=#ffddff

height=120
width=300
```

A `Config` method that is useful for selecting sets of property names is getKeys(*prefix, suffix*). The getKeys method will return a Vector of property names that match the *prefix* and *suffix* passed as parameters. Thus to select all label property names, one can use getKeys("",".label"), and to select all information about the three label, one can use getKeys("three. ", "").

A slightly modified example of the MyFrame class illustrates both lists and hierarchical data (Figure 6–3). We'll simply specify an arbitrary set of buttons rather than one. A new property, "buttons", will name the buttons, and the button properties will be prefixed with the button name. See Example 6–7.

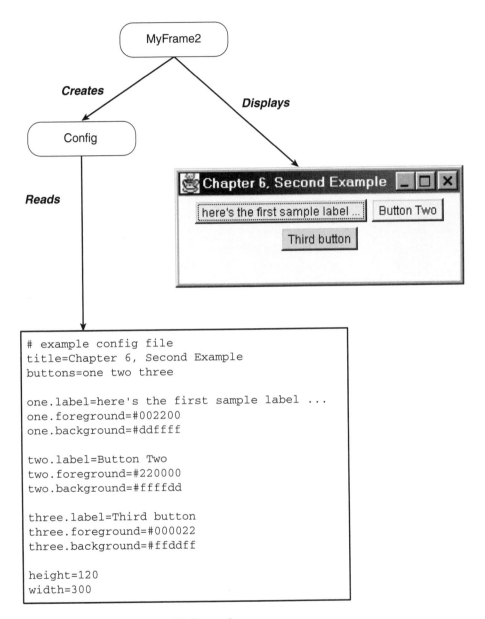

```
# example config file
title=Chapter 6, Second Example
buttons=one two three

one.label=here's the first sample label ...
one.foreground=#002200
one.background=#ddffff

two.label=Button Two
two.foreground=#220000
two.background=#ffffdd

three.label=Third button
three.foreground=#000022
three.background=#ffddff

height=120
width=300
```

Figure 6–3   Executing MyFrame2

Example 6–7: MyFrame2.java

```java
import java.awt.*;

/**
 * Chapter 6 Example illustrating hierarchy and lists.
 */
class MyFrame2 extends Frame {

    public MyFrame2(Config c) {
        super(c.get("title", "MyFrame Example"));
        String[] buttons = c.getList("buttons");
        setLayout(new FlowLayout());
        for (int j=0; j<buttons.length; ++j) {
            Button b = new Button(c.get(buttons[j]+".label", "?"));
            b.setBackground(Color.decode(
                c.get(buttons[j]+".background", "#000000")));
            b.setForeground(Color.decode(
                c.get(buttons[j]+".foreground", "#ffffff")));
            add(b);
        }
        setSize(c.getInt("width", 100), c.getInt("height", 100));
        show();
    }

    public static void main(String args[]) {
        if (args.length>0) {
            Config c = new Config(args[0]);
            new MyFrame2(c);
        } else {
            System.out.println("No config file specified");
        }
    }
}
```

6.1.3 Persistence

In some situations, a program may wish to alter some of the information in the configuration file so that it can remember things from one program instantiation to another. This is called persistent information. Since configuration files are based on the built-in Java class Properties, which has a method for saving property files, it is very simple to do. However, writing out configuration files using this method has two major disadvantages:

1. Comments in the original configuration file are lost. In addition, blank lines are removed.

2. The order of the property names is arbitrary. Any organization of properties will be lost.

If a Java program were to write out the configuration file in Example 6–6, the resulting file would be disorganized and comments would be lost, as shown in Example 6–8.

Example 6–8: myconfig2.txt as Saved by the Property Class

```
#Config
#Tue Jan 25 19:40:12 EST 2000
width=300
height=120
three.label=Third button
three.background=#ffddff
two.background=#ffffdd
one.background=#ddffff
title=Chapter 6, Second Example
two.foreground=#220000
one.foreground=#002200
two.label=Button Two
one.label=here's the first sample label ...
buttons=one two three
three.foreground=#000022
```

There's nothing easy you can do to fix this annoyance. You can rewrite the Property class to preserve the original organization of the file, but this will be difficult if the program adds and removes properties. You can divide up your properties into persistent and nonpersistent ones, so that at least the nonpersistent ones won't have this problem. Or you can use an alternative storage mechanism, such as a database, or some other language, such as XML (see Section 6.2).

6.1.4 *Dynamic Behavior*

Sometimes the information we'd like to encode is not easily specified in a simple string or number. For example, selecting the behavior for a specific button in a GUI can be as arbitrary as the underlying code permits. If the behavior is limited or restricted, one can devise a representation and build that into the code. Using the underlying implementation language to express the behavior is not always possible. In some languages without dynamic loading or compilation, it is nearly impossible to make arbitrary actions a run-time variability. Since the Java language allows dynamic loading, one can load new arbitrary behavior at run time.

Let's say one wants to express the behavior of a GUI button using Java code, one could add some code to a configuration file (Example 6–9):

Example 6–9: Dynamic Behavior as a Run-Time Variability

```
# action defines what to do when a button is clicked
two.action=System.out.println("I've been clicked!");
```

The program can take this chunk of code, generate a program with the code segment, compile the program, and dynamically load in the class file and attach it to the event listener for the GUI button. Although this is indirect, awkward, and somewhat inefficient, in some situations it can be useful.

6.2 | XML as a Configuration File

An alternative to Java property files is XML. Although XML is more complex than property files, XML has considerable advantages. It is a standard. Many other tools and systems can take advantage of the information in the XML files. In particular, XML-based editors make it easy to view and edit the data. See Chapter 5 for more information about XML.

Example 6–10 shows an example XML document using the same information found in the configuration file of Example 6–6.

Example 6–10: XML Configuration File

```
<?xml version="1.0"?>

<myconfig>
<title>Chapter 6, Third Example</title>
<buttons>one two three</buttons>

<button>
<name>one</name>
<label>here's the first sample label ...</label>
<foreground>#002200</foreground>
<background>#ddffff</background>
</button>

<button>
<name>two</name>
<label>Button Two</label>
<foreground>#220000</foreground>
<background>#ffffdd</background>
</button>

<button>
<name>three</name>
<label>Third button</label>
<foreground>#000022</foreground>
<background>#ffddff</background>
</button>

<width>300</width>
<height>120</height>

</myconfig>
```

Just as the `Config` class was created to make configuration files easier to use for our purposes, a Java class, called `Document`, will be used to read and store the information from an XML file. Except for this change, the structure of `MyFrame3` is identical to the previous two examples (Figure 6–4).

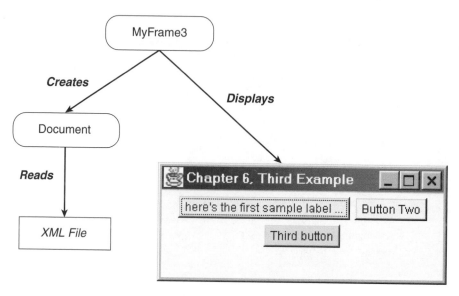

Figure 6–4   Executing MyFrame3

Unlike `Config`, the `Document` class is a standard class in the popular *Document Object Model* (DOM). Chapter 9 describes DOM in more detail, so in this chapter we will just identify a few methods that are needed for our purposes. Although the program in Example 6–11 looks a lot more complex than the two previous examples, most of the complexity is simply using the `Document` class.

- Instead of `getKeys` for retrieving a list, the `getElementsByTagName` is used. This method returns a `NodeList` of all nodes with a given element type name.

- The `get` and `getInt` methods from the `DOM_Util` class are used to retrieve specific value information from the XML document and are not further described here. Chapter 9 will discuss `DOM_Util` in more detail.

Example 6–11: MyFrame3.java

```java
import org.w3c.dom.*;
import java.awt.*;

/**
 * Chapter 6 Example using XML configuration file.
 */
class MyFrame3 extends Frame {

    public MyFrame3(Document c) {
        super(DOM_Util.get(c, "title", "MyFrame3 Example"));
        setLayout(new FlowLayout());
        NodeList blist = c.getElementsByTagName("button");
        for (int j=0; j<blist.getLength(); ++j) {
            Node bnode = blist.item(j);
            Button but = new Button(DOM_Util.get(bnode, "label", "?"));
            but.setBackground(Color.decode(
                DOM_Util.get(bnode, "background", "#000000")));
            but.setForeground(Color.decode(
                DOM_Util.get(bnode, "foreground", "#ffffff")));
            add(but);
        }
        setSize(DOM_Util.getInt(c, "width", 100),
                DOM_Util.getInt(c, "height", 100));
        show();
    }

    public static void main(String args[]) {
        if (args.length>0) {
            try {
                Document c = DOM_Util.readDocument(args[0]);
                new MyFrame3(c);
            } catch (Exception e) {
                System.out.println("Invalid config file: "+args[0]);
            }
        } else {
            System.out.println("No config file specified");
        }
    }
}
```

6.3 | The Play Domain with Run-Time Variabilities

The Play domain analysis was created to show off program-generation techniques and thus has many generation-time variabilities. But what if these were all run-time variabilities? How would we write the program differently?

The basic approach is a straightforward expansion of `MyFrame3` from the previous section. The configuration file will be XML and we'll use the language we defined for the Play domain in Chapter 5. Note that only Phase 1 will be considered. Phase 1 has no escapes to the Java language, so it is easy to read and act on all the XML data. Phase 2 would be more complex because of the escapes and the use of JavaBeans for Props.

The most straightforward approach is to read in an XML document and work directly from the XML data structures. For a simple example such as the Play domain, this approach works fine. However, we will use a different design that will work better for anything much more complicated than the Play domain. The approach is to create a new object, called `PlayData1`, which represents the Play domain data directly and simply. The play program will operate on the `PlayData1` object rather than the XML object. The chief disadvantage of this approach is the extra work required for defining and populating the `PlayData1` object. The primary advantage is that it makes the Play program itself simpler and easy to understand. A second advantage is that it provides an essential abstraction layer between the Play program and the data source. We can use non-XML data sources to populate `PlayData1` without having to change the Play program. It's also an excellent example of separation of concerns—namely, the separation between where the data comes from and what we do with the data (see Figure 6–5).

The `PlayData1` object represents the variabilities of Phase 1 of the Play domain analysis in a straightforward approach, as shown in Example 6–12. The XML details and conversion are saved until Chapter 9.

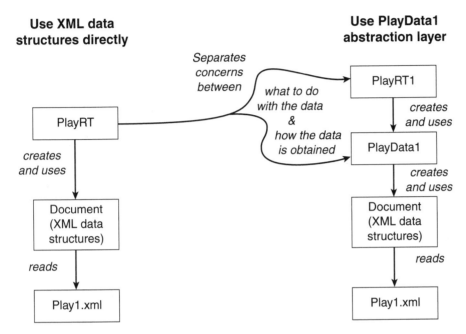

Figure 6–5   Two approaches to designing PlayRT (Run Time)

Example 6–12: PlayData1.java

```java
import org.w3c.dom.*;

class PlayData1 {
    public String name;
    public String title;
    public int width;
    public int height;
    public SceneData startScene;

    public PropData[] props;
    public SceneData[] scenes;

    public class PropData {
        public String name;
        public String label;     // initial value
        public ScriptData script; // only action script in Phase I
    }

    class SceneData {
        public String name;
        public String color;
```

```
        public PropData[] addprops;
    }

    class ScriptData {
        public SceneData nextScene;
        public TraitData[] traits;
    }

    class TraitData {
        public PropData prop;
        public String newValue;
    }

    public PlayData1(Document d) {
        convertDocument(d);
    }

    /** Convert XML data to PlayData1 */
    public void convertDocument(Document d) {
```
        details in Chapter 9
```
    }
}
```

The Play program, called PlayRT1, can now be written using the PlayData1 object rather than XML data structures, as shown in Example 6–13 and Figure 6–6. This program produces the behavior illustrated in Figure 5–9.

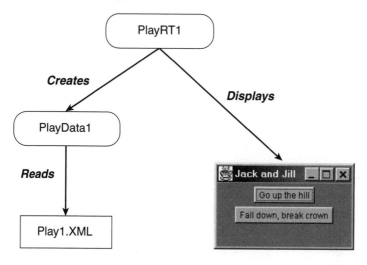

Figure 6–6 Executing PlayRT1

Example 6–13: PlayRT.java

```java
import org.w3c.dom.*;
import java.awt.*;
import java.awt.event.*;
import java.util.*;

/**
 * Play Domain with all Run-time variabilities using PlayData1
 */
class PlayRT1 extends Frame implements ActionListener {
    Hashtable prop2button = new Hashtable();// props to buttons
    Hashtable button2prop = new Hashtable();// buttons to props
    PlayData1 pd; // the internal representation of the Play Data

    /** Create and display a play based on PlayData1 */
    public PlayRT1(PlayData1 pd) {
        super(pd.title);
        this.pd = pd;
        setLayout(new FlowLayout());

        // create buttons and hash tables
        for (int j=0; j<pd.props.length; ++j) {
            PlayData1.PropData p = pd.props[j];
            Button b = new Button(p.label);
            b.addActionListener(this);
            prop2button.put(p, b);
            button2prop.put(b, p);
        }
        setSize(pd.width, pd.height);
        enterNewScene(pd.startScene);
        show();
    }

    /** Exit scene and enter a new one */
    void enterNewScene(PlayData1.SceneData scene) {
        removeAll();
        setBackground(Color.decode(scene.color));
        for (int j=0; j<scene.addprops.length; ++j) {
            Button b = (Button) prop2button.get(scene.addprops[j]);
            if (b!=null) {
                add(b);
            } else {
                error("No button for "+scene.addprops[j].name);
            }
        }
    }
```

```java
        show();
    }

    /** perform action when button is clicked */
    public void actionPerformed(ActionEvent e) {
        PlayData1.PropData p = (PlayData1.PropData)
                    button2prop.get(e.getSource());
        if (p==null) {
            error("No prop named "+e.getSource());
            return;
        }
        if (p.script==null) {
            return;
        }
        for (int j=0; j<p.script.traits.length; ++j) {
            PlayData1.TraitData td = p.script.traits[j];
            Button b = (Button) prop2button.get(td.prop);
            b.setLabel(td.newValue);
        }
        if (p.script.nextScene!=null) {
            enterNewScene(p.script.nextScene);
        }
    }

    static void error(String msg) {
        System.out.println("Error: "+msg);
    }

    public static void main(String args[]) {
        if (args.length>0) {
            try {
                // Read XML document
                Document c = DOM_Util.readDocument(args[0]);
                // Convert XML to PlayData1
                PlayData1 pd = new PlayData1(c);
                // Execute program
                new PlayRT1(pd);
            } catch (Exception e) {
                error("Invalid config file: "+args[0]);
            }
        } else {
            error("No config file specified");
        }
    }
}
```

To contrast the `PlayData1` approach with the more straightforward approach of using XML data structures, Example 6–14 shows the alternative `PlayRT` program that works directly from the XML data structures. Although it is just one object instead of two, the mixing of concerns makes it a more difficult program to maintain.[2]

Example 6–14: PlayRT.java, a Program Working Directly from XML Data Structures

```
package com.craigc.progen;
import org.w3c.dom.*;
import java.awt.*;
import java.awt.event.*;
import java.util.*;

/**
 * Play Domain with all Run-time variabilities, Phase I
 */
class PlayRT extends Frame implements ActionListener {
    Hashtable name2button = new Hashtable();// prop names to buttons
    Hashtable button2name = new Hashtable();// buttons to prop names
    Hashtable name2prop = new Hashtable();  // prop names to prop nodes
    Document doc; // the internal representation of the XML document

    public PlayRT(Document c) {
        super(DOM_Util.get(c, "title", "Play Example"));
        doc = c;
        setLayout(new FlowLayout());
        Node playNode = c.getDocumentElement();

        // initialize props and hash tables
        NodeList e = c.getElementsByTagName("prop");
        for (int j=0; j<e.getLength(); ++j) {
            Node bnode = e.item(j);
            String name = DOM_Util.getAttr(bnode, "name", "?");
            name2prop.put(name, bnode);
            Button b = new Button();
            setupProp(b, bnode);
```

---

[2]Maintenance is more difficult for a variety of reasons. A change to either the program being generated or to the XML structure may require understanding both parts even though only one aspect is being changed.

```
            b.addActionListener(this);
            name2button.put(name, b);
            button2name.put(b, name);
        }
        setSize(DOM_Util.getIntAttr(playNode, "width", 500),
                DOM_Util.getIntAttr(playNode, "height", 250));
        enterNewScene(DOM_Util.getAttr(playNode, "start", "?"));
        show();
    }

    void enterNewScene(String sceneName) {
        removeAll();
        NodeList e = doc.getElementsByTagName("scene");
        for (int j=0; j<e.getLength(); ++j) {
            Element snode = (Element) e.item(j);
            String name = DOM_Util.getAttr(snode, "name", "");
            if (name.equals(sceneName)) {
                // found the right scene, now add the props
                setBackground(Color.decode(DOM_Util.getAttr(snode,
                                              "color", "#ff0000")));
                NodeList e2 = snode.getElementsByTagName("addprop");
                for (int j2=0; j2<e2.getLength(); ++j2) {
                    Node pnode = e2.item(j2);
                    String pname = DOM_Util.getAttr(pnode, "name", "");
                    Button b = (Button) name2button.get(pname);
                    if (b!=null) {
                        add(b);
                    } else {
                        error("No prop named "+pname);
                    }
                }
                show();
                return;
            }
        }
    }

    /** perform action when button is clicked */
    public void actionPerformed(ActionEvent e) {
        String pname = (String) button2name.get(e.getSource());
        if (pname==null || pname.equals("")) {
            error("Invalid button prop");
            return;
        }
        Node bnode = (Node) name2prop.get(pname);
        if (bnode==null) {
```

```java
            error("No prop named "+pname);
            return;
        }
    NodeList e2 = ((Element)bnode).getElementsByTagName("script");
    // there should only be one action script for a prop
    for (int j=0; j<e2.getLength(); ++j) {
        Node snode = e2.item(j);
        // in phase 1, all scripts are Action scripts
        setupProp((Button)name2button.get(pname), snode);
        String nextScene = DOM_Util.getAttr(snode, "goto", "");
        if (nextScene!=null && !nextScene.equals("")) {
            enterNewScene(nextScene);
        }
        return; // only execute first script
    }
}


void setupProp(Button b, Node bnode) {
    // can't use getElementsByTagName here since there are nested
    // trait elements in script elements that shouldn't be used.
    for (Node n = bnode.getFirstChild(); n!=null;
                                    n = n.getNextSibling()) {
        if (n instanceof Element) {
            if (n.getNodeName().equals("trait") &&
              DOM_Util.getAttr(n, "name", "?").equals("Label")) {
                String pname = DOM_Util.getAttr(n, "prop", "");
                if (pname!=null && !pname.equals("")) {
                    b = (Button) name2button.get(pname);
                }
                if (b!=null) {
                    b.setLabel(DOM_Util.getContent(n));
                } else {
                    error("Configuration error");
                }
            } // ignore all other traits since this is only Phase 1
        }
    }
}


static void error(String msg) {
    System.out.println("Error: "+msg);
}

public static void main(String args[]) {
```

```
        if (args.length>0) {
            try {
                // read XML file and start up display
                Document c = DOM_Util.readDocument(args[0]);
                new PlayRT(c);
            } catch (Exception e) {
                error("Invalid config file: "+args[0]);
            }
        } else {
            error("No config file specified");
        }
    }
}
```

6.4 | Summary

Run-time variabilities provide the most flexibility at the latest binding time. A variety of techniques, such as property files, resource files, configuration files, XML files, and databases, can be used as input sources. If persistence is needed, then these can also be used as output. The run-time mechanisms described in this chapter can also be used to implement decisions made at other times. To increase flexibility and decrease maintenance difficulties, separate data input concerns from data usage concerns, as shown in Figure 6–5.

Compile-Time Variabilities

- Compile-time constants
- Object-oriented techniques
- Comparing run-time, compile-time, and generation-time variabilities

Compile-time variabilities are decisions made at compile time. Therefore such decisions cannot be either determined at generation time or changed at run time and must be part of the compiled program. Compile-time variabilities can be used and implemented in a number of ways,[1] including:

- **Compile-time constants**: Declaring identifiers as `final` makes them constant, so that in the hands of a good compiler they can be used to optimize a program.

- **Classic object-oriented techniques**: Base classes define the commonalities and subclasses can provide the variabilities, particularly compile-time behavior variabilities.

---

[1] We need to distinguish compile-time decisions from the mechanisms for implementing them. Run-time variabilities must be implemented with run-time mechanisms, but compile-time variabilities can be implemented using either compile-time or run-time mechanisms. For example, if we don't declare an identifier `final`, that doesn't mean it will be a run-time variability.

7.1 | Compile-Time Constants

Creating and using compile-time constants is a simple, effective, and common way to identify and remove mystery constants. To achieve separation of concerns, such compile-time constants can be placed in separate classes and files. Examples 7–1 and 7–2 show how to convert the examples from the previous chapter to this technique. A new class, MyConfig, is shown in Example 7–1. It has four final and static instance variables. The keyword, final, is used to identify those things that do not change. The keyword, static, identifies those things that belong to the class rather than the objects. In this example, it means there is no need to create an object for this class, since all it contains are static variables.

Example 7–1: MyConfig.java—an Example of Separating Compile-Time Constants from the Program

```
public class MyConfig {

    public static final int width = 300;
    public static final int height = 120;
    public static final String title = "MyFrame Example";
    public static final MyButton[] buttons = {
        new MyButton("xyz", "#000000", "#ffffff"),
        new MyButton("abc", "#000000", "#ffffff"),
        new MyButton("def", "#00ff00", "#ff00ff")

    };
}

class MyButton {
    String label;
    String foreground;
    String background;

    MyButton(String l, String fg, String bg) {
        label = l;
        foreground = fg;
        background = bg;
    }
}
```

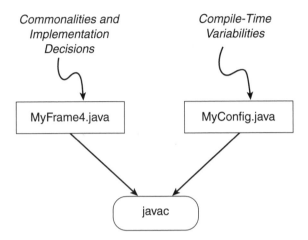

*Commonalities and
Implementation
Decisions*

*Compile-Time
Variabilities*

MyFrame4.java

MyConfig.java

javac

Figure 7–1 Separation of concerns at compile time

Note that the MyConfig class also uses the MyButton class, which uses neither static nor final variables. Although these variabilities are not explicitly defined as final, the intent is that this data does not change during run time. A compiler can use the data declared final for optimization, so it wouldn't be able to take advantage of the MyButton data. This is an example of favoring convenience and simplicity over efficiency.

The class MyFrame4 shows a program directly accessing the information from the MyConfig class (Figure 7–1). This simple example shows how we have effectively separated the *what* (MyConfig) from the *how* (MyFrame4).

Example 7–2: MyFrame4.java—Using Compile-Time Constants in MyConfig.java

```
import java.awt.*;

class MyFrame4 extends Frame {

    public MyFrame4() {
        super(MyConfig.title);
        setLayout(new FlowLayout());
        for (int j=0; j<MyConfig.buttons.length; ++j) {
            MyButton bdata = MyConfig.buttons[j];
```

```
            Button b = new Button(bdata.label);
            b.setBackground(Color.decode(
                bdata.background));
            b.setForeground(Color.decode(
                bdata.foreground));
            add(b);
        }
        setSize(MyConfig.width, MyConfig.height);
        show();
    }

    public static void main(String args[]) {
        new MyFrame4();
    }
}
```

Unfortunately the Java language is not one that makes it easy to do compile-time variabilities. We'd like to have a language that allows us to achieve separation of concerns *and* identification of constant data for optimization purposes. As Example 7–2 shows, it is sometimes inconvenient to try to make all your data final. In particular, let's examine the problems of trying to make the MyButton data truly `final`.

What we would like to say is that MyButton has three final variables, as shown in Example 7–3. Final data must be initialized at the time of declaring it, and it doesn't make sense to declare an uninitialized `final` variable. However, we want to have different final data for each instance of MyButton.

Example 7–3: MyButton with Final Data

```
class MyButton {
    final String label; // uninitialized final variables !!
    final String foreground;
    final String background;
}
```

This problem is not solved by subclassing, since the variables must be declared in the base class, not the subclasses. Interfaces do not provide a solution to this problem either. One way to solve the problem is to use arrays rather than objects, as shown in Example 7–4.

Example 7–4: MyConfig.java Using Arrays Instead of MyButton

```java
public class MyConfig {

    public static final int width = 300;
    public static final int height = 120;
    public static final String title = "MyFrame Example";
    public static final String[][] buttons = {
        { "xyz", "#000000", "#ffffff" },
        { "abc", "#000000", "#ffffff" },
        { "def", "#00ff00", "#ff00ff" }
    };
}
```

To the inexperienced programmer it might look as if Example 7–4 is much simpler and easier than Example 7–1. However, there are some major difficulties in using arrays over objects.

- You lose information about the structure of the object. For example, the `MyFrame4` program would use `MyConfig.buttons[j][0]` instead of `MyConfig.button[j].label`.

- The type of each element of the array must be the same. In Example 7–4 it worked only because each element just happened to be a `String`. Array representations won't work with mixed types such as `int` and `String`. You could use an array of `Objects`, use `Integer` instead of int, and use casting, but this is a rather awkward solution.

- Sometimes data must refer to other portions of the data (as we will see in the Play domain example later in this chapter). In such cases, it would be best to use an object reference. Using arrays would require using array indexes instead, which make the program much more difficult to write and maintain.

These difficulties are greatly reduced if you decide not to be picky about declaring compile-time variabilities as `final`. In that case, objects can be freely used and can be initialized at run time (just like MyButton in Example 7–1). Such an approach only removes the possibility of compile-time optimizations. On the other hand, one must wonder what its advantages are over run-time variabilities.

7.2 | Play Domain and Inheritance

Given the difficulties presented in the previous section, we can expect trouble trying to see what would happen if the Play domain generation-time variabilities were treated as compile-time variabilities instead. We will not attempt to define the Play data as final and instead will focus on the strengths of object-oriented approaches.

In an object-oriented approach we use inheritance to help us separate the common parts of a program from the variable parts. This means creating one or more base classes where the common methods are coded. Subclasses of the base classes specify the variations. In particular, base classes for a Play, Prop, and Scene will be created. Prop and Scene subclasses will contain data for each particular prop and scene (Figure 7–2).

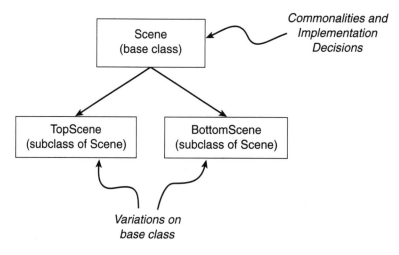

Figure 7–2 Using inheritance to separate concerns

Care must be taken to avoid some of the pitfalls of class initialization in the Java language. In addition to the `final` issues discussed in the previous section, we must also avoid the variable-shadowing problem. Consider Example 7–5.

Example 7–5: Base Classes for Scenes

```
public class Scene {
    String name;
    String color;
  ...
}
```

The base class for Scene defines two instance variables for storing the name and color of the scene. Our intention is that a subclass of Scene should provide values for these two variables.

Example 7–6: Shadowing—the Wrong Way to Extend Scene

```
public class BottomScene extends Scene {
    String name = "bottom";
    String color = "#8888aa";


  ...
}
```

The `BottomScene` class in Example 7–6 defines two variables that are distinct and separate from the two variables of the base class. This is called *shadowing*, because the variables in the subclass shadow or hide the variables in the superclass. The ways in which variables and methods are inherited in the Java language differ. Methods override inherited methods, but variables shadow superclass variables. Obviously we want to avoid this very confusing situation. To do so we can add an initializer block that will assign values to the variables in the superclass rather than shadowing them, as shown in Example 7–7.

Example 7–7: Extending Scene and Assigning Values to Scene Variables (Avoiding Shadowing)

```
public class BottomScene extends Scene {
    { name = "bottom";
      color = "#8888aa";
    }
  ...
}
```

Identifying what should be in the base class and the subclasses is challenging. Consider the method "enterScene", which will be invoked when entering a new scene. An example of "enterScene" is given in Example 7–8. Putting all of this code in the subclass takes "too much" of potential commonality out of the base class. In particular, examining the code reveals that the first line and the last two lines are common to all enterScene methods. Thus, a better division is to create a new method that we'll call "initScene" that captures the "variation" part of enterScene.

Example 7–8: A Possible enterScene Method for BottomScene

```java
public class BottomScene extends Scene {
    { name = "bottom";
      color = "#8888aa";
    }

    public void enterScene() {
        removeAll();
        add(upProp);
        add(fallProp);
        setBackground(Color.decode(color));
        show();
    }
}
```

The base class for the compile-time version of the Play domain (Phase 1) is given in Example 7–9. The Play1CT class is the base class for a play. It has two inner base classes for Props and Scenes. Common code has been identified in each of these three classes and provided as methods. In addition, methods for overriding with play specific code have been identified (actionPerformed and initScene).

Example 7–9: Play1CT.java

```java
import java.awt.*;
import java.awt.event.*;

public class Play1CT extends Frame {
    public String playname;
    public String title;
    public int width = 500;
```

```
public int height = 250;
public Scene start = null;

public void init() {
    setTitle(title);
    setSize(width, height);
    setLayout(new FlowLayout());
    start.enterScene();
}

public class Prop extends Button implements ActionListener {
    String name;

    public Prop()
    {
        addActionListener(this);
    }

    public void actionPerformed(ActionEvent e) {
        // script is coded here
    }
}

public class Scene {
    public String name;
    public String color;

    public void initScene() {
        // initialization script coded here
    }

    public void enterScene() {
        removeAll();
        setBackground(Color.decode(color));
        initScene();
        show();
    }
}
}
```

The Jack and Jill play defined and used in the previous two chapters can now be specified as a subclass of `Play1CT` as shown in Example 7–10. Some minor observations need to be made about why this class was constructed the way it was.

- The `main` method must be defined in `JackAndJillCT` rather than `Play1CT` since we must create a `JackAndJillCT` object rather than just a `Play1CT`. Alternatively we could pass a parameter to a main method in `Play1CT` that specifies what play object to create.

- The `init` method in `Play1CT` should logically go into the constructor for `Play1CT`, but unfortunately such code would be executed before the `JackAndJillCT` object was fully created, and references to variables such as `width` and `title` would occur before they were properly initialized with the values specific to `JackAndJillCT`. Therefore this code has been put in a separate method and called after `JackAndJillCT` is fully initialized.

- For the same reasons as above, the constructor for `Prop` does not initialize the button's label. This initialization is done in the initializer block for the subclasses of `Prop`, at which point there is not much need for a separate variable for the label, since we call `setLabel` at the same time.

- The `start` variable in `JackAndJillCT` can't be initialized until after `bottomScene` is defined.

Example 7–10: JackAndJillCT

```
import java.awt.*;
import java.awt.event.*;

public class JackAndJillCT extends Play1CT {
    { playname = "JackAndJill";
      title = "Jack and Jill";
      width = 200;
      height = 120;
    }

    class UpProp extends Prop {
        { name = "up";
          setLabel("Go up the hill");
        }
```

```
    public void actionPerformed(ActionEvent e) {
        fetchProp.setLabel("Fetch a pail of water");
        topScene.enterScene();
    }
}

UpProp upProp = new UpProp();

class FetchProp extends Prop {
    { name = "fetch";
      setLabel("Fetch a pail of water");
    }

    public void actionPerformed(ActionEvent e) {
        setLabel("Fetch another pail");
    }
}

FetchProp fetchProp = new FetchProp();

class FallProp extends Prop {
    { name = "fall";
      setLabel("Fall down, break crown");
    }

    public void actionPerformed(ActionEvent e) {
        setLabel("Break crown");
        tumbleProp.setLabel("Tumble after");
        bottomScene.enterScene();
    }
}

FallProp fallProp = new FallProp();

class TumbleProp extends Prop {
    { name = "tumble";
      setLabel("Tumble down");
    }

    public void actionPerformed(ActionEvent e) {
        bottomScene.enterScene();
    }
}

TumbleProp tumbleProp = new TumbleProp();
```

```
class BottomScene extends Scene {
    { name = "bottom";
      color = "#8888aa";
    }

    public void initScene() {
        add(upProp);
        add(fallProp);
    }
}

BottomScene bottomScene = new BottomScene();

class TopScene extends Scene {
    { name = "top";
      color = "#dddddd";
    }

    public void initScene() {
        add(fetchProp);
        add(fallProp);
        add(tumbleProp);
    }
}

TopScene topScene = new TopScene();

{
  start = bottomScene;
}

public static void main(String[] args) {
    JackAndJillCT p = new JackAndJillCT().init();
}
}
```

The strength of the OO approach becomes more apparent in Phase 2 when escapes become more plentiful. An escape is easily implemented as a method override in a subclass. The OO approach also easily accommodates many different props (particularly by using JavaBeans), multiple events, and traits. However, the OO approach in this particular example shows one of the disappointing aspects of using compile-time variabilities. The division between the base class and subclasses is not as clean or nice looking as run-time variabilities (using property files or XML files) and generation-time variabilities. The language design of Java does not lend itself very well to separating concerns along the lines that we wish. The issues of shadowing, limitations on `final`, and the manner in which classes are constructed and initialized, all contribute to less than ideal circumstances for creating subclasses with only the information we want.

7.3 | Comparing Run-Time, Compile-Time, and Generation-Time Variabilities

Chapter 6 showed how the Play domain would be constructed if its variabilities were all run-time variabilities. The previous section of this chapter showed what would happen if they were compile-time variabilities instead. The next few chapters show the case for generation-time variabilities. In this section we give a brief comparison of these three architectures.

With run-time variabilities, the information is typically stored in an external file (properties file, XML file, database, ...) and read by the program. With compile-time variabilities the information is incorporated into the program (using separate objects or subclasses). With generation-time variabilities, the information is read by a program generator that creates a custom-made program (Figure 7–3).

The run-time and generation-time approaches are similar in that they both cleanly separate the variabilities from the program and are unconstrained by how that information is expressed. In fact the same language, such as XML, could be used for either run-time or generation-time approaches. Compile-time variabilities, however, must somehow be expressed in the implementation language. This constraint limits the expressibility of the variabilities. Another complicating factor in the compile-time approach is that it may drastically affect the

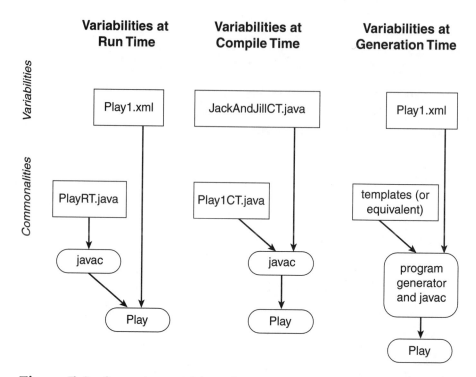

Figure 7–3 Separating variabilities from the program at three different times

architecture of the program. The architecture is used to achieve separation of concerns. Such an architecture may conflict with other design objectives. This does not occur using generation-time variabilities, because the approach is not concerned with achieving separation of concerns in the generated program. That separation of concerns is made at a higher level. Thus the generated programs are unconstrained architecturally.

Chapter 8 describes three different styles of generated programs. The architectures of these programs are unsuitable for compile-time variabilities, because the generated program does not separate concerns (Figure 7–4). The third approach in Chapter 8, the table-driven approach, with some tweaking could be transformed to a pure compile-time approach, but the program would be very difficult to maintain.

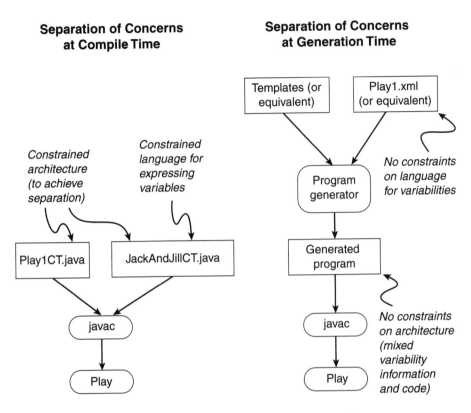

Figure 7–4 Comparison between Compile-Time and Generation-Time Variabilities

For these reasons, the compile-time approach is the weakest among the three. Thus, a domain analysis should usually distinguish between run-time and application-development-time variabilities. The application-development-time variabilities can be chosen to use either compile-time or generation-time mechanisms. If the application-development-time variabilities are sufficiently simple or amenable to compile-time approaches, then that is the preferred approach. But once these variabilities reach a certain level of complexity, the advantages of program generators outweigh those of a simpler compile-time approach.

7.4 | Preprocessing-Time Variabilities

Preprocessing time occurs just before compilation time, where pre-processors may be used to expand macros. For example, the C pre-processor can be used to do considerable work integrating variabilities into a program from separate header files. More importantly, C++ templates can be used to create an entire new level of programming, sometimes referred to as static metaprogramming in C++ (see the Czarnecki and Eisenecker reference at the end of this chapter). The Java language has neither a preprocessor nor templates, so this tech-nology is not easily available. A major criticism since Java 1.0 came out was the lack of parameterized types or template facilities. Although such a facility would not be as complete a solution as that found in Chapters 8 through 12, it would be much better than the compile-time support shown in this chapter.

7.5 | Summary

Compile-time variabilities are decisions made at compile time. The compiler may take advantage of this information to optimize pro-grams. Unfortunately, the Java language does not provide ideal facili-ties for simultaneously separating concerns between variabilities and commonalities and thus limits what can be accomplished. Compile-time variabilities may also be implemented with run-time mechanisms, but then you would lose any potential compile-time optimizations.

Further Reading

Krzysztof Czarnecki and Ulrich Eisenecker, *Generative Programming: Methods, Tools, and Applications*, Addison-Wesley, 2000.

The Styles of Generated Programs

- ▮ "What to generate?" versus "How to generate?"
- ▮ Comparing handcrafted and generated programs
- ▮ Three styles of generated programs:
  OO-driven style, code-driven style,
  and table-driven style

8

There are many ways to write a program. Specifications generally don't spell out everything, so a programmer has some choice over details and perhaps features. Even programs that are functionally identical (meaning you get exactly the same results) may have very different program structures and code. Sometimes these differences result in performance differences. Sometimes these differences result in programs that are considered easier to understand and change. A good program is correct, performs well (in terms of time and/or space), and is easy to change.

In this chapter we focus on the program to be generated, rather than the program that does the generation. Chapters 9 through 12 will focus on the generator program (Figure 8–1).

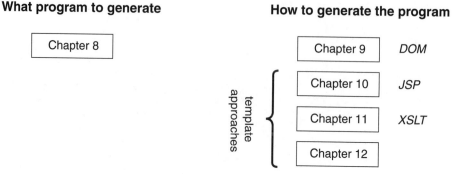

Figure 8–1　What and how for Chapters 8–12

8.1 | Comparing Handcrafted and Generated Programs

There is a major difference in style between manually crafted programs and generated programs. Humans design both, but there are different engineering principles at work (Figure 8–2).

When writing programs by hand, these are important guiding principles:

- **Design for change**: Software engineers use abstractions, useful comments, good variable names, good structure, and object-oriented techniques. These techniques decrease the cost of future changes required for maintenance, enhancements, and reuse.

- **Correctness**: Software engineers strive for functionally correct programs and programs that do reasonable things even under unreasonable circumstances. Software engineers may use defensive programming techniques (assertions, invariants, redundancy, fault tolerance) and

Handcrafted Programs One of a kind		Generated Programs One of a family
Great care and diligence are required to ensure the handcrafted program can be changed and maintained.	**Design for Change**	Specifications are changed; programs are not changed, but regenerated, so there is only minor concern about the program's appearance.
Great care and diligence are required to ensure the handcrafted program performs correctly.	**Correctness**	Generator's track record inspires confidence; correctness efforts are focused on the specifications, not the generated program.
As a handcrafted program, the performance can be fine-tuned to this application; however, such efforts may conflict with Design for Change and Correctness.	**Performance**	Although broad performance issues across the whole family can be used to create an efficient program, there are few or no provisions for fine-tuning a specific application.

Figure 8–2   Comparing handcrafted and generated programs

social processes for improving correctness (reviews, audits, testing, quality assurance).

■ **Performance**: Software engineers try to minimize required resources, such as code, data, network traffic, and CPU time. Improving performance usually increases program complexity and thus indirectly makes programs harder to change and less likely to be correct.

The guiding principles are the same when designing generated programs, but the emphasis is different.

■ **Design for change**: This is less important for generated programs. Just as almost no one cares about the style of assembly-language output of a compiler, few people look at generated programs. The output of an optimizing compiler may be very difficult to read; likewise the output of an optimizing program generator may be nearly impossible to decipher. It is more important that the specifications and program generator be designed for change than that the generated program be designed for change.

■ **Correctness**: This is at least as important for generated programs. New program generators are as likely to be as buggy as any other new program. Fortunately, once program generators have a proven track record, the generated programs are more likely to be correct than new handcrafted programs. Correctness efforts are therefore shifted to the specifications rather than the generated program.

■ **Performance**: This is sometimes less important and sometimes more. In most cases, people are willing to sacrifice performance to increase productivity. In other cases, program generators may be able to more quickly and accurately produce an efficient program by using standard techniques, such as Huffman encoding for reducing space requirements, or to make the appropriate trade-offs between time and space in selecting data representations and algorithms. A distinct advantage is that the generated programs can be designed to be efficient with less concern about the program's structure or readability.

As a result of the differences between the objectives between designing handcrafted and generated programs, it would be unfair to judge a generated program with the same criteria one would judge a handcrafted program. A generated program has to be correct and efficient, but it doesn't have to be a "pretty" program.

8.2 | Comparing Three Styles of Generated Programs

In this chapter we will examine three different styles of programming that may be adopted by program generators (Figure 8–3). A *JackAndJill program* is one that implements the JackAndJill specification (see Example 5–8 in Chapter 5). Chapters 6 and 7 showed run-time and compile-time variations of the JackAndJill program. The Chapter 7 compile-time program can be considered the typical handcrafted program. This chapter shows three JackAndJill programs generated by three different program generators. The examples in this chapter tend to show the end points of a spectrum. In real life, a program generator would employ a combination of all three styles. In all three programs, Java inner classes are used to create one self-contained class.

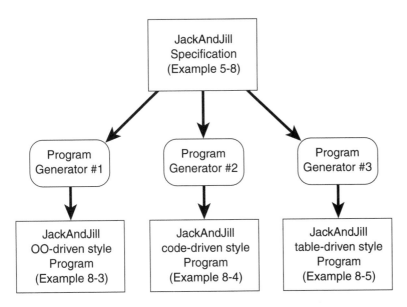

Figure 8–3 Three styles of generated programs

8.2.1   *OO-Driven Style*

The OO-driven style uses object-oriented techniques for organizing the program structure. However, unlike the OO style program in Chapter 7 (compile-time version), its organization does not have to be focused on separating the common and variable parts of a program. The program design can be based on other principles and concerns, such as performance issues or other design goals. For example, you could use this design approach to maximize the ease with which you can evolve to Phase 2. Classes are created for both Scenes and Events. Props are not explicitly identified as a separate class, since in Phase 2 any JavaBean will be usable as a prop. Although the OO example will look cluttered and overdone, this is simply a result of a small specification and seeing only Phase 1 features. Examining a more sophisticated specification with Phase 2 features will show off the OO style to full advantage. The chief disadvantage of the OO style is that it is usually slightly more difficult to create and less efficient than the code-driven style.

8.2.2   *Code-Driven Style*

Many program generators use a code-driven approach to creating programs because it is the easiest and most natural way. This approach means generating the code and directly embedding data wherever it's needed. Unlike the OO style (which also embeds data wherever needed), a code-driven approach doesn't worry too much about program structure, but rather focuses on simple efficient code. As you look at the code-driven example (Section 8.4), you'll note that there are far fewer classes. Code related to events is put in a single class rather than spread among different classes for different events. Likewise, scenes are not objects, and a single method handles entering a new scene. The chief advantage of this approach is simplicity and efficiency.

8.2.3 *Table-Driven Style*

The table-driven style shows a clean separation between the data and the code. All data from the specification are stored in tables, arrays, and other data structures. The code simply refers to the tables to retrieve the data rather than have the data embedded directly in the code. A table-driven approach is a classic software engineering technique, but probably is taken to an extreme in program generators, where tables can become arbitrarily complex. The chief advantages of a table-driven approach are:

- The code can be put in a library and doesn't have to be generated. This makes it easier to change the behavior of the code without having to change the program generator or regenerate the code.

- The data could just as easily be determined at run time as at code-generation time, making it easy to change the binding times for variabilities. In fact, it's possible to replace the program generator with a run-time parser that creates and populates the tables dynamically.

- The table-driven approach is probably the most space efficient. Sometimes the code-driven approach generates lots of space-consuming code, which a table-driven approach can avoid. The space efficiency is somewhat offset by a slower program, since data must now be looked up in data structures.

The chief disadvantages of the table-driven style are:

- The table-driven approach is harder to implement, requiring data structure design, accessing data, and keeping track of indices and other bookkeeping trivia.

- Table-driven code is harder to debug. A debugger works very nicely in a code-driven style program, since the line number also gives lots of information about the state of the program.

- Escapes to the underlying implementation language are more difficult to implement with a table-driven approach. Although the examples in this chapter do not show escapes, you should have no difficulty seeing where to put those escapes in the OO-driven and code-driven examples, but may find it hard to figure out how to incorporate escapes in the table-driven approach.

8.2.4   *Program Notes Common to All Three Styles*

To understand the generated programs you will need to be familiar with the Jack and Jill play described in Chapter 5. The XML specification is given in Example 5–8 and examples of its use in Section 5.7 (see Figure 5–9). The Jack and Jill play provides examples of some of the subtle nuances of the Play domain. Each program that purports to implement the Jack and Jill play (or any other play in the Play domain) must correctly implement each of the items noted below.

- The program must make sure that a prop value retains its state from one scene to another. For example, clicking on the fall button changes its label, which is used in all subsequent scenes.

- The program must make sure that each scene displays all the props that it includes.

- The label of a prop can be set in two different places. First, the initial value is determined by the trait in the prop definition. Second, a label can be changed when a script is executed. For example, when the program starts, the fetch prop is initialized to "Fetch a pail of water." When the fetch button is clicked, the script changes the label to "Fetch another pail." Finally, whenever the top scene is entered via the up button, the fetch prop's label is set to "Fetch a pail of water."

- A script can make changes to any prop, not just the prop it is associated with. For example, clicking on the "fall" button changes the label for the tumble prop.

- A script can redirect the program to a new scene. If there is no "goto" attribute, then the program does not change the scene. For example, clicking the "up" prop will change the scene to the top scene, but clicking on the fetch button should not alter the scene.

- The program must make sure the background color is set for each scene, including the default color if no background is specified.

- The program must make sure that the title of the play is the frame's title and that the width and height are properly used for the size of the frame. User actions may dynamically change the width and height of the frame over time.

In all three programs, all props are represented as AWT[1] buttons. The scenes are represented as AWT containers. AWT components, such as buttons, can be put in only one container at a time. Props may appear in multiple scenes, but cannot simultaneously be in multiple scenes. Since only one scene is shown at a time, this is not an issue. What is an issue is that upon entry a new scene must be recreated from scratch by explicitly adding all props.

---

[1]Abstract Window Toolkit is the standard Java GUI component library.

8.3 | OO-Driven Style

The OO-driven style creates a new class for each scene and script where custom code may be generated in its methods. Each scene has the method "setup" which is used to create a scene in the current frame. Each script is represented as a Java event listener. In Phase 1 this is just action events on buttons. In Phase 2 this is easily extended to arbitrary props and events. In contrast, the code-driven and table-driven programs lump all scripts in a single method.

Several different design approaches could have been taken, but we'll just briefly describe some of the alternatives with respect to prop objects. Each prop object in Phase 1 is a button with a single trait (the label) and single event, a mouse click that calls the `ActionListener` object. One way to set this up is shown in Example 8–1. An explicit class is declared for the action event and attached to the `fallProp` button in an initialization block.

Example 8–1: Fall Prop Implementation Using Named Inner Classes

```
class FallPropAction {
    actionPerformed(ActionEvent e) {
        fallProp.setLabel("Break crown");
        tumbleProp.setLabel("Tumble after");
        enterNewScene(bottomScene);
    }
}


Button fallProp = new Button();

{   fallProp.setLabel("Fall down, Break crown");
    fallProp.addActionListener(new FallPropAction());
}
```

An alternative is to use anonymous inner classes. An anonymous inner class is the declaration of a new unnamed class as part of an expression. This is shown in Example 8–2, where the second parameter to the new `ButtonProp` constructor creates a new object of a new class that implements `ActionListener`. The new unnamed class provides the single method required to implement `ActionListener`. A base class for all prop buttons is defined which includes a constructor object that is passed the initial label and the script as an `Action-Listener` object. The `fallProp` object can now be declared and initialized with one statement.

Example 8–2: Fall Prop Implementation Using Anonymous Inner Classes

```
class ButtonProp extends Button {
    ButtonProp(String label, ActionListener script) {
        super(label);
        addActionListener(script);
    }
}

ButtonProp fallProp = new ButtonProp("Fall down, break crown",
    new ActionListener() {
        public void actionPerformed(ActionEvent evt) {
            fallProp.setLabel("Break crown");
            tumbleProp.setLabel("Tumble after");
            enterNewScene(bottomScene);
        }
    });
```

It is logical to ask the difference between the handcrafted OO style JackAndJill program in Chapter 7 and the OO-driven style generated program shown in Example 8–3. The most important difference is that the Chapter 7 design was structured to support separation of concerns between common code in the base class `Play1CT` and the variabilities of the subclass `JackAndJillCT`. This separation is not necessary in the generated program because the separation of concerns occurs at a higher level. The generated program can be structured in accordance with other goals. This structural difference is illustrated in Figure 7–4. The implications of this difference are:

- The generated program is structured as one major class instead of two, resulting in the ability to consolidate information associated with particular objects in one place instead of two.

- The generated program has a single scene method, setup, whereas the handcrafted program had to introduce the auxiliary method initScene to adequately separate common parts from variable parts.

- The generated program initializes props in a more natural way. In the handcrafted version, the props were awkwardly initialized in a static initialization block. The awkwardness is caused by a combination of Java shadowing of variables and the reluctance to separate object-specific initialization code to a separate object. Also very importantly, the generated program has the option to structure itself to take advantage of declaring data to be "final," unlike the handcrafted program (although we didn't do this in the example).

Example 8–3: OO-Driven Style JackAndJill Program

```java
package com.craigc.progen;
import java.awt.*;
import java.awt.event.*;

public class JackAndJillPlay1 extends Frame {

    /** base class for all button props */
    class ButtonProp extends Button {
        ButtonProp(String label, ActionListener script) {
            super(label);
            addActionListener(script);
        }
    }

    /* The Props for JackAndJillPlay ******************/

    ButtonProp upProp = new ButtonProp("Go up the hill",
        new ActionListener() {
            public void actionPerformed(ActionEvent evt) {
                fetchProp.setLabel("Fetch a pail of water");
                enterNewScene(topScene);
            }
        });
    ButtonProp fetchProp = new ButtonProp("Fetch a pail of water",
```

```
        new ActionListener() {
            public void actionPerformed(ActionEvent evt) {
                fetchProp.setLabel("Fetch another pail");
            }
        });
ButtonProp fallProp = new ButtonProp("Fall down, break crown",
        new ActionListener() {
            public void actionPerformed(ActionEvent evt) {
                fallProp.setLabel("Break crown");
                tumbleProp.setLabel("Tumble after");
                enterNewScene(bottomScene);
            }
        });
ButtonProp tumbleProp = new ButtonProp("Tumble down",
        new ActionListener() {
            public void actionPerformed(ActionEvent evt) {
                enterNewScene(bottomScene);
            }
        });

/* The Scenes for JackAndJillPlay *****************/

/** base class for all scenes */
class Scene extends Panel {
    void setup() {};    // used to setup a scene on entry
};

class BottomScene extends Scene {
    void setup() {
        removeAll();    // remove any old props
        setLayout(new FlowLayout());
        add(upProp);
        add(fallProp);
        setBackground(Color.decode("#8888aa"));
    }
}

class TopScene extends Scene {
    void setup() {
        removeAll();    // remove any old props
        setLayout(new FlowLayout());
        add(fetchProp);
        add(fallProp);
        add(tumbleProp);
        setBackground(Color.decode("#dddddd"));
    }
}
```

```
      BottomScene bottomScene = new BottomScene();
      TopScene topScene = new TopScene();

      /* Creating and starting up the JackAndJillPlay **/

      Scene currentScene;

      public JackAndJillPlay1() {
          super("Jack and Jill #1");
          setSize(300, 120);

          // start scene
          enterNewScene(bottomScene);
      }

      public void enterNewScene(Scene scene) {
          removeAll();   // remove previous scene if any
          currentScene = scene;
          scene.setup();
          add(scene);
          show();
      }

      public static void main(String[] args) {
          new JackAndJillPlay1();
      }
  }
```

8.4 | Code-Driven Style

The code-driven style of program generation is a very basic and intuitive generation technique (Example 8–4). Simply output the code needed to do the job, throwing in information from the specification where it is needed. In some ways this style of program is easier to follow. In comparison with the OO-driven style there is less structure.

The code is more compact, and from a handcrafted point of view difficult to change. For example, to add a new prop would require changes to many different parts of the code. But then again, we don't fret over that issue, since generated programs are not (or shouldn't be) directly changed. Specifications are changed; generated programs are regenerated.

Example 8–4: Code-Driven JackAndJill Program

```java
package com.craigc.progen;
import java.awt.*;
import java.awt.event.*;

class JackAndJillPlay2 extends Frame {

    /* The Props for JackAndJill ****************/

    Button upProp = new Button("Go up the hill");
    Button fetchProp = new Button("Fetch a pail of water");
    Button fallProp = new Button("Fall down, break crown");
    Button tumbleProp = new Button("Tumble down");

    /* The Events in the JackAndJill **************/

    class PropEvent implements ActionListener {
        public void actionPerformed(ActionEvent evt) {
            Object prop = evt.getSource();
            if (prop==upProp) {
                fetchProp.setLabel("Fetch a pail of water");
                enterNewScene("top");
            } else if (prop==fetchProp) {
                fetchProp.setLabel("Fetch another pail");
            } else if (prop==fallProp) {
                fallProp.setLabel("Break crown");
                tumbleProp.setLabel("Tumble after");
                enterNewScene("bottom");
            } else if (prop==tumbleProp) {
                enterNewScene("bottom");
            } else {
                System.out.println("Invalid prop");
            }
        }
    }
```

```java
/* Creating and starting up the JackAndJill ****/

String currentScene;

public JackAndJillPlay2() {
    super("Jack and Jill");
    setSize(200, 120);
    setLayout(new FlowLayout());

    // initialize props
    PropEvent a = new PropEvent();
    upProp.addActionListener(a);
    fetchProp.addActionListener(a);
    fallProp.addActionListener(a);
    tumbleProp.addActionListener(a);

    // start scene
    enterNewScene("bottom");
}

public void enterNewScene(String scene) {
    removeAll();   // remove previous scene
    currentScene = scene;
    if (scene.equals("bottom")) {
        add(upProp);
        add(fallProp);
        setBackground(Color.decode("#8888aa"));
    } else if (scene.equals("top")) {
        add(fetchProp);
        add(fallProp);
        add(tumbleProp);
        setBackground(Color.decode("#dddddd"));
    } else {
        System.out.println("Invalid scene: "+scene);
    }
    show();
}

public static void main(String[] args) {
    new JackAndJillPlay2();
}

}
```

8.5 | Table-Driven Style

The table-driven approach to program generation is to separate the data from the code. The specification information is stored in specially designed data structures (called "tables" for historical reasons) and the code refers to the data structures to retrieve data when appropriate.

In this example, all data from the specification file is stored in variables, tables, and data structures. Each prop and scene is given a unique index number. Trait values (except the initial values) are all stored in a single string array, and most other arrays are just integers, usually indexes into other tables. Some tables, such as `propLabels` and `sceneColors`, are easy to decipher, whereas others, such as `propActions`, are much more difficult. Figure 8–4 describes how `propActions` work.

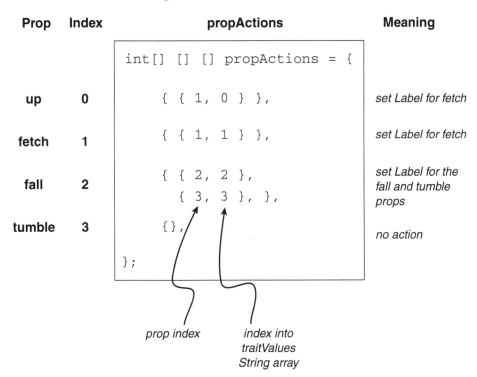

Prop	Index	propActions	Meaning
		`int[] [] [] propActions = {`	
up	0	`{ { 1, 0 } },`	*set Label for fetch*
fetch	1	`{ { 1, 1 } },`	*set Label for fetch*
fall	2	`{ { 2, 2 },` `  { 3, 3 }, },`	*set Label for the fall and tumble props*
tumble	3	`{},`	*no action*
		`};`	

prop index   *index into traitValues String array*

Figure 8–4   The design of the propActions array

As Figure 8–4 shows, the table-driven approach is not easy to figure out. If this were a handcrafted program, it would be difficult to maintain. Consider the changes that would be required if one were to remove the fetch prop. Many prop indexes would require changes, and many different arrays would require simultaneous alterations (prop-Names, propLabels, propActions, nextScene, sceneProps, and scenePropInit). If these changes were not made completely or consistently the program would be likely to behave in unintended ways. But as a generated program, these issues do not arise because changes occur at the specification level and the program is simply regenerated. Unlike humans, the program generator is good at remembering tedious details and will make changes consistently and completely.

Example 8–5: Table-Driven JackAndJill Program

```
package com.craigc.progen;
import java.awt.*;
import java.awt.event.*;

class JackAndJillPlay3 extends Frame {

    /* The Prop and Scene tables ******************/

    final static String title = "Jack and Jill #3";
    final int width = 300;
    final int height = 120;
    final int startScene = 0; // bottom

    // String[] propNames = { "up", "fetch", "fall", "down" };

    // initial labels
    final String[] propLabels = {
        "Go up the hill",
        "Fetch a pail of water",
        "Fall down, break crown",
        "Tumble down",
    };

    // map props to actions after each prop's action event
    final int[][][] propActions = {
        { { 1, 0 } },  // fetch "Fetch a pail of water"
        { { 1, 1 } },  // fetch "Fetch another pail"
        { { 2, 2 },    // fall "Break crown"
          { 3, 3 }, }, // tumble "Tumble after"
```

```
    {},
};

// map props to next scene
final int[] nextScene = {
    1,  // top
    -1, // none
    0,  // bottom
    0,  // bottom
};

// String[] sceneNames = { "bottom", "top" };

// map scenes to list of props to add for that scene
final int[][] sceneProps = {
    { 0, 2 },    // up fall
    { 1, 2, 3 }, // fetch fall tumble
};

final String[] sceneColors = {
    "#8888aa",
    null,
};

final String[] traitValues = {
    "Fetch a pail of water",
    "Fetch another pail",
    "Break crown",
    "Tumble after",
};

/* The Events in the JackAndJillPlay *******************/

class PropEvent implements ActionListener {
    int propnum;    // what prop this listener listens for

    public PropEvent(int j) {
        propnum = j;
    }

    public void actionPerformed(ActionEvent evt) {
        for (int j=0; j<propActions[propnum].length; ++j) {
            props[propActions[propnum][j][0]].setLabel(
                traitValues[propActions[propnum][j][1]]);
        }

        if (nextScene[propnum] >= 0) {
            enterNewScene(nextScene[propnum]);
```

```
        }
      }
    }

    /* Creating and starting up the JackAndJillPlay *********/

    int currentScene;
    Button[] props; // the props

    public JackAndJillPlay3() {
        super(title);
        setSize(width, height);
        setLayout(new FlowLayout());

        // initialize props
        props = new Button[propLabels.length];
        for (int j=0; j<propLabels.length; ++j) {
            props[j] = new Button();
            props[j].setLabel(propLabels[j]);
            props[j].addActionListener(new PropEvent(j));
        }

        // start scene
        enterNewScene(startScene);
    }

    public void enterNewScene(int scene) {
        removeAll();  // remove previous scene if any
        currentScene = scene;
        for (int j=0; j<sceneProps[scene].length; ++j) {
            add(props[sceneProps[scene][j]]);
        }
        String bg = sceneColors[scene];
        setBackground(Color.decode(bg==null?"#dddddd":bg));
        show();
    }

    public static void main(String[] args) {
        new JackAndJillPlay3();
    }
}
```

One advantage a table-driven approach has over the OO or code-driven approaches is that the data can be separate from the code. This separation might be desirable to avoid generating and compiling the same code whenever the data changes. In Example 8–5, everything above the class `PropEvent` is the data section and is unique for each specification. Everything below `PropEvent` (including `PropEvent`) is the code section, which is invariant—that is, it remains the same for all specifications. A more efficient way of structuring the program-generation process is to remove the invariant code section, compile it, and link it in only when the program is run, as illustrated in Figure 8–5.

The code section can be put in a separate class or a superclass, compiled in advance, and stored in a jar file. This separation would also make it possible to change and test the code section without having to regenerate and recompile the data section.

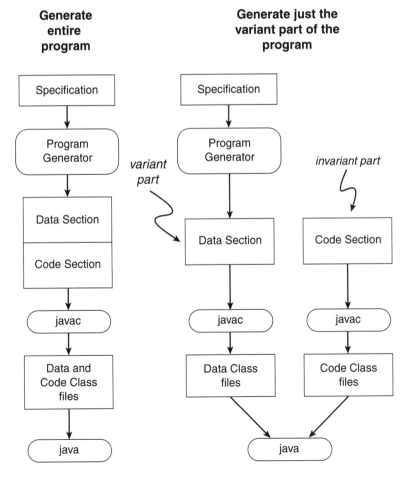

Figure 8–5 Comparing whole and partial program generation

On the surface, the separation of data and code is similar to the OO approach in Chapter 7, but there is a difference. The table-driven approach described here is made from arrays and indexes, an error-prone method if done by hand. The Chapter 7 example uses objects and object references, yielding a more structured and easy-to-understand program. Using arrays and final values will result in somewhat more efficient code.

The separation of data from code also makes possible the creation of systems that can dynamically change the specification at run time. Only the tables need to be altered, since the code is invariant. In fact, it would be possible to convert generation-time variabilities to run-time variabilities by creating and populating the tables at run time.

8.5.1   *Phase 2 Issues*

When the table-driven approach is extended to Phase 2, two new issues arise. In addition to being more complex, a table-driven approach may encounter large tables and arbitrary escapes to Java code.

In Phase 1, scripts can only be associated with props. In Phase 2, scripts can also be associated with props in specific scenes. Thus some tables, such as nextScene and propActions, will have to be adjusted by adding a new dimension indexed by the scene. Consider the old nextScene declaration in Example 8–6.

Example 8–6: Table nextScene in Phase 1

```
// map props to next scene
final int[] nextScene = {
     1,   // top
    -1,   // none
     0,   // bottom
     0,   // bottom
};
```

One possible data structure for Phase 2 is shown in Example 8–7. This is a two-dimensional array indexed by a prop index and a scene index. The data structure shows a simple change: the fourth prop, `tumble`, when clicked in the bottom scene, will take the user to the top scene rather than remain in the bottom scene. All other props are unaltered; they always go to the same scene regardless of where the prop was clicked.

**Example 8–7: Table nextScene in Phase 2, a Table
That May Grow Too Large**

```
// map (props,scenes) to next scene
final int[][] nextScene = {
    {  1,  1 },    // top
    { -1, -1 },  // none
    {  0,  0 },    // bottom
    {  1,  0 },    // bottom or top
};
```

This data structure grows by the product of the number of scenes and props. When there are just a few scenes and props, the array size is reasonable, but when the number of scenes and props grow, the table becomes much too large. A play with 100 scenes and 100 props creates a table with 10,000 entries. Sparse matrix representations save space for such tables. The `nextScene` array could be broken into two separate arrays. The first array could be the same one used in Phase 1 and would represent the default next scene for each prop. A second array could be an enumeration of the exceptions to the default. This representation would grow linearly as the play specification grew (Example 8–8).

Example 8–8: Tables That Grow Linearly with the Specification

```
// map props to the next default scene
final int[] nextScene = {
     1,     // top
    -1,     // none
     0,     // bottom
     0,     // bottom
};

// list of nextScene exceptions (prop, scene, nextScene)
final int[][] nextSceneExceptions = {
    { 3, 0, 1 },  // tumble prop in bottom scene, goto top scene
};
```

The second major difficulty with Phase 2 is handling Java code that appears in scripts or other places. Escapes cannot be simply stuck into simple arrays, but a variety of techniques retain the simple efficiency of tables while still having escapes. One approach is to number the escapes and use those indexes in tables. An escape method could execute the code associated with a given escape index.

Example 8–9: A Method with Escape Code Allowing Escape Indexes to Be Used in Tables

```
// escape code
void escape(int escapeIndex) {
    switch (escapeIndex) {
    case 0: ... escape code ... break;
    case 1: ... escape code ... break;
    ...
    default: error("escape index error");
    }
};
```

8.6 | Summary

The design of handcrafted programs and generated programs follow different paths. Handcrafted programs should be easy to understand and change. In a program-generation system, the need for understanding and change occurs at the specification level, not the program level. This results in greater flexibility in the design of generated programs. Three styles of generated programs are presented in this chapter. The OO-approach favors highly structured OO techniques. The code-driven approach favors straightforward code with embedded data. The table-driven approach puts data in a separate data section that is used by the code section. A typical program generator will use some combination of these three techniques.

Using DOM to Generate Programs

- Domain Object Model

- How to select the right approach:
  Pure DOM, DOM to Custom, and SAX to Custom

- Analysis and transformations

he Document Object Model (DOM) is a W3C standard[1] that describes itself as follows:

> The Document Object Model is a platform- and language-neutral interface that will allow programs and scripts to dynamically access and update the content, structure, and style of documents.

The DOM standard provides standard Java interfaces. An XML document is represented as a tree-structured object of nodes. Each node represents a portion of the document. There are nodes for each part of an XML document, including attributes, elements, and entities. The DOM provides standard interfaces for moving around the

---

[1] *http://www.w3.org/DOM.* Copyright® World Wide Web Consortium (Massachusetts Institute of Technology, Institut National de Recherche en Informatique et en Automatique, Keio University). All Rights Reserved.

tree (parent, children, and sibling) as well as getting specific information about each node, such as the name and value. The DOM also includes interfaces for creating new nodes and adding, changing, or removing nodes from the tree.

A typical program generator using XML input requires an XML parser to convert an XML file to a DOM object. Optionally, some analysis and even transformations may take place on the DOM object, and finally a program is generated (Figure 9–1). This is the classic structure of all program generators as described in Chapter 1.

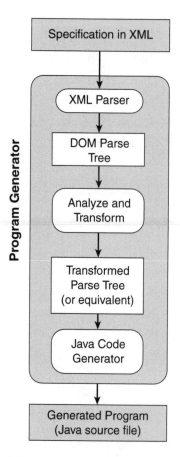

Figure 9–1   Using XML files and DOM to build a program generator

9.1 | Reading and Storing the Specification Using XML Parsers

There are three general approaches for parsing and storing the specification information as illustrated in Figure 9–2. We'll examine all three approaches and then provide guidance for choosing the best one for a given situation.

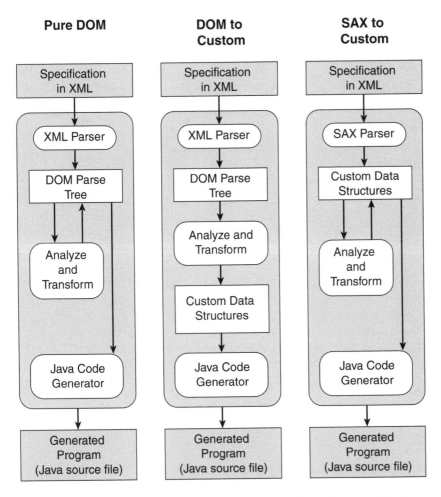

Figure 9–2 Three approaches to reading and storing specifications

9.1.1   *Pure DOM Approach*

The pure DOM approach uses a standard XML parser to create DOM data structures. Transformation and analysis are performed directly on these DOM data structures, and the code generator works directly on the DOM data structures. The pure DOM approach is the simplest of the three approaches, requiring the least amount of work.

The first step in creating a DOM-based program generator is to read and parse the XML file (Example 9–1). XML Parsers creating DOM objects are available from a variety of sources including IBM's alphaWorks,[2] Apache,[3] and Sun.[4] Three imports are required. An import for the DOM interfaces is provided by W3C, another is for IBM's parser,[5] and finally the standard Java IO package is used for reading a file.

Example 9–1: Read and Parse an XML File

```
import com.ibm.xml.parser.Parser;
import org.w3c.dom.*;
import java.io.*;

public class DOM_Util {

    ...

    /** Read and parse an XML file */
    public static Document readDocument(String filename)
                    throws Exception {
        InputStream is = new FileInputStream(filename);
        Parser parser = new Parser(filename);
        return parser.readStream(is);
    }
}
```

---

[2] http://www.alphaworks.ibm.com
[3] http://xml.apache.org
[4] http://java.sun.com/xml
[5] This example uses IBM's XML parser. This book has no code that depends on IBM's parser. Isolating dependencies on the parser to a single method or class makes it easy to substitute a different parser.

Once the DOM data structure is in memory, code can be written to analyze and transform the structure as will be described in Section 9.2. Finally the code generator obtains information directly from the DOM data structure.

9.1.2   *DOM to Custom Approach*

Just as in the pure DOM approach, a standard XML parser is used to create the DOM data structures. The difference occurs after parsing and creating the DOM data structures. During the analysis and transformation phase, new custom data structures are created. The code generator uses the new data structures rather than the original DOM data structures. This approach requires designing and creating the new data structures. Section 9.4 contains an example. Figure 6–5 also illustrates a comparison between a pure DOM approach and a DOM to Custom approach.

9.1.3   *SAX to Custom Approach*

An alternative parsing technique can be used to circumvent DOM entirely. SAX[6] (Simple API for XML) can be used to create custom XML parsers. Rather than providing a parse tree API, the SAX API provides an event-based interface. Methods are called during parsing so that any parse tree or other data structures can be built during the parsing phase. SAX could be used to create the DOM tree. Some implementations do this. SAX could be used to generate code directly without creating any data structures. Using SAX is more efficient than using DOM, since you can ignore any part of the XML document that is not needed. The DOM approach parses the entire XML file and creates an in-memory object representing the entire XML file. For large XML documents this is not desirable, if only a small portion of the document is needed.

---

[6]http://www.megginson.com/SAX

9.1.4 *Selecting the Best Approach*

Selecting the best approach is based on the two decisions shown in Figure 9–3.

First, should the code generator use custom data structures to get specification information? There are three reasons for considering custom data structures. First, you might be concerned about separation of concerns between where the data comes from and what to do with the data. In Section 6.3 the same issue arose in the context of run-time variabilities. If alternative data sources are required or expected in the future, then it may be desirable to use custom data structures rather than DOM. Otherwise, you will need to convert other data sources to DOM.

The second reason to prefer custom data structures is that they will make reading, writing, and modifying easier during the code-generation phase. Rather than using the DOM methods during code generation, you can use custom methods to get exactly what you want. Using DOM

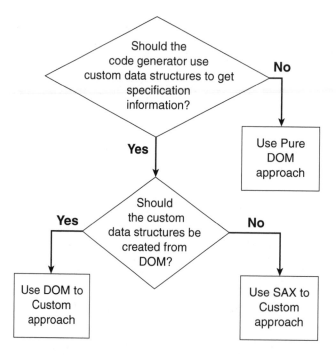

Figure 9–3 Decisions for selecting best approach

methods may require a lot of traversing and sorting through the DOM data structures to get what you want. In the Play example, a pure DOM approach adds about 30% more code to the code-generation phase. That doesn't mean a pure DOM approach is more expensive; you still have to design and create the custom data structures. The breakeven point between the cost of designing and creating custom data structures and the cost of more complex code-generation code will depend on how large these components are or will become. In a small program generator, it is better to use a pure DOM approach. The larger the code-generation phase gets, the more likely it is that you will need custom data structures.

The third reason to prefer a custom data structure is performance. Using DOM data structures on a large XML document can become expensive, particularly if you are only using a small portion of the document to generate a program. Thus for performance reasons you might want to avoid using DOM structures. In that case, you will be forced to create your own custom data structures, and you will also want to use SAX.

Now, let's consider the second decision: Should the custom data structures be created from DOM? This one is a bit more straightforward. Despite its name, a SAX implementation is going to be more complex than using DOM. It requires thinking about how to do the processing while parsing. In particular, you will not have access to the whole parse tree while parsing, so if cross-referencing is required to create the data structures, you will have some complex coding to do. However, SAX parsers are generally faster and require less memory than DOM, since only those parts of the XML document that you need are stored. How do you decide whether performance is an issue? In many XML implementations the decision between using SAX and DOM is critical. Fortunately, that is not the case with program generators. Almost all program generators will be fast enough using DOM, so the default choice should simply be to use DOM and to consider SAX only if there is sufficient evidence that performance will be an issue. Let's consider the reasons.

When one asks about the performance of a program generator, there are many different aspects to consider. These include the performance of the generated code, the performance of the code generator, and the performance of the combination of code generator and compiler. If the code generator is seldom used relative to the generated code, then it is more important to put effort into improving the performance of the generated code rather than the code generator. If you find that the code generator is used frequently during the development phase and is taking too long to support a rapid development cycle, then and only then should effort be put into improving the code-generator performance. Even in this case, it may not be clear how this effort should be deployed. Some program generators output large amounts of code that must be compiled. The compiler may take more time than the code generator. The code generator may be able to generate code faster than the compiler can compile it. In this case improving the performance of the code generator may not make much difference in the total time to generate and compile a program. Other techniques may be more effective. For example, it may be more effective to minimize the generated code by converting a code-driven approach to a table-driven approach. It may make sense to split the generated code into variant and invariant portions and move the invariant portions from the code generator to a jar file.

Finally, you may actually encounter a situation in which using DOM is too inefficient. This is likely to happen in situations where the program specifications are just a small portion of a large XML document. Using SAX will allow you to ignore most of the XML document and just extract the information necessary for the code generator.

9.2 | DOM Analysis and Transformations

Once the XML document is parsed and available as an object, one can optionally perform analysis and transformations on the object. Analysis includes:

- **Checking for errors**: Look for nonsyntactic errors in the specification. For example, make sure that appropriate names are declared, that there are no missing parts, and that all parts are used in their proper way.

- **Warnings**: Look for common mistakes or potential problems that are not explicitly wrong. This could include, for example, container objects with no elements, such as scenes with no props.

- **Model analysis**: Analyze the deeper semantic meanings of the specification. It may require constructing a model, some scenarios, and checking for potential problems. Finite state machine analysis, for example, could include looking for sinks (states or sets of states that one cannot leave), disconnected states (states that cannot be reached from the start states), or ambiguous transitions between states.

- **Performance analysis**: Examine the specification for ways in which it will be used to determine an optimal structure/code for the generated program. This may include, for example, a determination of whether some kind of information encoding is appropriate (such as Huffman encoding) to minimize certain performance parameters (such as traffic or memory).

The kinds of transformations that could occur include:

- **Expansion of abbreviations**: Often specifications provide abbreviations or shortcuts. To avoid complex code generation it is often easier to expand these abbreviations to their full description. This kind of transformation may fill in additional elements, default values, or references to other parts of the specification.

■ **Expansion to canonical forms**: Some specification languages allow a variety of ways to say the same thing. To avoid complex code generation, it is often easier to simply transform such parts to a standard form (sometimes called a canonical form).

■ **Optimizations**: Transform the object. For example, common subtrees may be detected so that code is generated just once and then reused in other locations. For example, place the code for a common subtree in a method that is called from each of the places it is used. Other transformations may be used to optimize other constraints such as memory, time, or traffic.

Much of the syntactic error checking can be expressed using a DTD.[7] In such a situation, a validating parser will automatically check for validity as well as well-formedness. DTDs are not powerful enough, though, to express all possible constraints. For example, a DTD can ensure that certain attribute names are properly declared and referenced throughout the document (using ID and IDREF). However, if this information were designed as elements rather than attributes, then a DTD would not be able to automatically check for these relationships.

9.2.1 *The DOM API*

The DOM API for Java is a set of classes and methods. The Java DOM classes and methods used in this book are briefly described in Tables 9–1 through 9–5.

---

[7]Document Type Definitions are described in Section 5.8.

Table 9–1 DOM Java Classes

Class	Description
Node	Represents a node in the parse tree. Each node represents some piece of information from the XML document.
Element extends Node	Represents an element node of the parse tree.
Document extends Node	Represents the document node of the parse tree, which is the root node. Its first child is the root element node.
Attr extends Node	Represents an attribute node of the parse tree (typically a child of an element node).
CharacterData extends Node	Represents a node that has character data associated with it such as comments and data content.
Text extends Character Data	Represents a node that has just character data of the XML document.
NodeList	An interface representing a list of nodes (returned by getElementsbyTagName).

Table 9–2 Node Methods

public String **getNodeType**();	Returns the type of the node, such as ELEMENT_NODE, ATTRIBUTE_NODE, TEXT_NODE, etc.
public String **getNodeValue**();	Returns the value of the node. For example, if the node is a text node, the value returned is the character data that makes up the node.
public Node **getFirstChild**();	Returns the first child node of the current node. Returns null if there are no children.
public Node **getNextSibling**();	Returns the next sibling node of the current node or null if there are no more siblings.

Table 9–3 Element Methods

`public String getTagName();`	Returns the element-type name of the XML element.
`public String getAttribute( String name);`	Returns the value of the attribute whose name is name.
`public NodeList getElementsByTagName( String name);`	Returns a list of all elements in the subtree of the current element whose element type name is name.

Table 9–4 Document Methods

`public Element getDocumentElement();`	Returns the top-level element node in an XML document.

Table 9–5 Node List Methods

`public int getLength();`	Returns the number of nodes in the node list.
`public Node item(int index);`	Returns a node from the node list (zero-based indexed).

9.2.2 *A Simple Analysis Example*

To illustrate the DOM API and a simple analysis, consider the XML document with four friend elements shown in Example 9–2.

Example 9–2: XML Document with Four Friends

```
<?xml version="1.0"?>
<mydoc>
<friend>joe</friend>
<friend phone="928735">jill</friend>
<friend phone="123d34">june</friend>
<friend phone="928735">jane</friend>
</mydoc>
```

Figure 9–4 shows how a simple XML document is parsed into a series of Node objects forming a parse tree.

In Example 9–3 we show a simple program that reads the XML document looking for three types of errors:

Friend elements with no phone attribute (missing attribute error)

Phone numbers with invalid characters (invalid phone number error)

Unique phone numbers for each friend element (duplicate phone error)

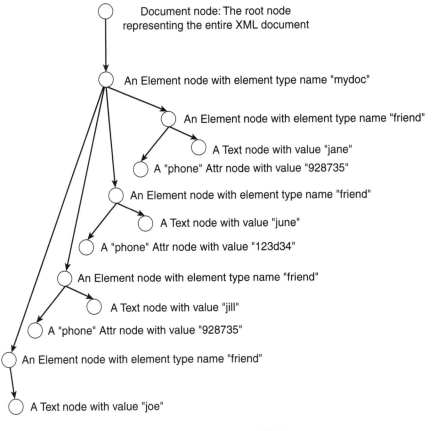

Figure 9–4   DOM parse tree for a simple XML document

Example 9–3: A Simple Program Checking for Errors in an XML Document

```java
import com.ibm.xml.parser.Parser;
import org.w3c.dom.*;
import java.io.*;
import java.util.*;

public class Checker {
    int errorcount = 0;
    Document doc;

    /** Verify that every "friend" element has a unique
        phone attribute with numeric characters */
    public void check() {
        Hashtable phones = new Hashtable(); // map phones to nodes
        NodeList nodes = doc.getElementsByTagName("friend");
        for (int j=0; j<nodes.getLength(); ++j) {
            Element n = (Element) nodes.item(j);
            String phone = n.getAttribute("phone");
            if (phone==null || phone.length()==0) {
                error("No phone for friend: "+n);
            } else {
                for (int k=0; k<phone.length(); ++k) {
                    char c = phone.charAt(k);
                    if ("0123456789".indexOf(c) == -1) {
                        error("Invalid character in phone: "+phone);
                        break;
                    }
                }
                if (phones.get(phone)==null) {
                    phones.put(phone, n);
                } else {
                    error("duplicate phone: "+phone);
                }
            }
        }
    }

    /** Emit error messages */
    public void error(String m) {
        ++errorcount;
        System.out.println("Error: "+m);
    }

    /** Read and parse an XML file */
```

```
    public Checker(String filename)
                    throws Exception {
        InputStream is = new FileInputStream(filename);
        Parser parser = new Parser(filename);
        doc = parser.readStream(is);
    }

    public static void main(String[] args) throws Exception {
        Checker c = new Checker(args[0]);
        c.check();
        if (c.errorcount==0) {
            System.out.println("No errors");
        } else {
            System.out.println("Sorry, there were "
                            +c.errorcount+" errors.");
        }
    }
}
```

9.3 | Program Generation from the DOM

Once the XML document is parsed, analyzed, and perhaps transformed, it is time for code generation. This is straightforward in principle but becomes messy with details. The messiness leads to difficult-to-read programs, which you will find in the remainder of this chapter. Don't despair, because the next three chapters will show alternative ways to tame this messiness by replacing the unreadable code-generation code with templates.

A typical code generator is simply a series of print statements with occasional flow of control statements for repetition or conditional code. The peculiarities of the program language may dictate either messier or less messy code. As an example, let's examine the generation of an array of elements. In the Java language[8] one can put a comma after every array element or a comma between every two elements. The two array declarations in Example 9–4 are both syntactically valid and mean the same thing:

---

[8]Also true in C and C++, but not other languages such as Pascal.

Example 9–4: Two Syntactic Ways of Declaring an Array

```
int[] widths = { 3, 4, 5 };
int[] heights = { 3, 4, 5, };
```

To generate the above two arrays one must write code something like that shown in Example 9–5. Note that the second array is easier to generate.

Example 9–5: Code to Generate the Arrays in Example 9–4

```
out.print("int[] widths = {");
for (int j=0; j<widthData.length; ++j) {
        out.print(" "+widthData[j]);
        if (j<widthData.length-1) {
                out.print(",");
        }
}
out.println(" };");

out.print("int[] heights = { ");
for (int j=0; j<heightData.length; ++j) {
        out.print(heightData[j]+", ");
}
out.println("};");
```

These kinds of situations occur in other places as well. Consider the mutually exclusive choice structure such as that shown in Example 9–6.

Example 9–6: Mutually Exclusive Choice

```
if (x==firstChoice) {
    ...
} else if (x==secondChoice) {
    ...
} else if (x==thirdChoice) {
    ...
}
```

It will be easier to generate the equivalent code (assuming x is a constant and the choices are all different), as shown in Example 9–7.

Example 9–7: Mutually Exclusive Choice Alternative Code

```
if (x==firstChoice) {
    …
}
if (x==secondChoice) {
    …
}
if (x==thirdChoice) {
    …
}
```

The second example is easier to generate but incurs a slight performance penalty. So there is a choice to either make the code generator somewhat more complicated or to have the generated code slightly more inefficient. These kinds of choices occur very frequently.

9.4 | The Play Program Generator using DOM

We now present the Play program generator using DOM. We first provide a simple utility base class that defines utility methods for retrieving information from the DOM tree (Example 9–8). These methods are straightforward and are useful in other generation programs as well.

Example 9–8: The DOM_Util Class

```
package com.craigc.progen;
import com.ibm.xml.parser.Parser;
import org.w3c.dom.*;
import java.io.*;

/**
 * XML DOM Utility Class
 */
public class DOM_Util {
```

```java
/** Get an attribute value from a node, using default if no node */
public static String getAttr(Node n, String attrName,
                                         String defaultVal) {
    if (n instanceof Document) {
        n = ((Document) n).getDocumentElement();
    }
    String v = null;
    if (n instanceof Element) {
        v = ((Element)n).getAttribute(attrName);
    }
    if (v==null || v.equals("")) {
        return defaultVal;
    }
    return v;
}


/** Find and get an integer attribute value */
public static int getIntAttr(Node n, String tagName,
                                 int defaultValue) {
    String s = getAttr(n, tagName, "");
    return Config.parseInt(s, defaultValue);
}


/** Find and get content of a node, or defaultValue if not found */
public static String get(Node n, String tagName,
                             String defaultValue) {
    if (n instanceof Document) {
        n = ((Document) n).getDocumentElement();
    }
    if (n instanceof Element) {
        NodeList nodes = ((Element)n).getElementsByTagName(tagName);
        if (nodes.getLength()==0) {
            return defaultValue;
        } else {
            return getContent(nodes.item(0));
        }
    } else return defaultValue;
}


/** Find and get an integer value */
public static int getInt(Node n, String tagName, int defaultValue) {
    String s = get(n, tagName, "");
    return Config.parseInt(s, defaultValue);
}
```

```
/** Get content of a node */
public static String getContent(Node n) {
    StringBuffer buf = new StringBuffer();
    getContent1(n, buf);
    return buf.toString();
}

private static void getContent1(Node n, StringBuffer buf) {
    for (Node c = n.getFirstChild(); c!=null;
                                c = c.getNextSibling()) {
        if (c instanceof Element || c instanceof EntityReference) {
            getContent1(c, buf);
        } else if (c instanceof Text) {
            buf.append(c.getNodeValue());
        }
    }
}

/** Read and parse an XML file */
public static Document readDocument(String filename)
                throws Exception {
    InputStream is = new FileInputStream(filename);
    Parser parser = new Parser(filename);
    return parser.readStream(is);
}
}
```

The DOM_Util class provides utility methods for accessing information from the DOM data structures. The get method is used to get the data associated with a node in the parse tree (similar to the get methods used in the Config classes of Chapter 6). The get method will search the parse tree for the first occurrence of a particular type of node and return the content of that node. The getContent method is used to obtain the content of an element (or any node). The getAttr method obtains the value of an attribute of an element, and getIntAttr method returns the value as an integer.

We'll use the DOM-to-custom approach. That is, our program will read the XML Play specification in as a DOM data structure and then converted to a custom data structure. In Chapter 6, a Play specification in XML was read in at run time. In this chapter we will read the same file in at generation time. The Play specification was converted to an object of type `PlayData1` in Chapter 6. This data structure is reused here instead of the XML DOM data structures, because it makes the code-generation part easier to understand. The transformation from DOM data structures to PlayData1 is shown in Example 9–9.

Example 9–9: The PlayData1 Class

```
package com.craigc.progen;
import org.w3c.dom.*;

public class PlayData1 extends HandlerBase {
    public String name;
    public String title;
    public int width;
    public int height;
    public SceneData startScene;

    public PropData[] props;
    public SceneData[] scenes;

    public class PropData {
        public String name;
        public String label;      // initial value
        public ScriptData script; // only action script in Phase I
    }

    public class SceneData {
        public String name;
        public String color;
        public PropData[] addprops;
    }

    public class ScriptData {
        public SceneData nextScene;
        public TraitData[] traits;
    }

    public class TraitData {
        public PropData prop;
        public String newValue;
    }

    public PropData findProp(String n) {
        for (int j=0; j<props.length; ++j) {
            if (props[j].name.equals(n)) {
```

```
                return props[j];
            }
        }
        return null;
    }


    public SceneData findScene(String n) {
        for (int j=0; j<scenes.length; ++j) {
            if (scenes[j].name.equals(n)) {
                return scenes[j];
            }
        }
        return null;
    }


    public PlayData1(Document d) {
        convertDocument(d);
    }


    public PlayData1(String filename) throws Exception {
        convertDocument(DOM_Util.readDocument(filename));
    }

    /** Convert XML data using DOM to PlayData1 */
    public void convertDocument(Document d) {
        Element playNode = (Element) d.getDocumentElement();
        title = DOM_Util.get(playNode, "title", "Play Example");
        width = DOM_Util.getIntAttr(playNode, "width", 500);
        height = DOM_Util.getIntAttr(playNode, "height", 250);
        name = DOM_Util.getAttr(playNode, "name", "Unknown");

        // First must create data structures for all props & scenes
        // before doing scripts or traits

        // Create SceneData
        NodeList e = playNode.getElementsByTagName("scene");
        scenes = new SceneData[e.getLength()];
        // first create all scenes
        for (int j=0; j<e.getLength(); ++j) {
            Node bnode = e.item(j);
            SceneData n = new SceneData();
            n.name = DOM_Util.getAttr(bnode, "name", "?");
            n.color = DOM_Util.getAttr(bnode, "color", "?");
            scenes[j] = n;
        }
```

```
        // Create PropData
        e = playNode.getElementsByTagName("prop");
        props = new PropData[e.getLength()];
        for (int j=0; j<e.getLength(); ++j) {
            Node bnode = e.item(j);
            PropData n = new PropData();
            n.name = DOM_Util.getAttr(bnode, "name", "?");
            n.label = getLabel(bnode);
            props[j] = n;
        }

        for (int j=0; j<e.getLength(); ++j) {
            props[j].script = getScript(e.item(j), props[j].name);
        }

        // next do addprops & scripts with goto next scene
        e = playNode.getElementsByTagName("scene");
        for (int j=0; j<e.getLength(); ++j) {
            Element bnode = (Element) e.item(j);
            // Create AddPropData
            NodeList e2 = bnode.getElementsByTagName("addprop");
            scenes[j].addprops = new AddPropData[e2.getLength()];
            for (int j2=0; j2<e2.getLength(); ++j2) {
                Node anode = e2.item(j2);
                String pname = DOM_Util.getAttr(anode, "name", "?");
                scenes[j].addprops[j2] = findProp(pname);
            }
        }
        startScene = findScene(DOM_Util.getAttr(playNode,
                                  "start", "?"));
    }

    /** Gets label value of trait if any */
    String getLabel(Node n) {
        // ==> wrong way
        return DOM_Util.get(n, "trait", null);
        // return "?";
    }

    ScriptData getScript(Node n, String dname) {
        NodeList e = ((Element)n).getElementsByTagName("script");
        // only include the Action script
        for (int j=0; j<e.getLength(); ++j) {
            Element snode = (Element) e.item(j);
            // assume first and only script is Action script
            ScriptData sd = new ScriptData();
            sd.nextScene = findScene(DOM_Util.getAttr(snode,
                                                "goto", ""));
```

```
            NodeList e2 = snode.getElementsByTagName("trait");
            sd.traits = new TraitData[e2.getLength()];
            for (int j2=0; j2<e2.getLength(); ++j2) {
                Node tnode = e2.item(j2);
                sd.traits[j2] = new TraitData();
                sd.traits[j2].prop = findProp(
                        DOM_Util.getAttr(tnode, "prop", dname));
                sd.traits[j2].newValue = DOM_Util.getContent(tnode);
            }
            return sd;
        }
        return null;
    }
}
```

We are ready for the full program generator for the code-driven style example previously discussed in Chapter 8. This program generator has no analysis or transformations, so it simply reads the XML document and generates the program (Example 9–10).

Example 9–10: The PlayGen1.java Class

```java
package com.craigc.progen;
import java.io.*;

/**
 * Generator for Play domain, phase I
 */
public class PlayGen1 extends DOM_Util {

    public static void main(String args[]) {
        PlayData1 d = null;
        PrintWriter out;
        if (args.length>1) {
            try {
                // read and parse Play specification
                d = new PlayData1(args[0]);

                // open up output file
                out = new PrintWriter(new FileOutputStream(args[1]));
            } catch (Exception e) {
                System.out.println("Exception: "+args[0]);
                e.printStackTrace();
                return;
            }
        } else {
```

```java
            System.out.println("Usage: PlayGen1 xml-file output-file");
            return;
        }

        out.println("package com.craigc.progen;");
        out.println("import java.awt.*;");
        out.println("import java.awt.event.*;");
        out.println("");
        out.println("class "+d.name+"Play2 extends Frame {");
        out.println("    ");
        out.println("    /* The Props for "+d.name+" *************/");
        out.println("    ");
        for (int j=0; j<d.props.length; ++j) {
            PlayData1.PropData prop = d.props[j];
            out.println("    Button "+prop.name+"Prop = new Button(\""
                +prop.label+"\");");
        }
        out.println("");
        out.println("    /* The Events in the "
                            +d.name+" *************/");
        out.println("");
        out.println("    class PropEvent implements ActionListener {");
        out.println("        public void actionPerformed(ActionEvent "
                                    +"evt) {");
        out.println("            Object prop = evt.getSource();");
        for (int j=0; j<d.props.length; ++j) {
            PlayData1.PropData prop = d.props[j];
            out.print("            ");
            if (j!=0) {
                out.print("} else ");
            }
            out.println("if (prop=="+prop.name+"Prop) {");
            if (prop.script!=null) {
                for (int k=0; k<prop.script.traits.length; ++k) {
                    String pname = prop.script.traits[k].prop==null
                        ? prop.name : prop.script.traits[k].prop.name;
                    out.println("            "
                        +pname+"Prop.setLabel(\""
                        +prop.script.traits[k].newValue+"\");");
                }
                if (prop.script.nextScene!=null) {
                    out.println("            enterNewScene(\""
                        +prop.script.nextScene.name+"\");");
                }
            }
        }
    }
```

```
out.println("                } else {");
out.println("                    System.out.println("
                                +"\"Invalid prop\");");
out.println("               }");
out.println("            }");
out.println("        }");
out.println("    ");
out.println("    /* Creating and starting up the "+d.name
                                                +" ****/");
out.println("    ");
out.println("    String currentScene;");
out.println("    ");
out.println("    public "+d.name+"Play2() {");
out.println("        super(\""+d.title+"\");");
out.println("        setSize("+d.width+", "+d.height+");");
out.println("        setLayout(new FlowLayout());");
out.println("    ");
out.println("        // initialize props");
out.println("        PropEvent a = new PropEvent();");
for (int j=0; j<d.props.length; ++j) {
    PlayData1.PropData prop = d.props[j];
    out.println("        "+prop.name
                        +"Prop.addActionListener(a);");
}
out.println("");
out.println("        // start scene");
out.println("        enterNewScene(\""+d.startScene.name
                                        +"\");");
out.println("    }");
out.println("");
out.println("    public void enterNewScene(String scene) {");
out.println("        removeAll();  // remove previous scene");
out.println("        currentScene = scene;");
for (int k=0; k<d.scenes.length; ++k) {
    PlayData1.SceneData scene = d.scenes[k];
    out.print("        ");
    if (k!=0) {
        out.print("} else ");
    }
    out.println("if (scene.equals(\""+scene.name+"\")) {");
    for (int p2=0; p2<scene.addprops.length; ++p2) {
        PlayData1.PropData prop2 = scene.addprops[p2];
        out.println("            add("+prop2.name+"Prop);");
    }
    out.println("            setBackground(Color.decode(\""
        +scene.color+"\"));");
}
```

```
            out.println("            } else {");
            out.println("                System.out.println(\"Invalid scene: \""
                                                          +"+scene);");
            out.println("            }");
            out.println("            show();");
            out.println("        }");
            out.println("");
            out.println("    public static void main(String[] args) {");
            out.println("        new "+d.name+"Play2();");
            out.println("    }");
            out.println("}");
            out.close();
    }

    public static String genScript(PlayData1.PropData n,
                                   PrintWriter out) {
        if (n.script==null) {
            return "";
        }
        for (int j=0; j<n.script.traits.length; ++j) {
            genTrait(n.script.traits[j], n, "                ", out);
        }
        return n.script.nextScene==null ? "" : n.script.nextScene.name;
    }

    public static void genTrait(PlayData1.TraitData trait,
            PlayData1.PropData prop, String indent, PrintWriter out) {
        String propName = trait.prop==null?prop.name:trait.prop.name;
        out.println(indent+propName+"Prop.setLabel(\""
                            +trait.newValue+"\");");
    }
}
```

9.5 | Summary

A program generator typically consists of three parts: the parser, the analyzer/transformer, and the code generator. An XML document can be read and parsed using either DOM data structures or custom data structures using SAX. For most program generators it is sufficient and easier to use DOM rather than SAX. The analyzer/transformer will examine the XML document for problems and may perform some transformations. The transformations may include the creation of custom data structures. Finally, the code generator will use either the DOM or custom data structures for generating a program.

Further Reading

H. Maruyama, K. Tamura, and N. Uramoto, *XML and Java, Developing Web Applications*, Addison-Wesley, 1999.

A. Nakhimovsky and T. Myers, *Java XML Programming with Servlets and JSP,* Wrox, 1999.

Using Java Server Pages to Generate Programs

▮ Dynamic generation of Web pages (and programs)

▮ Chart Applet Program Generator

▮ JSP as a program generator

ava Server Pages are used to dynamically create Web pages. We can also use them to generate programs, with the side benefit that they can be delivered over the Internet.

10.1 | Applets and Servlets

When the Java programming language first appeared in 1995, the most visible aspect was the applet, a Java program that was delivered over the Internet and executed inside the Web browser (Figure 10–1).

At the time, the Java language was not seriously considered as a server-side language, but that changed quickly. Soon Java servlets were being deployed. A Java servlet is a Java class executed in the Web server rather than browser. Although a servlet can do many different things, the most important for our purposes is the ability to dynamically create customized Web pages as shown in Figure 10–2.

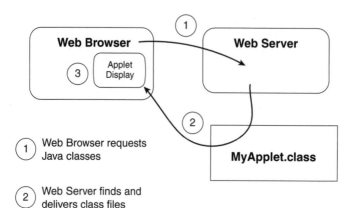

1. Web Browser requests Java classes

2. Web Server finds and delivers class files

3. Web Browser executes Applet on the client machine

Figure 10–1   Applet mechanics

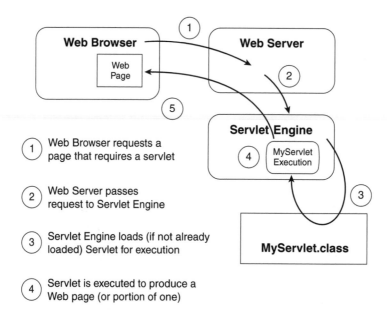

1. Web Browser requests a page that requires a servlet

2. Web Server passes request to Servlet Engine

3. Servlet Engine loads (if not already loaded) Servlet for execution

4. Servlet is executed to produce a Web page (or portion of one)

5. The dynamically created Web page is delivered to the browser

Figure 10–2   Servlet mechanics

Let's take a look at a simple servlet that outputs the current date and the value of the x parameter if any. Figure 10–3 shows two possible pages served by this applet. The first page has no x parameter, while the second has an x parameter with value "hi".

A servlet that implements these dynamic HTML pages is given in Example 10–1. Notice the method doGet, which services a Web browser request to return a Web page. The code inside the method has a certain similarity to program generators. This shouldn't come as a surprise to faithful readers of previous chapters, since dynamic generation of Web pages is no different in concept from program generation.

Example 10–1: A Servlet Creating a Simple HTML Page

```java
import java.io.*;
import java.util.Date;
import javax.servlet.*;
import javax.servlet.http.*;

public class Example10 extends HttpServlet
{
    /** Handle the GET method by building a simple Web page. */
    public void doGet (HttpServletRequest request,
                       HttpServletResponse response)
        throws ServletException, IOException {
            PrintWriter out;

            // set content type
            response.setContentType("text/html");

            // write the Web page
            out = response.getWriter();

            out.println("<HTML><HEAD><TITLE>");
            out.println("Example Servlet");
            out.println("</TITLE></HEAD>");
            out.println("<BODY>");
            out.println("<H3>The time is " + new Date() + "</H3>");
            String x = request.getParameter("x");
            if (x==null) {
                out.println("There is no x parameter");
            } else {
                out.println("The x parameter is "+x);
            }
            out.println("</BODY></HTML>");
            out.close();
        }
}
```

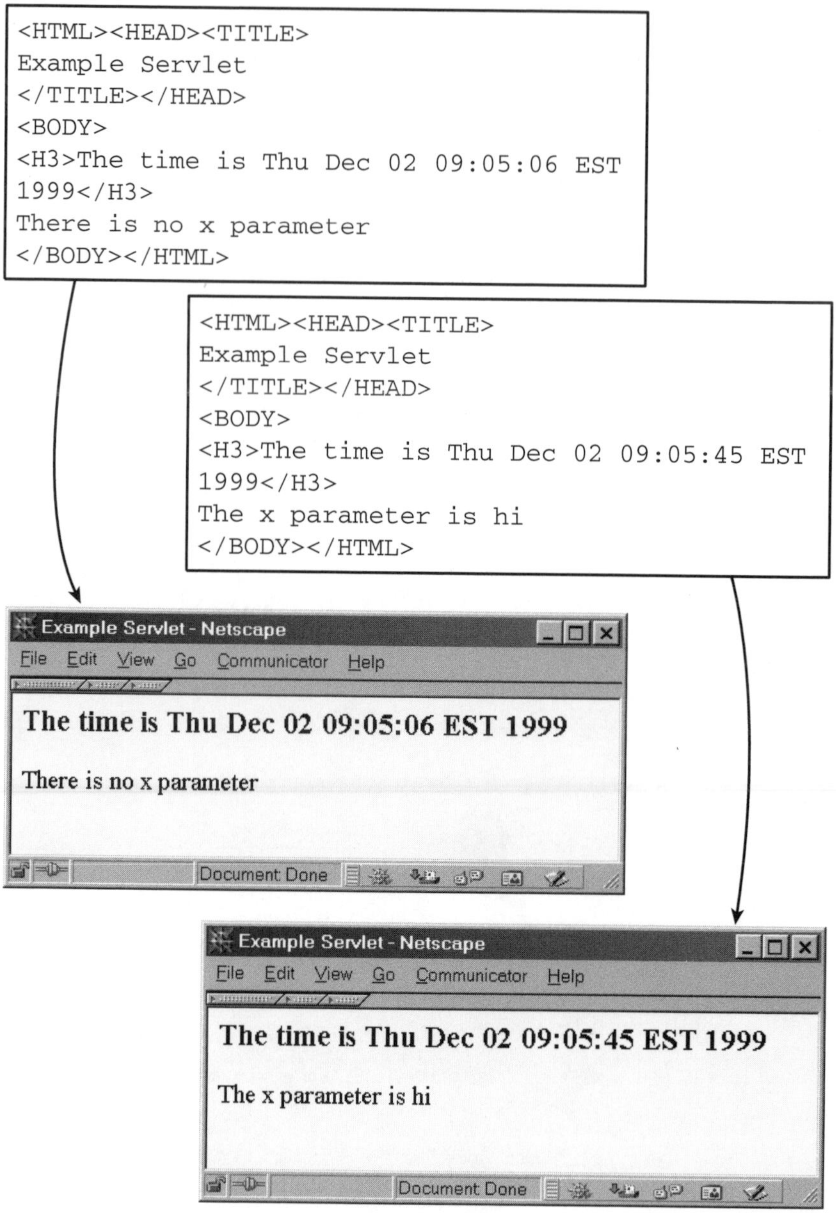

```
<HTML><HEAD><TITLE>
Example Servlet
</TITLE></HEAD>
<BODY>
<H3>The time is Thu Dec 02 09:05:06 EST
1999</H3>
There is no x parameter
</BODY></HTML>
```

```
<HTML><HEAD><TITLE>
Example Servlet
</TITLE></HEAD>
<BODY>
<H3>The time is Thu Dec 02 09:05:45 EST
1999</H3>
The x parameter is hi
</BODY></HTML>
```

Example Servlet - Netscape

File Edit View Go Communicator Help

The time is Thu Dec 02 09:05:06 EST 1999

There is no x parameter

Document Done

Example Servlet - Netscape

File Edit View Go Communicator Help

The time is Thu Dec 02 09:05:45 EST 1999

The x parameter is hi

Document Done

Figure 10–3 Two different Web pages served by the same servlet

10.2 | Java Server Pages

As you can imagine, writing the code for the above servlet day in and day out can become quite tedious. Sun Microsystems developed a simpler way to develop these dynamically created pages, called Java Server Pages (JSP[1]). A Java Server Page is a file that looks like an HTML file. In addition to HTML code, a JSP file also has escapes to Java code embedded within the delimiters, "<%" and "%>". The Java escapes are executed to produce the dynamic portions of the HTML page. Example 10–2 shows the equivalent of the previous servlet.

Example 10–2: A Simple JSP Showing Current Time and a Counter

```
<%@ import = "java.util.Date;" %>
<HTML><HEAD><TITLE>
Example 10
</TITLE></HEAD>
<BODY>
<H3>The time is <%=new Date()%></H3>
<% String x = request.getParameter("x");
   if (x==null) {
%>
There is no x parameter
<% } else { %>
The x parameter is <%=x%>
<% } %>
</BODY>
</HTML>
```

A JSP file may contain the kinds of escapes shown in Table 10–1.

Table 10–1: Escapes in a JSP File

Syntax	Example
<%@ *Java-directive* %>	<%@ import="java.util.Date" %>
<%! *Java-declaration* %>	<%! int x = 3; %>
<% *Java-code* %>	<% if (x==null) { %>
<%= *Java-expression* %>	<%=new Date()%>
<%− *comment* −%>	<%− comments and notes −%>

---

[1] Active Server Pages (ASP) is the original inspiration for Java Server Pages.

The Java-directives are used for such things as imports (as in the example) and to control such things as buffering, optional error pages, and thread safeness. Java-declarations are used to declare instance variable and methods in the generated class. Java-code is mostly used for flow of control over the generated code, and as such each escape may have part of a statement. In Example 10–2, the *if* statement is broken into three fragments which are used as the boundaries between the *then* and *else* parts. Java-expressions are used to compute values that are embedded in the generated Web page, and are probably the most used and useful escape. The comment escape is redundant, since the Java-code escape can include comments, or HTML comments can be used. The only difference between these kinds of comments is how far they go with respect to processing. JSP comments are filtered out when the JSP file is translated to Java-code. Java comments are removed when the Java-code is compiled, and HTML comments are retained until display time.

You can think of the JSP file as a specification for a servlet. In particular, you can think of the above JSP file as the specification for the previously given servlet. Although a separate class is created (as a subclass of `HttpJspPage` which is a subclass of `HttpServlet`), the relevant servlet context remains the same, so you can think of the JSP page as representing an `HttpServlet` class. A number of implicit objects are available as listed in Table 10–2. Most of these objects are directly available in a servlet and are thus made available in a JSP file as well.

Table 10–2: Javax.Servlet Variables

javax.Servlet Variables	*Meaning*
`ServletRequest` `request;`	This is the servlet input. It includes information information about origin, parameters, and other information about the request.
`ServletResponse` `response;`	This is the servlet output. It includes information about the type and content of the response.

(continued)

Table 10–2: Javax.Servlet Variables *(Continued)*

javax.Servlet Variables	*Meaning*
`jsp.PageContext pageContext;`	This provides facilities such as access to namespaces, APIs, and mechanisms for including other JSP files.
`http.HttpSession session;`	The session object (if any). It contains information associated with the user of the request, and its lifetime may extend over multiple requests.
`ServletContext application;`	The servlet context obtained from the servlet configuration object. This information is global to all service calls.
`jsp.JspWriter out;`	The output stream where the generated page is created.
`ServletConfig config;`	The `ServletConfig` for the JSP which provides access to configuration information.

Most of these objects are not used if you are using JSP to generate Java programs. One that may be used often is the `out` object. It is sometimes simpler to output text using `out` in long Java-code sections. The following three JSP segments are equivalent.

```
<% if (x==null) { %>5<% } else {%>6<% } %>

<% out.print(x==null?"5":"6"); %>

<%=x==null?"5":"6"%>
```

The only other object in Table 10–2 that might be used is the `request` object. This object provides access to information about the original URL request including parameters, remote IP address, and cookies.

JSP files are typically processed dynamically inside the servlet engine. When a request is received for a JSP file, the servlet engine will translate the JSP file to a Java servlet program, compile it, and execute it as shown in Figure 10–4. The servlet engine is typically smart enough to cache the servlet program so that it doesn't have to translate and compile it for every request. However, if it is cached, the JSP file will still be checked to see if it has been changed since the last compile. This makes it very easy for JSP writers to modify and test their Web pages.

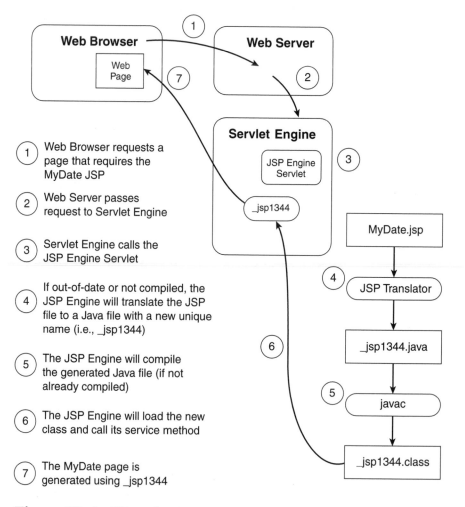

Figure 10–4 JSP mechanics

JSP, then, is an important example of a program generator in general use over the Internet. It is a very simple specification language consisting simply of static text to output to a Web page and escapes to the underlying implementation language. There are no high-level abstractions and no language structure to speak of. The escapes provide maximal flexibility but at the same time minimal leverage. The importance of JSP in this book is that it provides a very simple way to use "templates" to create program generators. Although JSP was designed and implemented for Web pages, there is no reason in principle that it can't be used to deliver other things. In particular, it can be used to deliver Java programs. Example 10–3 is a JSP file that delivers a simple program instead of an HTML page.

Example 10–3: A Simple JSP That Delivers a Java Program (Instead of HTML Page)

```
<%@ import = "java.util.Date;" %>
<pre>
import java.util.Date;

class MyProgram {

    public static main(String[] args) {
        System.out.println("This program was generated"
            +" <%=new Date()%>");
        System.out.println("This output was created "+new Date());
<% String x = request.getParameter("x");
    if (x==null) {
%>
        System.out.println("There was no x parameter.");
<% } else { %>
        String x = "<%=x%>";
        System.out.println("The x parameter was "+x);
<% } %>
    }
}
```

The `<pre>` tag is used to deliver preformatted text.[2] No other HTML tags are used, and just the text of the program is delivered. Example 10–4 is a program delivered by this JSP file.

---

[2]Alternatively, one can use response.setContentType method or the contentType JSP directive.

Example 10–4: A Java Program Delivered by the JSP File in Example 10–3

```
import java.util.Date;

class MyProgram {

    public static main(String[] args) {
        System.out.println("This program was generated"
            +" Thu Dec 02 09:55:11 EST 1999");
        System.out.println("This output was created "+new Date());

        String x = "hi";
        System.out.println("The x parameter was "+x);

    }
}
```

Note that Example 10–3 can be confusing, since it uses Java-code on two different levels. One is the program generator itself, which includes the first import, `new Date()` expression and `String x` declaration, and the other is the program itself, which includes the second import, `new Date()` expression and `String x` declaration. It is useful to employ different colors or fonts to distinguish between these two levels with when you view them, so they don't get mixed up. Example 10–5 shows the JSP file again, this time with the program-generator parts in a different font. Notice how much easier it is to read.

Example 10–5: An Easier-to-Read Version of Example 10–3

```
<%@ import = "java.util.Date;" %>
<pre>
import java.util.Date;

class MyProgram {

    public static main(String[] args) {
        System.out.println("This program was generated"
            +" <%=new Date()%>");
        System.out.println("This output was created "+new Date());
<% String x = request.getParameter("x");
   if (x==null) {
%>
        System.out.println("There was no x parameter.");
```

```
<% } else { %>
        String x = "<%=x%>";
        System.out.println("The x parameter was "+x);
<% } %>
    }
}
```

10.2.1 *The Entity-Reference Annoyance*

HTML (and XML) documents use certain characters to identify markup information. In particular the ampersand, "&", is used to identify entity references, and the less-than character, "<", is used to identify tags. Unfortunately, Java programs also use these two characters as operators, which typically must be escaped using an entity reference. Each entity reference begins with the ampersand character followed by an identifier and ending with a semicolon. Some standard predefined entity references are listed in Table 10–3.

Table 10–3: Predefined Entity References

Entity Reference	*Character*	*Description*
&lt;	<	Less than
&amp;	&	Ampersand
&quot;	"	Quote
&gt;	>	Greater than
&apos;	'	Apostrophe

What this means is that a Java program cannot be written exactly the way you would under normal circumstances. Each special symbol should be replaced with the corresponding entity reference. In practice only the ampersand and less-than symbols need to be replaced, but to be completely safe in all circumstances, the greater-than symbol and quote should also be replaced with entity references. Example 10–6 shows how one ought to express a Java expression such as "x < 5 && y < 5".

Example 10–6: Using Entity References Rather Than Ampersands and Less-Than Symbols

```
<pre>
    if (x &lt; 5 &amp;&amp; y &lt; 5) {
        ...
    }
```

10.2.2   JSP XML Syntax

JSP version 1.1 provides an alternative syntax to the <% ... %> syntax that is compatible with XML. Using the alternative syntax, a JSP file can be created that will also be an XML file. Translating Example 10–5 would result in the equivalent file shown in Example 10–7 (keeping the same font styles for readability purposes). Note that XML namespaces are used; in this case the namespace is "jsp".

Example 10–7: A Simple JSP That Delivers a Java Program Using Different Font and Color for the Program-Generator Parts

```
<jsp:root
xmlns:jsp="http://java.sun.com/products/jsp/dtd/jsp_1_2.dtd">

<jsp:directive.page import = "java.util.Date;" />
<pre>
import java.util.Date;

class MyProgram {

    public static main(String[] args) {
        System.out.println("This program was generated"
            +" <jsp:expr>new Date()</jsp:expr>");
        System.out.println("This output was created "+new Date());
<jsp:scriptlet>
    String x = request.getParameter("x");
    if (x==null) {
</jsp:scriptlet>
        System.out.println("There was no x parameter.");
```

```
<jsp:scriptlet> } else { </jsp:scriptlet>
        String x = "<jsp:expr>x</jsp:expr>";
        System.out.println("The x parameter was "+x);
<jsp:scriptlet> } </jsp:scriptlet>
    }
}
</pre>
</jsp:root>
```

Translating between these formats is not difficult to do. This makes it possible to store, edit, and manipulate JSP files as if they were XML files.

10.3 | Chart Applet Program Generator

A Chart Applet is a Java program that will display data in some kind of chart (bar chart, line chart, pie chart, …) typically embedded on a Web page. A Chart Applet Program Generator (CAPG) is a program generator that will create customized chart applets. The important ideas illustrated by CAPG are as follows.

Form Input: Web-based forms are used to provide the specifications for the Chart Applet.

Skinny Applet: A small customized chart applet is created to satisfy the needs of the application. This avoids bloated code while still retaining a full range of features. Only the selected features are created and downloaded.

Roles and Separation of Concerns: Most projects require a variety of roles, and even in this simple example the clean separation of roles can be illustrated.

Variable Binding Times of Variabilities: Some variabilities may determine the binding time of other variabilities. CAPG shows a couple of variabilities whose binding time may be either at generation time or at run time.

The process for creating and using programs over the Web varies in some details from other program generators, as shown in Figure 10–5. A Web page with a form is used to specify the customized chart applet (called chartgen.html). A developer selects a chart applet and then clicks on the "Generate Chart Applet" button. The request with form information is sent to the server, where a JSP file (newchart.jsp) is used to generate a program and returns the program source code as a Web page. The developer copies the code to a file, compiles it, and uploads it along with a new html page that uses the customized applet (mychart.html). The roles in this process include the following.

Domain Engineer: Designs and implements CAPG including the chartgen.html page and newchart.jsp file.

Chart Designer: Determines what kind of chart applet to create using the chartgen.html page.

Web Page Designer: Creates a Web page with embedded charts using customized chart applets from the chart designer. The Web page designer determines the data sources and label sources.

User: Reads the Web page with embedded charts and, if permitted, can alter one or more settings to change the data display

The Chart Applet Program Generator (CAPG) will create an applet for displaying a simple chart based on data from a database or other source. General-purpose chart applets are available for this purpose, but they often include many features that are not used and can cause a longer-than-necessary download time. CAPG will create a customized chart applet that contains only what is used for a specific Web page.

The process is shown in Figure 10–5. Jill is the domain engineer who created CAPG, consisting of the chartgen.html Web page for specifying a custom chart applet and newchart.jsp. John is a chart designer who uses CAPG to select the styles and features for a chart. When he clicks on the "Generate Chart Applet" button, the request

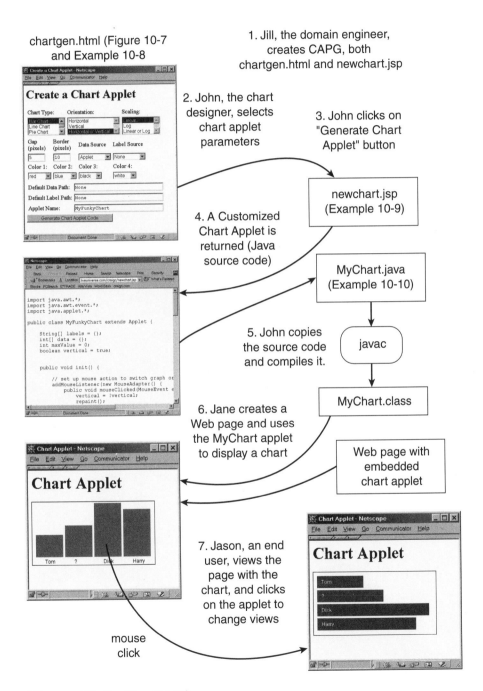

Figure 10–5 The CAPG process

goes to the Web server, which passes the request to the servlet engine, which in turn passes it to the JSP engine. The JSP engine will translate newchart.jsp to a Java class, compile it, and execute it to return the customized Java source code for the requested applet. This source code is returned in a Web page, which John can copy and paste to a file in his own development environment. John compiles the applet and makes it available to Web page designers.

Jane is a Web page designer who is writing a report, needs to insert a chart, and decides to use John's custom applet. She installs her page and the class file for the applet on her Web site. Finally, Jason reads the report, observes the chart, and uses the mouse to dynamically change his view of the chart.

The CAPG story began, like any good program generator, with a domain analysis that resulted in the variabilities described in Table 10–4. These variabilities are representative of a chart applet program generator, not a definitive set. The example implements only the bar-chart type and orientation and leaves many other features unimplemented.

Table 10–4: CAPG Variabilities

Variability	Range	Description
Chart Type	Bar Chart Line Chart *etc...*	This determines what kind of chart to use for displaying the data.
Orientation	Horizontal Vertical Horizontal or Vertical	The orientation of the chart. If "Horizontal or Vertical" is selected, then the user can switch between the two orientations.
Scaling	Linear Log Linear or Log	Chart scaling (if applicable). If "Linear or Log" is selected, then the user can switch between the scalings.
Gap	0–1000	Number of pixels between chart elements.

(continued)

Table 10–4: CAPG Variabilities *(Continued)*

Variability	Range	Description
Border	0–1000	Number of pixels used on borders.
Data Source	Applet Database JavaBean Fake it	Where does the chart data come from?
Label Source	Applet Database JavaBean Fake it None	Where do the chart labels come from?
Color1, Color2, Color3, Color4	Color range	The colors to use for various chart elements.
Default Data Path	None A URL (if database) JavaBean Name	If the applet parameter does not specify the source of the chart data, then this value is used.
Default Label Path	None A URL (if database) JavaBean Name	If the applet parameter does not specify the source of the chart labels, then this value is used.
Applet Name	A string	The name of the applet.

The orientation and scaling variabilities are unique in that the binding time varies. The chart designer can explicitly select an orientation (vertical or horizontal) and scaling (linear or log), or the chart designer can defer the decision to the end user who can select the orientation and scaling with appropriate mouse clicks. Some situations may require fixed orientation and scaling—for example, Web pages that describe the chart assuming it is displayed in a specific manner. In other situations, the end user may have control over these features. When these features can be selected at run time, the customized applet will be required to have the code to implement these features. Let's examine the situation for the orientation variability. If the orientation is fixed, then the customized applet will only need the code for drawing the applet in that one orientation. If the orientation is determined at run time, then the applet will be required to have the code for both orientations. In addition, the applet must have the code to allow the user to select the orientation. In the simplest case, this may be implemented as just a mouse click on the applet. By examining newchart.jsp in Example 10–9 you can see that the differences between these variations.

There are seven places in newchart.jsp (Example 10–9) that generates different code based on the value of the `orient` variable, including the instance variable "`boolean vertical`", adding a mouse listener, and the paint code. The difference in the amount of code is significant for such a small program. This example does not implement variations for scaling, chart type, data source, or label source. When you add in all these possibilities as well, the range of source code that can be generated multiplies considerably (Figure 10–6). If all of these features were deferred to run time, the applet would be very large. For these reasons, generated chart applets can support a potentially very wide and powerful set of features and yet still be small and efficient.

10.3.1   *Web Form Input*

These variabilities can be expressed as a straightforward Web-based form that a chart designer can fill out. The form is shown in Figure 10–7, and a portion of the HTML is shown in Example 10–8.

Example 10–8: Excerpts from HTML Form for CAPG Specification

```
<html><head><title>Create a Chart Applet</title></head>
<body>
<h1>Create a Chart Applet</h1>
<form method=post action=newchart.jsp>
<table>

<tr>
<td>Chart Type:</td>
<td>Orientation:</td>
<td>Scaling:</td>
</tr>
```

```
<tr>

<td><select name="type" size=3>
<option value=1 selected>Bar Chart</option>
<option value=2>Line Chart</option>
<option value=3>Pie Chart</option>
<option value=4>Area Chart</option>
<option value=5>3D Bar Chart</option>
<option value=6>Scatter Plot</option>
</select></td>

...

</table>
<input type=submit value="Generate Chart Applet Code">
</form>
</body>
</html>
```

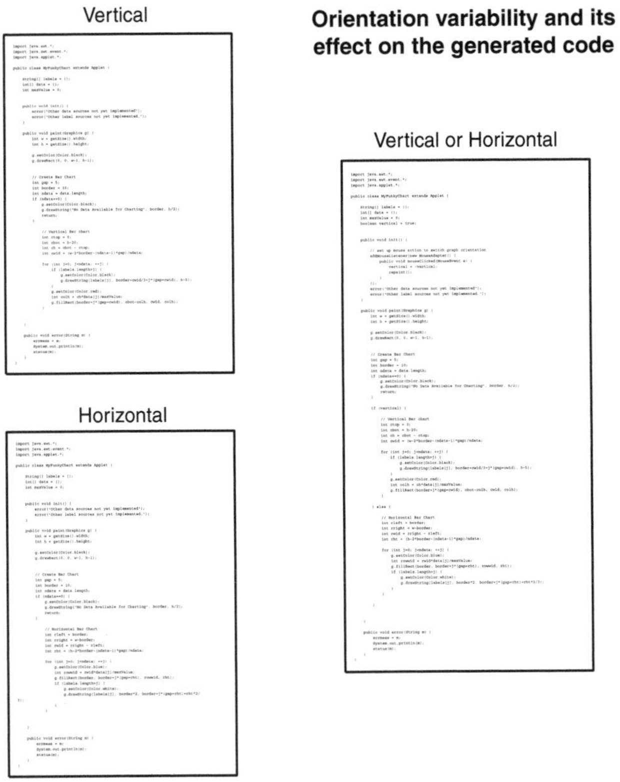
Vertical
Orientation variability and its effect on the generated code
Vertical or Horizontal
Horizontal

Figure 10–6 Code to implement different orientation settings

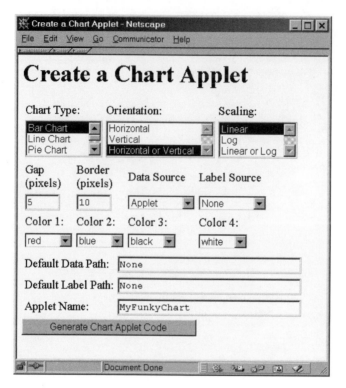

Figure 10–7 CAPG specification form

The complete JSP file, newchart.jsp, for producing the customized chart applet is shown in Example 10–9.

An enhancement to newchart.jsp that is worth considering is to return a working applet as well as the source code. To accomplish this, a new JSP file should be created that will call newchart.jsp twice—first to generate the program for return to the user, and then to generate the program to a file on the server. This file can be compiled and the class stored in the appropriate directory. In addition to returning the Java source code, a Web page with the embedded applet will also be returned. This allows the chart designer not only to get the source code, but also to try out the chart applet.

Example 10–9: newchart.jsp File for Creating a Custom Chart Applet

```jsp
<pre>
<%
      String name = request.getParameter("name");
      String type = request.getParameter("type");
      String orient = request.getParameter("orient");
      String scale = request.getParameter("scale");
      String gap = request.getParameter("gap");
      String border = request.getParameter("border");
      String data = request.getParameter("data");
      String label = request.getParameter("label");
      String datasource = request.getParameter("datasource");
      String labelsource = request.getParameter("labelsource");
      String color1 = request.getParameter("color1");
      String color2 = request.getParameter("color2");
      String color3 = request.getParameter("color3");
      String color4 = request.getParameter("color4");
%>
import java.awt.*;
import java.awt.event.*;
import java.applet.*;

public class <%=name%> extends Applet {

    String[] labels = {};
    int[] data = {};
    int maxValue = 0;
  <% if (orient.equals("3")) { %>boolean vertical = true;
    <% } %>

    public void init() {
      <% if (orient.equals("3")) { %>
        // set up mouse action to switch graph orientation
        addMouseListener(new MouseAdapter() {
            public void mouseClicked(MouseEvent e) {
                vertical = !vertical;
                repaint();
            }
        });
      <% } %>

      <% if (data.equals("4")) { %>
        // fake data
        int[] fakeData = { 14, 20, 34, 30 };
```

```
      data = fakeData;
      maxValue = 35;
 <% } else { %>
      error("Other data sources not yet implemented");
 <% } %>

 <% if (label.equals("2")) { %>
      // read labels from applet parameters
      labels = new String[data.length];
      for (int j=0; j&lt;labels.length; ++j) {
          labels[j] = getParameter("label"+j);
          if (labels[j]==null || labels[j].equals("")) {
              labels[j] = "?";
          }
      }
 <% } else { %>
      error("Other label sources not yet implemented.");
 <% } %>
 }

 public void paint(Graphics g) {
      int w = getSize().width;
      int h = getSize().height;

      g.setColor(Color.black);
      g.drawRect(0, 0, w-1, h-1);

 <% if (type.equals("1")) { %>
      // Create Bar Chart
      int gap = <%=gap%>;
      int border = <%=border%>;
      int ndata = data.length;
      if (ndata==0) {
          g.setColor(Color.black);
          g.drawString("No Data Available for Charting", border, h/2);
          return;
      }
 <% if (orient.equals("3")) { %>
      if (vertical) {
 <% }
      if (orient.equals("3") || orient.equals("2")) {
 %>
          // Vertical Bar chart
          int ctop = 0;
          int cbot = h-20;
          int ch = cbot - ctop;
          int cwid = (w-2*border-(ndata-1)*gap)/ndata;

          for (int j=0; j&lt;ndata; ++j) {
```

```
              if (labels.length>j) {
                  g.setColor(Color.<%=color3%>);
                  g.drawString(labels[j],
                      border+cwid/3+j*(gap+cwid), h-5);
              }
              g.setColor(Color.<%=color1%>);
              int colh = ch*data[j]/maxValue;
              g.fillRect(border+j*(gap+cwid), cbot-colh, cwid, colh);
          }
  <% }
      if (orient.equals("3")) {
  %>
      } else {
  <% }
      if (orient.equals("3") || orient.equals("1")) {
  %>
          // Horizontal Bar Chart
          int rleft = border;
          int rright = w-border;
          int rwid = rright - rleft;
          int rht = (h-2*border-(ndata-1)*gap)/ndata;

          for (int j=0; j&lt;ndata; ++j) {
              g.setColor(Color.<%=color2%>);
              int rowwid = rwid*data[j]/maxValue;
              g.fillRect(border, border+j*(gap+rht), rowwid, rht);
              if (labels.length>j) {
                  g.setColor(Color.<%=color4%>);
                  g.drawString(labels[j], border*2,
                      border+j*(gap+rht)+rht*2/3);
              }
          }
  <% }
      if (orient.equals("3")) {
  %>
      }
  <% } %>
  <% } else { %>
      g.setColor(Color.black);
      g.drawString("Chart Style not yet implemented.", border, h/2);
  <% } %>
  }

  public void error(String m) {
      errmess = m;
      System.out.println(m);
      status(m);
  }
}
```

An example chart applet, with the orientation set to vertical, as produced by the newchart.jsp file is shown in Example 10–10. Also the data source has been set to "fake", and the label source comes from the applet parameters.

Example 10–10: MyChart.java (with Orientation Set to Vertical)

```java
import java.awt.*;
import java.awt.event.*;
import java.applet.*;

public class MyChart extends Applet {

    String[] labels = {};
    int[] data = {};
    int maxValue = 0;

    public void init() {
        // fake data
        int[] fakeData = { 14, 20, 34, 30 };
        data = fakeData;
        maxValue = 35;

        // read labels from applet parameters
        labels = new String[data.length];
        for (int j=0; j<labels.length; ++j) {
            labels[j] = getParameter("label"+j);
            if (labels[j]==null || labels[j].equals("")) {
                labels[j] = "?";
            }
        }
    }

    public void paint(Graphics g) {
        int w = getSize().width;
        int h = getSize().height;

        g.setColor(Color.black);
        g.drawRect(0, 0, w-1, h-1);


        // Create Bar Chart
        int gap = 5;
```

```
        int border = 10;
        int ndata = data.length;
        if (ndata==0) {
            g.setColor(Color.black);
            g.drawString("No Data Available for Charting", border, h/2);
            return;
        }


            // Vertical Bar chart
            int ctop = 0;
            int cbot = h-20;
            int ch = cbot - ctop;
            int cwid = (w-2*border-(ndata-1)*gap)/ndata;

            for (int j=0; j<ndata; ++j) {
                if (labels.length>j) {
                    g.setColor(Color.black);
                    g.drawString(labels[j],
                            border+cwid/3+j*(gap+cwid), h-5);
                }
                g.setColor(Color.red);
                int colh = ch*data[j]/maxValue;
                g.fillRect(border+j*(gap+cwid), cbot-colh, cwid, colh);
            }


    }

    public void error(String m) {
        errmess = m;
        System.out.println(m);
        status(m);
    }
}
}
```

To use the custom chart applet, the applet's HTML code is embedded in some Web page (see Example 10–11). The resulting Web page is presented at the bottom of Figure 10–5 and it shows the two views that the chart applet displays. A mouse click on the applet will change the chart display. Also note that label1 is purposely omitted to show the effect on the applet display.

Example 10–11: An HTML Page Using a Custom Chart Applet

```
<html><head><title>Chart Applet</title></head>
<body>
<h1>Chart Applet</h1>
<applet code=MyChart.class width=300 height=150>
<param name=label0 value=Tom>
<param name=label2 value=Dick>
<param name=label3 value=Harry>
<param name=label4 value=Jack>
What, no Java!
</applet>
</body>
</html>
```

10.3.2 XML Input

We will now consider specification input that is an XML file rather than a Web form. Two different ways of specifying the XML file are given. In the first example the XML specification is read from an accessible file using a URL. In the second case, the XML file is copied to a text area on the Web form and passed to the JSP as part of the URL.

The two forms in Figures 10–8 and 10–9 can be used as the input to a JSP file that accesses the XML file using the parameter information.

10.4 | The JSP Translator, a Simple Program Generator

The JSP Translator is an example of a program generator in widespread use. It translates a JSP file (the specification) into a Java

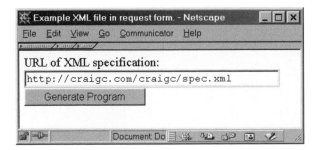

Figure 10–8   Form asking for URL of XML file

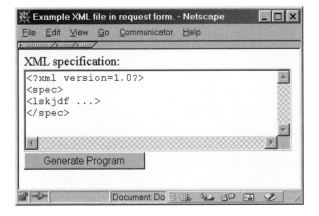

Figure 10–9   Form asking for XML specification

program, as shown in Figure 10–10. It is a simple but general-purpose program generator, little more than the program generator in Chapter 1 with escapes. The input is a template language with escapes to the Java language. The input can be pure XML using the JSP XML syntax.

The translation from a JSP file to a Java program is defined by the Java Server Pages Specification. The generated Java program will have the form shown in Example 10–12.

Example 10–12: Java Program Generated by the JSP Translator

```
Imports

class _jspXXXX extends SuperClass {

    declarations

    public void _jspService(ServletRequest request,
                            ServletResponse response)
                        throws ServletException, IOException {
                    declare implicit objects such as ...
            JSPWriter out = pageContext.getOut();

                        translated code

            out.flush();
        }
    }
}
```

Java directives such as `<%@ import="java.util.Date" %>` are placed in the *imports* area. Java-declarations, such as as `<%! int x=5; %>` are placed in the *declarations* area. The SuperClass is determined by the JSP Engine (or possibly overridden by the user with a Java-directive). And finally the bulk of the JSP file is translated and placed in the *translated code* area. Segments of text without Java escapes are enclosed in quotes (with suitable escapes for quote characters) and passed to `out.print`. Java-code, such as `<% if (x==null) { %>` are placed in the *translated code* area without changes. Java-expressions such as `<%=x%>` are passed to `out.print` (after suitable conversion to strings).

10.5 | Play Domain Program Generator

Let's revisit the Play domain program generator developed in the previous chapter using DOM (Example 10–13). The final program in Example 9–10 was difficult to read. Using JSP can make it somewhat easier to read. We'll use the same font for the program-generator parts to make reading even easier. As in Example 9–10, we will use the Play-Data1 data structures from Example 9–9.

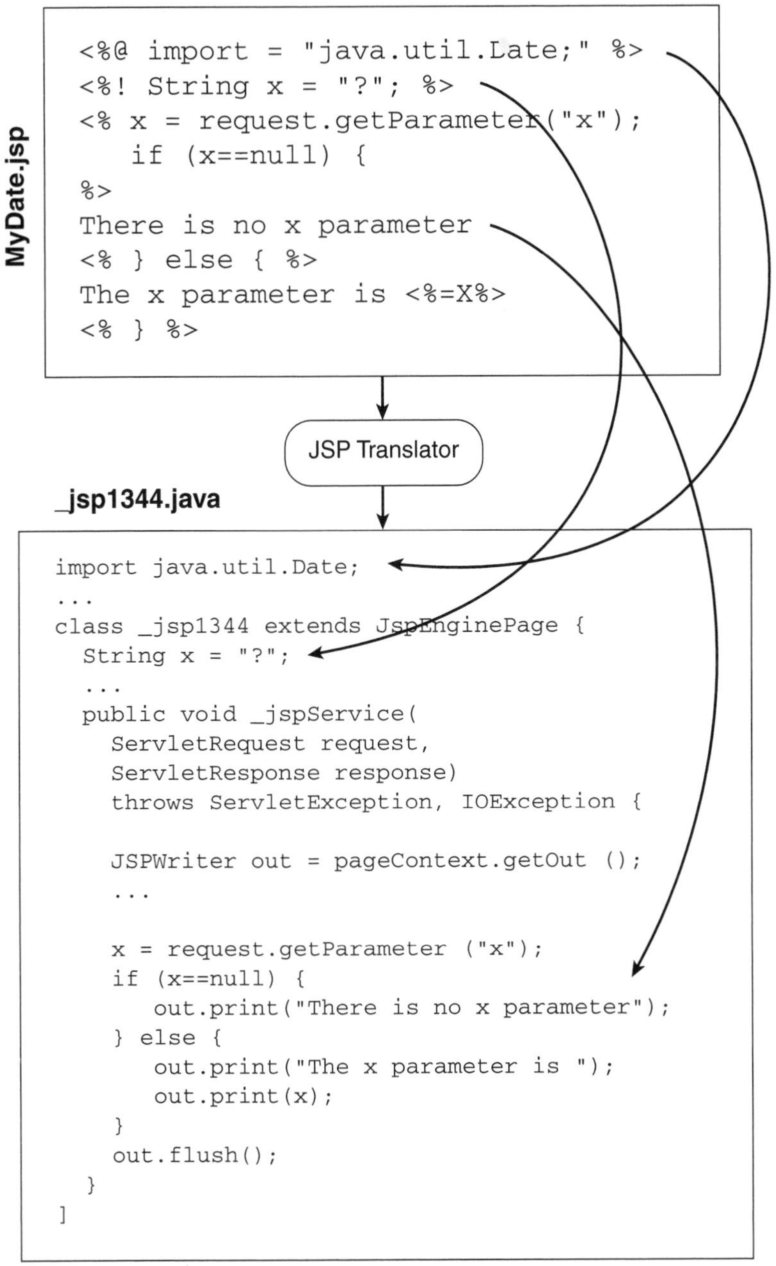

MyDate.jsp

```
<%@ import = "java.util.Late;" %>
<%! String x = "?"; %>
<% x = request.getParameter("x");
    if (x==null) {
%>
There is no x parameter
<% } else { %>
The x parameter is <%=X%>
<% } %>
```

JSP Translator

_jsp1344.java

```
import java.util.Date;
...
class _jsp1344 extends JspEnginePage {
  String x = "?";
  ...
  public void _jspService(
    ServletRequest request,
    ServletResponse response)
    throws ServletException, IOException {

    JSPWriter out = pageContext.getOut ();
    ...

    x = request.getParameter ("x");
    if (x==null) {
       out.print("There is no x parameter");
    } else {
       out.print("The x parameter is ");
       out.print(x);
    }
    out.flush();
  }
]
```

Figure 10–10   Example JSP translation

Example 10–13: Play Domain Program Generator Using JSP

```
<pre>
<%@ import = "java.io.*" %>
<% PlayData1 d = null;
   String filename = request.getParameter("xmlfile");
   if (filename==null || filename.equals("")) {
     filename = "/home/craig/progen/play/play1.xml";
   }
   try {
      // read and parse Play specification
      d = new PlayData1(filename);
   } catch (Exception e) {
     out.println("Exception: "+e.getMessage());
     e.printStackTrace(out);
   }
%>


import java.awt.*;
import java.awt.event.*;

class <%=d.name%>Play2 extends Frame {
    /* The Props for <%=d.name%> ***************/

<% for (int j=0; j<d.props.length; ++j) {
       PlayData1.PropData prop = d.props[j];
%>
    Button <%=prop.name%>Prop = new Button("<%=prop.label%>");
<% } %>

    /* The Events in the <%=d.name%> **************/

    class PropEvent implements ActionListener {
        public void actionPerformed(ActionEvent evt) {
            Object prop = evt.getSource();
<% for (int j=0; j<d.props.length; ++j) {
       PlayData1.PropData prop = d.props[j];
       out.print("              ");
       if (j!=0) {
           out.print("} else ");
       }
       out.println("if (prop=="+prop.name+"Prop) {");
       if (prop.script!=null) {
           for (int k=0; k<prop.script.traits.length; ++k) {
               String pname = prop.script.traits[k].prop==null
```

```
                          ? prop.name : prop.script.traits[k].prop.name;
                out.println("                        "
                    +pname+"Prop.setLabel(\""
                    +prop.script.traits[k].newValue+"\");");
            }
            if (prop.script.nextScene!=null) {
                out.println("                    enterNewScene(\""
                        +prop.script.nextScene.name+"\");");
            }
        }
    }
%>
            } else {
                System.out.println("Invalid prop");
            }
        }
    }


    /* Creating and starting up the <%=d.name%> ****/

    String currentScene;

    public <%=d.name%>Play2() {
        super("<%=d.title%>");
        setSize(<%=d.width%>, <%=d.height%>);
        setLayout(new FlowLayout());

        // initialize props
        PropEvent a = new PropEvent();
<% for (int j=0; j<d.props.length; ++j) {
        PlayData1.PropData prop = d.props[j];
%>
        <%=prop.name%>Prop.addActionListener(a);
<% } %>

        // start scene
        enterNewScene("<%=d.startScene.name%>");
    }

    public void enterNewScene(String scene) {
        removeAll();   // remove previous scene
        currentScene = scene;
<% for (int k=0; k<d.scenes.length; ++k) {
        PlayData1.SceneData scene = d.scenes[k];
        out.print("         ");
```

```
        if (k!=0) {
            out.print("} else ");
        }
        out.println("if (scene.equals(\" "+scene.name+"\")) {");
        for (int p2=0; p2<scene.addprops.length; ++p2) {
            PlayData1.PropData prop2 = scene.addprops[p2];
            out.println("                add("+prop2.name+"Prop);");
        }
%>
            setBackground(Color.decode("<%=scene.color%>"));
<% } %>
        } else {
            System.out.println("Invalid scene: "+scene);
        }
        show();
    }

    public static void main(String[] args) {
        new <%=d.name%>Play2();
    }
}
```

10.6 | Summary

JSP (Java Server Pages) is a technology for producing Web pages. In this book JSP is used to generate Java programs from templates. Templates have embedded Java code to determine the dynamic parts of the generated output. JSP provides a convenient way to build program generators and at the same time make them available over the Internet. The JSP engine itself is an example program generator, which translates JSP files to Java programs.

Using XPath and XSLT to Generate Programs

- XPath: a language for extracting information from XML documents
- XSLT: a language for transforming XML documents

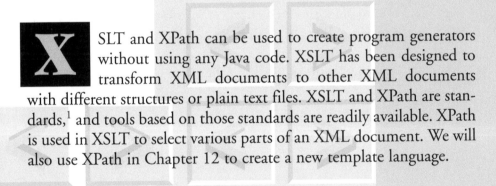

Chapter

11

XSLT and XPath can be used to create program generators without using any Java code. XSLT has been designed to transform XML documents to other XML documents with different structures or plain text files. XSLT and XPath are standards,[1] and tools based on those standards are readily available. XPath is used in XSLT to select various parts of an XML document. We will also use XPath in Chapter 12 to create a new template language.

11.1 | XPath

XPath is a language for identifying and selecting parts of an XML document. Although too complex to describe in its entirety here, it is worth describing in some detail, since we will also use it independently

---

[1]To be more precise, XSLT and XPath are W3C standards and are parts of the XML family of standards. XSLT is part of XSL (yet another XML standard) which also includes styling and formatting using cascading style sheets. Although used in XSLT, XPath is a separate standard because it is also used in XPointer (yet another XML standard).

of XSLT in the next chapter. In Chapter 9 we found that the DOM API has one method for finding parts of an XML document, namely:

```
NodeList getElementsByTagName(String x)
```

Given a DOM subtree (identified by an element), `getElements-ByTagName` returns a list of all element nodes with the element type name "x" found in the subtree. Although this was sufficient for our purposes in the Play domain, it is not expressive enough for more practical program generators. XPath provides a more powerful and succinct way of expressing exactly which nodes of the tree you want.

The full-unabbreviated XPath language provides a rich set of notations "using a straightforward but rather verbose syntax."[2] XPath also has abbreviations for the most commonly used notations, which we use in this book wherever possible.

Text data is conveniently normalized in XPath so that you will consistently get the same data characters independently of how they happened to be expressed in the XML document. For example, the character "<" can be expressed in the following ways in XML:

```
&lt;
<![CDATA[<]]>
&#60;
&#x3c;
```

The character could also be embedded in other entities, but no matter what way it is expressed, XPath will always treat it consistently.

11.1.1 XPath Trees

To show how XPath is used for precisely selecting certain parts of an XML document, we use an excerpt from the Play domain example (Example 11–1).

---

[2]This is how it is described in the XPath formal specification, XML Path Language (XPath) Version 1.0

Example 11–1: Excerpt from play1.xml

```xml
<?xml version="1.0"?>
<play name="JackAndJill" width="300" height="120" start="bottom">
  <title>Jack and Jill</title>

  <prop name="up">
    <trait>Go up the hill</trait>
    <script goto="top"/>
  </prop>
  <prop name="fetch"/>
  <prop name="fall"/>
  <prop name="tumble"/>
  <scene name="bottom"/>
  <scene name="top">
    <addprop name="fetch">
      <trait>Fetch another pail</trait>
    </addprop>
    <addprop name="fall"/>
    <addprop name="tumble"/>
  </scene>

</play>
```

Figure 11–1 shows this XML document as a tree. XPath trees consist of seven types of nodes.

1. Root node: This is the top of the tree, parent of the root element of the tree (just like the DOM).

2. Element nodes: Each element in the document is represented as a node of the tree.

3. Attribute nodes: Each attribute of an element is represented as a node.

4. Text nodes: Each sequence of data characters (after normalization) is represented as a node.

5. Namespace nodes: These nodes keep track of namespaces and their references (URIs). We don't consider these nodes in this book.

6. Comment nodes: Each comment is preserved as a node.

7. Processing instruction nodes: Each XML processing instruction is a node. These nodes are ignored in this book.

The tree shown in Figure 11–1 uses different shapes to represent the different nodes of the play1.xml document. Element nodes are in

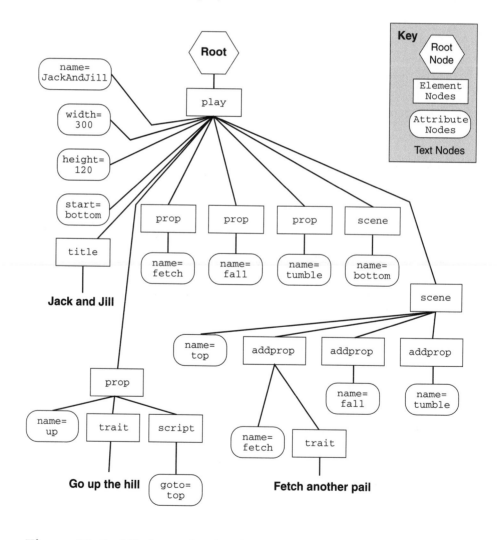

Figure 11–1 XPath tree for the play.xml excerpt

rectangles with the name of the element in the box and its children in order as they appear in the document. Attribute nodes in boxes with curved corners show both the attribute name and attribute value. Text nodes are not enclosed in a shape. This visual tree is useful for quickly understanding the XPath examples that follow.

11.1.2 *XPath Expressions*

XPath has four basic expression types.

1. Node set (a set of nodes of the XPath tree)

2. Boolean (true or false)

3. Number (floating-point numbers)

4. String (a sequence of UCS characters)

The first type, a node set, sometimes called a *location path,* is the most important one. The other three types are used in creating XPath predicates.

Each XPath expression is evaluated in an environment containing the following items, called the *context*.

1. A node of the XPath tree called the *context node*.

2. A pair of nonzero positive integers that specify the position of the context node in an ordered set of nodes. These numbers are called the *context position* and *context size*.

3. A set of variable bindings.

4. A function library.

5. The set of namespace declarations in scope for the expression.

11.1.3   *XPath Node-Set Expressions*

The most important XPath type is the node set. Node-set expressions return a set of nodes, possibly empty, many times with just one node, but possibly including many nodes. XPath uses a notation similar to UNIX path names (Table 11–1). An absolute location path begins with a slash ("/"). All other node-set expressions are relative location paths and are computed relative to the *context node*. For example, "/X/Y" means a grandchild of the root node, whereas "X/Y" means a grandchild of the context node.

Table 11–1: XPath Notations (*X* and *Y* are element type names).

Notation	Description
.	Self (the context node)
..	Parent of the context node
/	The root node
X	All *X* element children of the context node
*	All children elements of the context node
X/Y	All Y children elements of the *X* children elements of the context node
.//X	All *X* descendant elements of the context node
//X	All *X* elements in the document
@X	The *X* attribute of the context node
@*	All attributes of the context node
X[predicate]	All *X* children of the context node that satisfy *predicate*
text()	All text node children of the context node
X|Y	All *X* and *Y* children of the context node
ancestor::*X*	All *X* ancestor elements of the context node
id(*object*)	All node(s) whose unique IDs satisfy *object*

From earlier chapters, we know that access to certain parts of the XML document is required for generating the program. We provide expressions for those as well as others to demonstrate other XPath capabilities. The result of an XPath node-set expression is typically a set of nodes, possibly an empty set. Table 11–2 shows examples of node-set expressions and the value they would return for an example context node.

Table 11–2: Node-Set Expressions and Values Returned

Example (see Figure 11–1)	Context Node	Result
`//prop`	Any	All four `prop` elements
`//play/title`	Any	The title element node of the play
`//play/title/ text()`	Any	"Jack and Jill"
`//play/@name`	Any	"JackAndJill"
`addprop`	The top scene element	The three `addprop` children elements of the top scene element
`trait`	The top scene element	Empty set (there are no trait children of the top scene … there is one grandchild trait element, but it is not a child of the top scene)
`@width`	The play element	"300"
`@*`	The play element	All four attribute nodes of the play element: name, width, height, and start
`../@name`	The fetch addprop	"top", the name attribute of the parent

(continued)

Table 11–2: Node-Set Expressions and Values Returned *(Continued)*

Example (see Figure 11–1)	Context Node	Result
`.//text()`	The fetch addprop	"`Fetch another pail`", the only text node in this subtree (note that the period is needed to indicate the context node rather than the root)
`ancestor::prop/@name`	The trait element with text "Go up the hill"	"`up`", the name attribute of the `prop` ancestor element
`text()|@*`	The title element	"`Jack and Jill`", the only text or attribute child of the title element
`*`	The play element	All seven children elements of the play element (does not include the attributes or other types of nodes)

11.1.4   *XPath Number Expressions*

An XPath number expression returns a floating-point number. XPath number expressions include the operators and functions shown in Table 11–3.

Table 11–3: XPath Number Expressions

Notation or Function	Description
number	A numeric literal
x+y	Add
x-y	Subtract

(continued)

Table 11–3: XPath Number Expressions *(Continued)*

Notation or Function	Description
x mod *y*	Returns the remainder after a truncating division
x div *y*	Divide
x * *y*	Multiply
position()	Returns the context position
last()	Returns the context size
count(*node-set*)	Returns the number of nodes in the node set
string-length(*string*)	Returns the number of characters in string
number(*object*)	Convert object to a number
floor(*number*)	Returns the largest integer that is not greater than the number
ceiling(*number*)	Returns the smallest integer that is not less than the number
round(*number*)	Returns the closest integer to the number

11.1.5   *XPath String Expressions*

An XPath string expression returns a possibly empty sequence of characters. XPath string expressions include the functions listed in Table 11–4.

Table 11–4: XPath String Expressions

Notation or Function	Description
"*literal*"	A literal string
string(*object*)	Convert an object to a string; see notes below
concat(*string*, …)	The concatenation of all its arguments

XPath string functions also include various substring functions and ways of determining the names of nodes.

Any XPath value can be converted to a string, called its *string value*. The string function can explicitly perform this conversion, but in other places the conversion is implicit. The string value of a node set is the string value of the first node (in document order). The string value of a text node is the character data making up the node. The string value of an attribute is the value of the attribute. The string value of an element node is the concatenation of the string value of all its text nodes.

11.1.6 *XPath Boolean Expressions*

An XPath boolean expression returns true or false. XPath boolean expressions include the operators and functions shown in Table 11–5.

Table 11–5: XPath Boolean Expressions

Notation or Function	Description
true()	The true value
false()	The false value
x and *y*	Returns true if both x and y are true
x or *y*	Returns true if either x or y is true
not(*boolean*)	Returns true if *boolean* is false
boolean(*object*)	Converts *object* to boolean
x = *y*	Equals; see notes below
x != *y*	Not equal; see notes below
x < *y*	Less than (use < when used in attribute values)
x > *y*	Greater than; see notes below
x <= *y*	Less than or equal; see notes below
x >= *y*	Greater than or equal; see notes below

The comparison operators will automatically convert objects to other types so that any two objects can be compared. The rules are complex and depend on the type of the operands. When both operands are node sets, the comparison returns true if there exist nodes in both sets such that their string values are equal (which obviously is different from set equality). When one of the operands is a node set and the other is a string, the comparison will return true if there exists a node in the node set whose string value is equal to the other operand. For other obscure combinations, the XPath specification should be consulted. Examples of comparison are given in the following section.

11.1.7 *XPath Predicates*

Predicates are used to further restrict a set of nodes, sometimes called a filter. A predicate follows a node-set expression and is contained in square brackets as follows.

X [*predicate*]

The X returns a node set. Each node in the node set is evaluated as the context node for the predicate expression. If the predicate evaluates to true, then the node is retained, otherwise it is removed from the resulting node set. The next expression specifies all prop elements whose name attribute is "up."

```
//prop[@name="up"]
```

If the predicate expression results in a number, then it is compared to the position of x in the node set, where the nodes are in document order. In essence, a numeric predicate expression [n] is converted to [n=position()], where position is the function that returns the context position of x in the node set.

If the predicate expression is a node set, then it will return true if the set is not empty and false otherwise. Table 11–6 illustrates these rules with examples. In each case, the node set begins with all prop elements (because `//prop` selects all prop descendants of the root node). The predicate then selects some subset of this set of four nodes (using the example given in Figure 11–1). In some cases, such as the second example, the node set is used in further processing.

Table 11–6: Results Yielded by Rules

Example	Result
`//prop[3]`	The third `prop`, the `fall` prop, equivalent to `//prop[position()=3]`
`//prop[3]/@name`	The name attribute of the third `prop`: `fall`
`//prop[@name="fall"]`	All `prop` elements with attribute `name` equal to `fall`
`//prop[trait]`	All `prop` elements with at least one `trait` child element (only up)
`//prop[.//trait]`	All `prop` elements with at least one descendant `trait` element (only up)
`//prop[@peculiar]`	All `prop` elements with a `peculiar` attribute, in this case, an empty node set
`//prop[trait][@script]`	All `prop` elements that have a `trait` child element AND a `script` attribute (only up)
`//prop` `[trait[@peculiar]]`	All `prop` elements that have a `trait` child element with an attribute named `peculiar` (empty nodeset)
`//prop` `[@name=//addprop/@name]`	All `prop` elements whose `name` attribute is the same as some `addprop` element with the same `name` attribute (the `fall`, `fetch`, and `tumble` props)

Comparisons can be tricky because of the complex rules mentioned in the previous section. An example of a comparison between a node set and a string is the expression `//prop[trait="xyz"]`, which means the set of all props which have a `trait` element whose value is "xyz". Note that the subexpression "`trait`" returns a node set, which may include multiple elements (since a `prop` may have multiple `trait` children elements). The comparison will return true if at least one of those traits has a string value (the concatenation of all its text nodes) equal to "xyz".

An example of a comparison where both operands are node sets is the expression `//prop[trait=peculiar]`, which means the set of all `prop` elements which have a `trait` child and a `peculiar` child with the same string value.

The inequality comparison works similarly but is tricky because it is not the same as the negation of the equals comparison. The expression `//prop[trait!=peculiar]` means any `prop` which has a `trait` value different from one of its `peculiar` element values. This differs from the expression `//prop[not(trait=peculiar)]`, which means any `prop` in which all of its `trait` values differ from all of its `peculiar` values.

Another example is the expression,

```
//script[not(@goto =//scene/@name)]
```

This expression returns all `script` elements whose `goto` attribute value does not match a `scene name`.

11.1.8 XPath Variables

Every XPath expression is evaluated in a context that includes not only the context node, its position and size, but also a set of variable bindings. An XPath variable is an identifier (*QName* in XML namespace parlance) and a value, such as a node set, but it could also be a value of some other type. Other notations, such as XSLT, may use variables to make XPath more useful. XPath itself does not assign values to variables. Notations, such as XSLT, will create and assign values to variables, and these are passed to XPath for evaluating expressions.

As an example, let's consider the following set of variable bindings.

`fallprop` is assigned the "fall" prop

`xprop` is assigned the string "`fall`"

An XPath expression may include variable references, denoted as a dollar sign followed by the variable's identifier (Table 11–7). To evaluate an expression with variable references, one simply replaces the variable references with their values.

Table 11–7: Variable References

Example	Result
`$fallprop/trait`	The trait element of the fall prop, which is empty in our example
`//prop[@name=$xprop]`	All prop elements whose name attribute is the value of the `xprop` variable (in this case, just the "`fall`" prop)

11.2 | XSLT

XSLT is a language for describing the transformation of an XML document to another XML document or a plain text file. We will use XSLT to transform an XML document to Java source code files. An XSLT specification itself is an XML document whose element type names have the "`xsl`" namespace prefix. To show how XSLT works, we first summarize some of the basic XSLT element types, then show some example translations from the Play domain. As with XPath, we can give only a brief overview of XSLT, only enough to demonstrate how it can be used to create program generators (Figure 11–2).

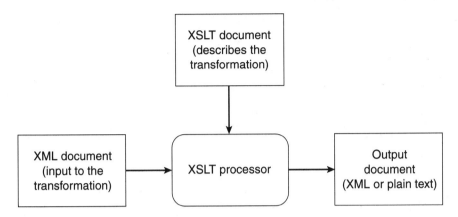

Figure 11–2   XSLT processing

11.2.1   *XSL Template*

The XSL template rule describes how to transform an XML element. The form of the rule is

```
<xsl:template match="pattern" ...>
template
</xsl:template>
```

The *pattern* is an XPath node-set expression that defines the set of potential nodes that the template can be applied to. Each node that matches is replaced with *template*. We'll continue to use Example 11–1 and Figure 11–1. An XSLT document has a root element "stylesheet" that defines version information. An xsl:output element is used to specify that we want plain text output rather than XML or HTML output. The main difference is that special characters like "less than" are not escaped.

Example 11–2 shows how to generate a simple "hello world" Java program. The match attribute says to replace the root of the XML tree with the Java program.

Example 11–2: Template Example

```
<?xml version="1.0"?>
<xsl:stylesheet version="1.0"
      xmlns:xsl="http://www.w3.org/1999/XSL/Transform">
<xsl:output method="text"/>
<xsl:template match="/">
class Hello {
    public static void main(String[] args) {
        System.out.println("Hello, World");
    }
}
</xsl:template>
</xsl:stylesheet>
```

In Example 11–2, the text appearing inside the template rule element is called the *template*, and in this case, since it is only character data, it will be copied directly to the output. It doesn't matter what the XML input document is. In the more general case, the template will be a combination of text to output and other XSLT tags. The matching node becomes the context node for any XPath expressions in the template. Any number of template rules can appear in the XSLT document. There are also default template rules that will be used if there is no appropriate rule in the XSLT document.

11.2.2   *XSL value-of*

The XSL `value-of` element type is used to compute and print a value on the output. In most cases, the computed value comes directly from the XML document. The form of the `value-of` element type is

```
<xsl:value-of select="expression"/>
```

The *expression* is an XPath expression that is converted to a string and sent to the output. To print the name attribute of the play, simply replace *expression* with "`/play/@name`". This expression will result in a node set consisting of just one attribute node. When it is converted to a string for printing, the value of the attribute will be used.

Let's modify the XSLT document of the previous section to create a
new "hello world" example which prints the `title` of the `play`
(Example 11–3). Also, the name of the class will come from the `name`
attribute of the `play` element.

Example 11–3: value-of Example

```
<?xml version="1.0"?>
<xsl:stylesheet version="1.0"
      xmlns:xsl="http://www.w3.org/1999/XSL/Transform">
<xsl:output method="text"/>
<xsl:template match="/">
class <xsl:value-of select="/play/@name"/> {
    public static void main(String[] args) {
        System.out.println("<xsl:value-of select="/play/title"/>");
    }
}
</xsl:template>
</xsl:stylesheet>
```

Note that the `value-of` element's content is never used, so you can
expect empty element tags for all `value-of` elements.

11.2.3   *XSL for-each*

The XSL for-each element type is used to output something for each
node in a node set. The general form of the for-each element type is

```
<xsl:for-each select="node-set-expression">
    optional-sorting-elements
  template
</xsl:for-each>
```

The *node-set-expression* is an XPath expression returning a set of
nodes. For each node in the set, the *template* is evaluated using the
node as the new context node. We'll extend Example 11–3 to also
generate a string variable for each prop (Example 11–4). The name of
the prop will be used to construct the name of the variable. The string
value will be the (first) trait element of the prop.

Example 11–4: for-each Example

```
<?xml version="1.0"?>
<xsl:stylesheet version="1.0"
    xmlns:xsl="http://www.w3.org/1999/XSL/Transform">
<xsl:output method="text"/>
<xsl:template match="/">
class <xsl:value-of select="/play/@name"/> {
    <xsl:for-each select="//prop">
    String <xsl:value-of select="@name"/>Prop
                = "<xsl:value-of select="trait"/>";
    </xsl:for-each>
    public static void main(String[] args) {
        System.out.println("<xsl:value-of select="/play/title"/>");
    }
}
</xsl:template>
</xsl:stylesheet>
```

Note carefully that the context node for the nested XPath expression trait is a node in the node set produced by the for-each select attribute. The resulting output of this transformation when applied to the play1.xml (Example 5–8) will result in the file shown in Example 11–5.

Example 11–5: Output with play1.xml as Input

```
class JackAndJill {

    String upProp
                = "Go up the hill";

    String fetchProp
                = "Fetch a pail of water";

    String fallProp
                = "Fall down, break crown";

    String tumbleProp
                = "Tumble down";

    public static void main(String[] args) {
        System.out.println("Jack and Jill");
    }
}
```

These three element types (template, value-of, for-each) are sufficient to do almost the whole program generator. Unfortunately, many more features may be needed to complete the job.

11.2.4   *XSL if*

The XSL if element type is used for conditionals, meaning output that is produced only under certain conditions. The XSL if element type has no provision for "else" parts. The form of the rule is

```
<xsl:if test="boolean-expression">
   template
</xsl:if>
```

The *boolean expression* is an XPath boolean expression. If it evaluates to true, then *template* is output, otherwise it is not output. In the simple example shown next (Example 11–6), the output of the Java program is the number of props. The conditional is used to output "prop" rather than "props" if there is exactly one prop.

Example 11–6: if Example

```
<?xml version="1.0"?>
<xsl:stylesheet version="1.0"
      xmlns:xsl="http://www.w3.org/1999/XSL/Transform">
<xsl:output method="text"/>
<xsl:template match="/">
class <xsl:value-of select="/play/@name"/> {
    public static void main(String[] args) {
        System.out.println("<xsl:value-of select="count(//prop)"/>"
              +" prop<xsl:if test="count(//prop)!=1">s</xsl:if>");
    }
}
</xsl:template>
</xsl:stylesheet>
```

11.2.5   *XSL choose*

A more complex multiway conditional provided by XSLT is the choose element type. The form of the choose element type is

```
<xsl:choose>
<xsl:when test="boolean-expression">
  template
</xsl:when>

... any number of additional when elements ...

<xsl:otherwise>
  template
</xsl:otherwise>
</xsl:choose>
```

Each *test* is evaluated in sequence until one of the tests returns a value of true, at which point the *template* content is evaluated. If none of the tests returns true, then the *otherwise* element is evaluated. The choose element type is a good choice for if-then-else constructs.

Example 11–7 shows how to produce different outputs depending on the type attribute value. Also, note that an XPath attribute value, like any other XML attribute value, can be delimited with single or double quotes, as demonstrated in the two test attributes.

Example 11–7: choose Example

```
<?xml version="1.0"?>
<xsl:stylesheet version="1.0"
      xmlns:xsl="http://www.w3.org/1999/XSL/Transform">
<xsl:output method="text"/>
<xsl:template match="/">
<xsl:for-each select="//prop">
  <xsl:choose>
  <xsl:when test='@type="string"'>
     string stuff for <xsl:value-of select="@name"/>
  </xsl:when>
  <xsl:when test="@type='int'">
     int stuff for <xsl:value-of select="@name"/>
  </xsl:when>
  <xsl:otherwise>
     otherwise stuff for <xsl:value-of select="@name"/>
```

```
    </xsl:otherwise>
    </xsl:choose>
  </xsl:for-each>
  </xsl:template>
  </xsl:stylesheet>
```

11.2.6   *XSL Variables*

In most cases, the context node is sufficient for keeping track of where you are in the XML source tree. Sometimes, however, you need to keep track of two or more places or items of information. At other times it may simply be convenient or efficient to store computed information in variables rather than recomputing every time the information is needed. XSLT provides the `variable` element type to assign values to variables as part of the XPath variable bindings. The form of the "variable" element type is

```
<xsl:variable name="qname" select="expression"/>
```

The *expression* is evaluated and stored as a variable binding in the XPath context. Variables may be needed when there are nested for-each elements, and the innermost template requires information from the context node of the outer for-each element.

In Example 11–8 a matrix of props and scenes is generated. For each combination of prop and scene, the prop name, the scene name, and the word "Included" are output if the prop is included in the scene. To accomplish this, two nested `for-each` elements are used, with the outermost one iterating over all props and the inner one iterating over all scenes. Within the inner `for-each`, the context node is a scene. Without a variable, there would be no way to determine information about the outer `for-each`. Therefore, we place a variable element in the outer `for-each` to store the value of the current prop node (whose value is indicated by a period) into a variable called "prop." In the inner loop, the prop node can now be easily referred to with the variable reference, "`$prop`". To determine if the prop is used in the scene, a comparison is made between "addprop/@name" and "$prop/@name". The expression "addprop/@name" selects all name attributes of all the addprops of the current context node which is the current scene. The "$prop/@name" expression selects the name attribute of the current prop node bound to the variable $prop. The comparison will return true if at least one addprop in the current scene matches the name of the prop node.

Example 11–8: Variable Example

```
<?xml version="1.0"?>
<xsl:stylesheet version="1.0"
      xmlns:xsl="http://www.w3.org/1999/XSL/Transform">

<xsl:template match="/">
<xsl:for-each select="//prop">
  <xsl:variable name="prop" select="."/>
  <xsl:for-each select="//scene">

Prop <xsl:value-of select="$prop/@name"/>
  Scene <xsl:value-of select="@name"/>
    <xsl:if test="addprop/@name=$prop/@name">
    Included
    </xsl:if>
  </xsl:for-each>
</xsl:for-each>
</xsl:template>
</xsl:stylesheet>
```

11.2.7   *XSL apply-templates*

The XSL apply-templates element type describes when the template rules should be processed. The form of the rule is

```
<xsl:apply-templates select="node-set-expression">
sorting or parameter elements
</xsl:apply-templates>
```

The *node-set-expression* defines the set of nodes whose template rules will be processed. If the `select` attribute is missing, then the node set will be the children elements of the context node. The nodes in the node set are processed in document order unless otherwise specified with a sorting element. For each node in the set, the template rules are examined and the best one is applied.[3] In Example 11–9, template rules describe how to transform not only the root-level node, but also other nodes in the tree. The `apply-templates` element is put where you want those rules applied. In the example, we use them to generate simple declarations for props and scenes.

Also note, as a change of pace, that the first template has been changed to match "`play`" instead of the root node. This has the effect of changing the context node to the play element node instead of the root node. The only place this makes a difference is the select attribute of the `apply-templates` element. The other XPath expressions are absolute paths where it won't make a difference. If the match attribute was left as the root document, then the select attribute of the `apply-templates` element would have to be rewritten, such as "`play/prop|play/scene`" or "`//prop|//scene`" or "`/play/prop|/play/scene`".

Example 11–9: Template Rule and apply-templates Example

```
<?xml version="1.0"?>
<xsl:stylesheet version="1.0"
    xmlns:xsl="http://www.w3.org/1999/XSL/Transform">

<xsl:template match="play">
class <xsl:value-of select="/play/@name"/> {
    <xsl:apply-templates select="prop|scene"/>
    public static void main(String[] args) {
        System.out.println("<xsl:value-of select="/play/title"/>");
    }
}
</xsl:template>

<xsl:template match="prop">
```

---

[3] Best means the highest priority template (more specific matches get higher priority). Consult the XSLT specification for further details.

```
      Prop <xsl:value-of select="@name"/>Prop = new Prop();
  </xsl:template>

  <xsl:template match="scene">
      Scene <xsl:value-of select="@name"/>Scene = new Scene();
  </xsl:template>
  </xsl:stylesheet>
```

The output of the above transformation (given as input the standard Play example in Example 5–8) is shown in Example 11–10.

Example 11–10: Output from apply-templates Example

```
class JackAndJill {

    Prop upProp = new Prop();

    Prop fetchProp = new Prop();

    Prop fallProp = new Prop();

    Prop tumbleProp = new Prop();

    Scene bottomScene = new Scene();

    Scene topScene = new Scene();

    public static void main(String[] args) {
        System.out.println("Jack and Jill");
    }
}
```

11.2.8 *XSL Text and Whitespace Issues*

The XSL text element type is used to directly output text. The form of the element type is

```
<xsl:text>
```
text
```
</xsl:text>
```

At first the `text` element type appears redundant, since *text* would be output regardless of whether it was wrapped inside the `text` element. However, whitespace characters are treated differently. If a text node created from a template contains only whitespace characters, then the text node is not included in the result tree. This makes sense, because in almost all cases such whitespace characters are used to format the XSLT file rather than the output file. In some circumstances, however, such whitespace characters are really needed to format the output. In such cases they can be wrapped in an XSLT `text` element to avoid stripping. Surprisingly enough, `text` elements can also be used to force the removal of whitespace characters, as we will see in Example 11–13. XSLT provides other mechanisms to control stripping, which are not discussed here. As shown elsewhere in this book, formatting is a particularly ugly problem when using templates, because we want to simultaneously format the template file as well as the output file, and XSLT doesn't inherently avoid the issue.

In Example 11–10, each prop and scene declaration is indented and double-spaced. Suppose we wanted to remove the blank lines between the declarations. First, let's examine why the blank lines are inserted. The problem lies in the template rules for prop and scene, so let's just look at the prop template rule (Example 11–11).

Example 11–11: Prop Template Rule That Outputs an Extra Blank Line

```
<?xml version="1.0"?>
...
<xsl:template match="prop">
    Prop <xsl:value-of select="@name"/>Prop = new Prop();
</xsl:template>
...
</xsl:stylesheet>
```

There are two text nodes that will be created from the template. The first one starts immediately after the greater-than sign that closes the template start-tag and ends with the start of the `value-of` element. This text node starts with a new-line character and the initial indentation (blanks or tabs). The other text node starts after the `value-of` element and ends just before the end-tag of the template rule. This text node thus includes the new line character immediately after the semicolon. So each declaration begins and ends with a new-line character. We can remove one of these new-line characters by simply removing one or the other, as shown in Example 11–12. Note that we end up with an XSLT file that is slightly harder to read because it is now formatted for the convenience of the output file, not the XSLT file.

Example 11–12: Prop Template Rule that Avoids an Extra Blank Line

```
<?xml version="1.0"?>
...
<xsl:template match="prop">
    Prop <xsl:value-of select="@name"/>Prop = new Prop();</xsl:template>
...
</xsl:stylesheet>
```

The `text` element can help us avoid this difficulty. In Example 11–13, the seemingly useless empty-element, `<xsl:text/>`, has been added to the end of the prop declaration line. Since it is an empty element tag, no additional text is output. However, it causes creation of a new text node between itself and the end-tag of the `template` element consisting of just whitespace characters (the lone new-line character) which is stripped.

Example 11–13: Using a text Element to Help Format Both Files

```
<?xml version="1.0"?>
...
<xsl:template match="prop">
    Prop <xsl:value-of select="@name"/>Prop = new Prop();<xsl:text/>
</xsl:template>
...
</xsl:stylesheet>
```

Let's examine one other common formatting issue and see how the `text` element helps solve it. Consider the same prop declaration, except that we'll consider it in the context of Phase 2, where the type attribute specifies the Java type of the prop. In that case, we want to replace the text "Prop" with a `value-of` element, as shown in Example 11–14. To keep it simple, we'll ignore initializing the variable.

Example 11–14: Phase 2 Example of a Prop Template

```
<?xml version="1.0"?>
...
<xsl:template match="prop">
    <xsl:value-of select="@type"/> <xsl:value-of select="@name"/>Prop;
</xsl:template>
...
</xsl:stylesheet>
```

Since the first nonstripped text node begins in the middle of a line, there is no longer an initial new-line character. This solves the double new-line character problem, but now new problems are introduced. There is no initial indentation (stripped out) and there is no blank character between the type name and variable name, because it too will be stripped out! You will get something like Example 11–15 (assuming the type attribute value is set to `Prop`).

Example 11–15: Output from Example 11–14 Prop Template

```
PropupProp;
PropfetchProp;
PropfallProp;
ProptumbleProp;
```

Adding a couple of `text` elements to preserve the indentation and blank character will solve this problem, as shown in Example 11–16.

Example 11–16: Phase 2 Example of a Prop Template with text Elements

```
<?xml version="1.0"?>
...
<xsl:template match="prop">
<xsl:text>    </xsl:text><xsl:value-of select="@type"/>
       <xsl:text> </xsl:text><xsl:value-of select="@name"/>Prop;
</xsl:template>
...
</xsl:stylesheet>
```

11.3 | Using XPath and XSLT in the Play Domain

Before showing the program generator for Play, it's worth taking a minute to examine one more XSLT file. XSLT is designed primarily for transforming XML files to other XML files or HTML. An example was given in Chapter 5, Figure 5–10. This view of a play specification was created employing XSLT using the file in Example 11–17. Note that HTML tags are embedded where needed with certain HTML tags, such as <br> requiring the more strict syntax, <br/>.

Example 11–17: viewplay.xsl

```
<?xml version="1.0"?>
<xsl:stylesheet xmlns:xsl="http://www.w3.org/1999/XSL/Transform"
             version="1.0">

<xsl:template match="/">
<html><head><title><xsl:value-of select="//play/title"/></title></head>
<body>
<h3>Play Specification</h3>
<br/>Title: <xsl:value-of select="//play/title"/>
<br/>Width: <xsl:value-of select="//play/@width"/>
<br/>Height: <xsl:value-of select="//play/@height"/>
<br/>Start Scene: <code><xsl:value-of select="//play/@start"/></code>

<table border="1" cellpadding="5">
<tr><th>Buttons</th><th>Scenes</th></tr>
<tr><td>
<xsl:for-each select="//play/prop">
<br/>Button: <code><xsl:value-of select="@name"/></code>
<xsl:for-each select="trait">
<br/>   <xsl:value-of select="@name"/>: "<code><xsl:value-of
select="."/></code>"
</xsl:for-each>
<xsl:for-each select="script">
<br/>   Script <xsl:value-of select="@name"/>:
<ol>
  <xsl:for-each select="trait">
      <li/>Change <xsl:value-of select="@name"/>
  <xsl:if test="@prop"> for Button <code><xsl:value-of
select="@prop"/></code></xsl:if>
```

```
            to "<code><xsl:value-of select="."/></code>"
      </xsl:for-each>
   <xsl:if test="@goto">
         <li/>Change to Scene <code><xsl:value-of select="@goto"/></code>;
   </xsl:if>
</ol>
<hr/>
</xsl:for-each>


</xsl:for-each>
</td><td valign="top">
<xsl:for-each select="//play/scene">
<br/>Scene: <xsl:value-of select="@name"/>
<br/>Background Color: <code><xsl:value-of select="@color"/></code>
<br/>
<ol>
   <xsl:for-each select="addprop">
         <li>Button <code><xsl:value-of select="@name"/></code>
         </li>
   </xsl:for-each>
</ol>
<hr/>
</xsl:for-each>
</td></tr></table>
</body>
</html>
</xsl:template>


</xsl:stylesheet>
```

Now, finally, let's look at the Play program generator using XPath and XSLT (Figure 11–3). For the file to fit nicely across the page, some lines had to be shortened. This was accomplished mostly by dividing start-tags across boundary lines where the new-line character would not be transferred to the output file.

Example 11–18: Play2.xsl

```
<?xml version="1.0"?>
<xsl:stylesheet xmlns:xsl="http://www.w3.org/1999/XSL/Transform"
            version="1.0"
              xmlns:xt="http://www.jclark.com/xt"
              extension-element-prefixes="xt">
<xsl:output method="text"/>
```

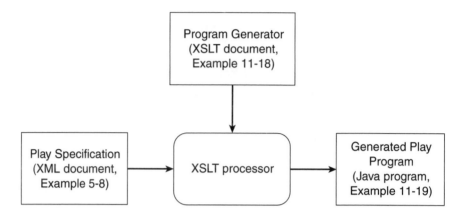

Figure 11–3   Process diagram for XSLT-based Play program generator

```
<xsl:template match="/">
import java.awt.*;
import java.awt.event.*;

class <xsl:value-of select="//play/@name"/>Play2 extends Frame {
    /* The Props for <xsl:value-of
        select="//play/@name"/> ***********/
<xsl:for-each select="//play/prop">
    Button <xsl:value-of select="@name"/>Prop
                = new Button("<xsl:value-of
select="trait"/>");<xsl:text/>
</xsl:for-each>

    /* The Events in the <xsl:value-of
        select="//play/@name"/> ********/

    class PropEvent implements ActionListener {
        public void actionPerformed(ActionEvent evt) {
            Object prop = evt.getSource();
<xsl:for-each select="//play/prop">
<xsl:text>                </xsl:text>
            <xsl:if test="position()!=1">
            } else </xsl:if>if (prop.equals(<xsl:value-of
                    select="@name"/>Prop)) {<xsl:text/>
                <xsl:apply-templates select="script/trait"/>
                <xsl:if test="./script/@goto">
```

```
                        enterNewScene("<xsl:value-of

select="script/@goto"/>");<xsl:text/>
                        </xsl:if>
</xsl:for-each>
                } else {
                    System.out.println("Invalid prop");
                }
            }
        }

    /* Creating and starting up the <xsl:value-of
                                    select="//play/@name"/> ****/

    String currentScene;

    public <xsl:value-of select="//play/@name"/>Play2() {
        super("<xsl:if
                test="count(//play/title)=0">No Title xx</xsl:if>
                    <xsl:value-of select="//play/title"/>");
        setSize(<xsl:value-of select="//play/@width"/>, <xsl:text/>
                    <xsl:value-of select="//play/@height"/>);
        setLayout(new FlowLayout());

        // initialize props
        PropEvent a = new PropEvent();
<xsl:for-each select="//play/prop">
<xsl:text>        </xsl:text>
        <xsl:value-of select="@name"/>Prop.addActionListener(a);
</xsl:for-each>
        // start scene
        enterNewScene("<xsl:value-of select="//play/@start"/>");
    }

    public void enterNewScene(String scene) {
        removeAll();  // remove previous scene
        currentScene = scene;
<xsl:for-each select="//play/scene">
<xsl:text>            </xsl:text>
                <xsl:if test="position()!=1">
        } else </xsl:if>if (scene.equals("<xsl:value-of
                                    select="@name"/>")) {<xsl:text/>
  <xsl:for-each select="addprop">
                    add(<xsl:value-of select="@name"/>Prop);<xsl:text/>
</xsl:for-each>
```

```
                      setBackground(Color.decode("<xsl:value-of
                                    select="@color"/>"));<xsl:text/>
</xsl:for-each>
        } else {
            System.out.println("Invalid scene: "+scene);
        }
        show();
    }

    public static void main(String[] args) {
        new <xsl:value-of select="//play/@name"/>Play2();
    }
}

</xsl:template>

<xsl:template match="trait">
<xsl:text>
                </xsl:text>
 <xsl:choose>
  <xsl:when test="@prop"><xsl:value-of select="@prop"/></xsl:when>
  <xsl:otherwise><xsl:value-of
      select="ancestor::addprop/@name | ancestor::prop/@name"/>
  </xsl:otherwise>
  </xsl:choose>Prop.setLabel("<xsl:value-of select="."/>");<xsl:text/>
</xsl:template>

</xsl:stylesheet>
```

The XSLT in Example 11–18, when applied to the standard Play specification (Example 5–8), will generate the file Example 11–19. The output file differs only slightly from previous generated programs.

Example 11–19: The Generated Program

```java
import java.awt.*;
import java.awt.event.*;

class JackAndJillPlay2 extends Frame {
    /* The Props for JackAndJill ***********/

    Button upProp
            = new Button("Go up the hill");
    Button fetchProp
            = new Button("Fetch a pail of water");
    Button fallProp
```

```java
        = new Button("Fall down, break crown");
Button tumbleProp
        = new Button("Tumble down");

/* The Events in the JackAndJill ********/

class PropEvent implements ActionListener {
    public void actionPerformed(ActionEvent evt) {
        Object prop = evt.getSource();
        if (prop.equals(upProp)) {
            fetchProp.setLabel("Fetch a pail of water");
            enterNewScene("top");
        } else if (prop.equals(fetchProp)) {
            fetchProp.setLabel("Fetch another pail");
        } else if (prop.equals(fallProp)) {
            fallProp.setLabel("Break crown");
            tumbleProp.setLabel("Tumble after");
            enterNewScene("bottom");
        } else if (prop.equals(tumbleProp)) {
            enterNewScene("bottom");
        } else {
            System.out.println("Invalid prop");
        }
    }
}

/* Creating and starting up the JackAndJill ****/

String currentScene;

public JackAndJillPlay2() {
    super("Jack and Jill");
    setSize(200, 120);
    setLayout(new FlowLayout());

    // initialize props
    PropEvent a = new PropEvent();
    upProp.addActionListener(a);
    fetchProp.addActionListener(a);
    fallProp.addActionListener(a);
    tumbleProp.addActionListener(a);

    // start scene
    enterNewScene("bottom");
}
```

```
public void enterNewScene(String scene) {
    removeAll();   // remove previous scene
    currentScene = scene;
    if (scene.equals("bottom")) {
            add(upProp);
            add(fallProp);
            setBackground(Color.decode("#8888aa"));
    } else if (scene.equals("top")) {
            add(fetchProp);
            add(fallProp);
            add(tumbleProp);
            setBackground(Color.decode("#dddddd"));
    } else {
        System.out.println("Invalid scene: "+scene);
    }
    show();
}

public static void main(String[] args) {
    new JackAndJillPlay2();
}
}
```

11.4 | Summary

XPath is an expression language for selecting nodes in an XML tree. An XSLT stylesheet is an XML document that specifies how to transform XML documents into other XML documents, HTML documents, or plain text documents. XSLT, which uses XPath, is used in this chapter to create a Play domain program generator. This shows how Java program generators can be created solely from XML tools without using the Java language.

Crafting Your Own Template Language

- What's wrong with using JSP or XSL?

- Let's create our own template language!

- Bootstrapping: implementing the template language using the template language

12

C hapters 10 and 11 examined the use of JSP and XSLT as
template languages in the construction of program generators. This chapter examines what a template language
might look like if we crafted our own. It will show that the cost of
building one from scratch or using one like the one crafted in this
chapter is rather small, and the benefits to be gained such as increased
readability readily justify the costs. Before doing so, it is worth evaluating JSP and XSLT to help provide guidance in our own design.

12.1 | Evaluating JSP and XSLT

The JSP and XSLT approaches to program generation are reasonable
and effective. Nevertheless, they do have some disadvantages that
should be examined. Both have the considerable advantage that they
use common freely available software tools for creating program generators; there is no need to buy or create proprietary software. However,

neither JSP or XSLT was designed to be used for building program generators, and as a consequence both have some drawbacks when used for that purpose.

JSP is designed to create Web pages on the fly with dynamic content. Dynamic content is provided by escapes to the Java language. JSP files are installed in a (Web) server environment and passed sufficient context information about the request to enable sophisticated Internet applications that span over multiple requests. Typically program generators are batch-oriented jobs and in many cases are part of a larger scheme for translating software programs to object code. Also, typically input to JSP comes from request parameters, not files. Consequently, the major drawbacks of JSP are the following.

1. **Server Context**: JSP works in the context of a server, often not needed, and somewhat of a hindrance for most program generators. Although such a context can be useful for some situations, such as delivery over the Internet, in other situations it becomes very awkward to integrate with other system building tools.

2. **Awkward Input**: JSP input is assumed to come from request parameters rather than the command line and files. Request parameters can be used instead of command-line arguments and even files. Reading of files may be awkward if they are located on other machines. The DOM API can be used for reading XML files. Although not limited to XML input, JSP also does not provide any facilities for other kinds of input.

XSLT is designed to transform XML files into either HTML or other XML files. XSLT also provides a means for generating plain text files, but the design of XSLT is not focused on plain text file generation. Like JSP, XSLT is also designed with the intent of creating Web pages, but not exclusively, and not necessarily as part of a Web server. XSLT can be deployed on the server side, the client side, or as a standalone facility. The major drawbacks of XSLT are the following.

1. **Limited Java Escapes**: XSLT does not provide direct escapes to the Java language for controlling the template. There are provisions for extending the XPath function library, but such functions only extend the XPath features and do not extend or control the XSLT features. It is assumed that XSLT features are sufficient to generate almost anything you want. Unfortunately, this may exclude sophisticated program generators that use complex data structures, optimization techniques, or other kinds of transformations.

2. **Wordy Template Controls**: XSLT is a verbose language and consequently often obscures the underlying structure of the program being generated.

3. **Entity References**: Special characters must be appropriately escaped. The most obvious is the less-than character, which is often needed in program generation.

JSP and XSLT do have significant strengths. The most powerful feature of XSLT is XPath, which provides a concise and powerful means of extracting exactly the information you want from an XML document. JSP provides a very simple and effective way of allowing the Java language to control the output of the generator. Is there a way to combine the strengths of JSP and XSLT while removing their disadvantages?

12.2 | TL—A New Template Language

Before embarking on designing a new template language, it is reasonable to carefully consider the goals of the language. We will only consider program-generator templates using the Java language as the underlying implementation language (but not necessarily as the output language) and XML as the input specification language. JSP and

XSLT provide excellent starting points, and since we've identified some strengths and weakness in these approaches, we can quickly and briefly state the major design goals for the new template language. Let's call the new template language TL.

1. TL should have a concise and powerful expression language for accessing information from an XML document. The language should allow one to easily navigate through the XML tree and to select specific subsets of elements and attributes.

2. TL should have a concise way to insert information from the XML specification into the generated output. It should have concise ways to iterate over elements of the specification. It should have conditional generation. This goal says that the common things needed for program generation should be simple to express.

3. TL should have a way to express complex and unusual iteration and other flow-of-control constructs. As these things are not common, it is not necessary that they be easily expressed.

4. TL should have full and direct access to the complete range of Java features. These include the ability to integrate with other components and libraries.

5. TL should provide access to the DOM API. This could be used to perform transformations directly on the XML tree.

6. TL should allow control over whitespace characters, without unduly obscuring the program generation.

7. TL should minimize disruptive escaping of characters in the programming language.

8. TL should be executable from a command-line processor with command-line arguments specifying the input and output files. This allows program generators to be easily incorporated into software construction tools such as make. It's also important that such program generators also be usable from other Java objects; in particular, templates should be able to use other templates.

9. TL should allow program generators with multiple inputs and outputs. This permits a specification to be organized in multiple files and permits a generated program to span multiple files. Multiple outputs are also important for generating noncode files such as documentation, test scripts, and other files.

10. TL should be easily converted to and from XML so that the full range of XML tools can be applied to templates. The XML version of JSP is an example of this feature.

11. TL should have an option to allow compilation or interpretation mode. Some features may not be available if interpretation mode is used.

To achieve these goals, a design and the rationale are presented organized by the numbered goals above.

12.2.1 *Use XPath*

We are truly lucky that XPath provides exactly what we need to meet this goal. XPath is a recent addition to the XML family of standards. It arose as a result of recognizing that two other standards, XSL and XPointer, required a similar set of features. The standards committee agreed to a common solution, which resulted in XPath. It shouldn't be too surprising, therefore, to see XPath as a possibly useful element in other tools and standards as well. Therefore, XPath will be an essential element of our new template language.

To integrate XPath into TL, we will need to specify the context of XPath expression evaluation. As with XSLT, we'll need a means to specify variable bindings, context node, size, and position. Unfortunately, at the time of this writing XPath does not yet have an API for integration as a component into other tools and solutions. Thus, we will use our own homegrown API. This API will require a new class and methods for loading a DOM tree, establishing a context, including variable bindings, and evaluating XPath expressions. An overview of this API is given in Table 12–1. The new class is called XPathContext.[1] The XPathContext API includes methods for getting and setting the various elements making up the context, evaluating XPath expressions, and pushing and popping the context for applications that have nested scopes such as XSLT and our new template language.

Table 12–1: API Overview

Method Signature	Description
XPathContext(String filename)	Create a new XPath context using the XML source in filename as the document, the root element as the context node, and position and size as 1.
XPathContext(Document d, Node n, int position, int size)	Create a new XPath context for document d with context node n, and context position and size.
public void setDocument (Document d)	Establishes the XML document.
public void setPosition(int n)	Sets context position to n.
public void setSize(int n)	Sets context size to n.
public void setNode(Node n)	Sets the context node.

(continued)

---

[1] The API must also be extended to include function libraries and namespace declarations as described in the XPath specification.

Table 12–1: API Overview *(Continued)*

Method Signature	Description
`public void setVariable (String var, Object x)`	Sets value of variable. The type of x must be a `Boolean`, `Double`, `String` or `NodeList`. If x is `null`, the variable is removed from the context.
`public Document getDocument()`	Returns the XML document.
`public int getPosition()`	Returns the context position.
`public int getSize()`	Returns the context size.
`public Node getNode()`	Returns the context node.
`public Object getVariable(String var)`	Returns the value of a variable or null if the variable is not found.
`public Object eval(String path)`	Evaluates the XPath expression and returns either a `Boolean`, `Double`, `String`, or `NodeList`.
`public boolean evalBoolean(String path)`	Evaluates the XPath expression and converts to boolean according to the XPath specification.
`public String evalString(String path)`	Evaluates the XPath expression and converts to `String` according to the XPath specification.
`public NodeList evalNodeSet(String path)`	Evaluates the XPath node-set expression.
`public double evalNumber(String path)`	Evaluates the XPath expression and converts it to a number according to the XPath specification.
`public void push(Node n, int position, int size)`	Save current node, position, and size on a stack, and make the parameters the new context node, position, and size.
`public void pop()`	Restore the old context node, position, and size from the stack.

12.2.2 *Syntax for Common Constructions*

The common constructions used in program generators include inserting values, iterating over elements of the specification, and conditional expressions. It is worth examining these three constructs in JSP and XSLT. Example 12–1 shows all three constructs in a typical situation. Each prop in the specification with a name attribute generates a declaration. The JSP example uses some simple method calls to reduce the complexity of the DOM API.

Example 12–1: Common Constructs in JSP

```
<% NodeList props = spec.getElementsByTagName("prop");
   for (int j=0; j<props.getLength(); ++j) {
       Node prop = props.item(j);
       String propName = getAttrValue(prop, "name");
       if (propName!=null) {
%>
   Button <%=getAttrValue(prop, "name")%>Prop;
<%     }
   } %>
```

Example 12–2: Common Constructs in XSLT

```
<xsl:for-each select="//prop">
    <xsl:if test="@name">
    Button <xsl:value-of select="@name"/>Prop;
    </xsl:if>
</xsl:for-each>
```

The design decisions to consider for the new template language are whether to use the syntax of JSP, XSLT, or something new. Although XSLT is verbose, in Example 12–2 it is much simpler because of XPath. What if we add XPath to JSP? This would result in something like Example 12–3.

Example 12–3: Common Constructs in JSP with XPath

```
<% NodeList props = spec.evalNodeSet("//prop");
   int len = props.getLength();
   for (int j=0; j<len; ++j) {
```

```
        Node prop = props.item(j);
        XPathContext c = new XPathContext(spec, prop, j, len);
        if (c.evalBoolean("@name")) {
%>
    Button <%=c.eval("@name")%>Prop;
<%      }
    } %>
```

Example 12–3 is an improvement over Example 12–1 but is still more complex than the XSLT in Example 12–2. The reason for its complexity is that, although we added XPath, it is not integrated with the constructs such as <%=*expression*%>, where the *expression* is a Java language expression rather than an XPath expression. Similarly, there is no explicit construct for iterating over elements of an XPath expression. To make these explicit constructs in JSP, let's invent new JSP constructs with the new character "#" to indicate the new XPath constructs. This is shown in Example 12–4 without further explanation of the new constructs.

Example 12–4: Common Constructs in JSP Extended with Explicit JSP Constructs for XPath

```
<%#for "//prop" %>
    <%#if "@name" %>
    Button <%# "@name" %>Prop;
    <%#end-if%>);
<%#end-for %>
```

This is a considerable improvement in readability (once you understand that # is used to escape to XPath constructs). To provide further simplification over either JSP or XSLT, let's consider a more specialized language that gets away from the syntactic structure of either JSP or XSLT.

One problem of using the JSP or XSLT syntax is the use of the less-than symbol, a character that is commonly used in the Java language. If our primary intent is to generate Java programs, it makes sense to select a character that is used rarely in Java to distinguish these escapes from regular Java programs. Three characters meet this criterion, namely, sharp, the at symbol, and the dollar symbol. Any of these will work, but we'll select the sharp symbol, since the other two are used in XPath.[2]

Next, we need to consider what the form of the constructs should be. Some possibilities for values are the following.

```
#//props
#//props#
#(//props)
#"//props"
#"//props"#
```

The first one has the flaw that it will be difficult to determine where the XPath expression ends. We must remember that these expressions may occur anywhere, and there might not be whitespace following the expression. The remaining examples do not have this problem. The second example terminates with a sharp symbol. However, it will be difficult to provide other constructs that don't conflict with XPath expression, and it may be difficult to parse. Therefore, we need some additional syntax to help us provide other constructs. The third example uses parentheses to identify XPath expressions, but this also has the drawback that it is inconsistent with the syntax of expressions in XSLT. Adopting the use of either single or double quotes will make it much easier to translate to other forms without worrying about such technicalities. Thus, the fourth example, which uses quotes, is a better form. We may also want to adopt the fifth form to provide further redundancy and readability, by using the sharp symbol to provide both beginning and ending delimiters for all TL constructs.

Following this convention, the syntax we'll adopt for the three common constructs will be as follows.

```
#"xpath-expression"#
#for "xpath-expression"# template #end#
#if "xpath-expression"# template #else# template #fi#
```

---

[2] The dollar symbol and at symbol are used in XPath to denote variables and attributes. The sharp symbol is used by the C preprocessor and was often used for conditional compilation, an activity suggesting the need for a program generator, so perhaps it is historically appropriate to use the sharp symbol for this purpose.

Using these three constructs will result in Example 12–5.

Example 12–5: Common Constructs in the New Template Language

```
#for "//prop" #
    #if "@name" #
    Button #"@name"#Prop;
    #fi#
#end#
```

Like JSP, the readability of the language is greatly improved by using different fonts (and colors), as shown in Example 12–6.

Example 12–6: Common Constructs in the New Template Language Using Different Fonts

```
#for "//prop" #
    #if "@name" #
    Button #"@name"#Prop;
    #fi#
#end#
```

We need to make another change to the "for" construct. One problem with having a single implicit context node is the inability to refer to multiple nodes at the same time. XPath provides this capability with variable bindings, and we can use these variables to solve the problem. First, let's consider the following example, where we wish to generate a line of code for each addprop in each scene, using the name attributes of both the scene and the "addprop." Unfortunately, in Example 12–7, the first "@name" refers to the "addprop" node, not the scene node.

Example 12–7: Nested For Constructs with Erroneous @name Reference

```
#for "//scene" #
    #for "//addprop"#
        #"@name"#Scene.addProp(#"@name"#Prop);
    #end#
#end#
```

By allowing each "for" loop to use a named loop variable, we can easily solve this problem. The variable name will also be used as the name of the loop variable in the Java code. This allows easy access to the context node. The syntax we choose for this is shown below.

#for *var* "*xpath-expression*" # *template* #end#

Example 12–7, rewritten with `for` variables, now looks as shown in Example 12–8.

Example 12–8: Nested For Constructs with Named Loop Variables

```
#for scene "//scene" #
    #for "//addprop"#
        #"$scene/@name"#Scene.addProp(#"@name"#Prop);
    #end#
#end#
```

Whenever a language like this is proposed, many people have a negative reaction to the syntactic choices that were made. The syntactic choices made in this chapter are not important. It is easy to parameterize the delimiters of the new template language. Thus, if someone would like a syntax that looks like JSP, all she would have to do is provide a new set of delimiter symbols. If we parameterize the delimiters, we may also wish to parameterize the keywords as well.

This language will also appear to be abandoning XML as syntax for template languages. As will be shown shortly, an XML form of the language is also presented, just as JSP has an XML form.

12.2.3 *Escapes to the Java Language*

The new template language will also require escapes to the Java language for more powerful control over the generated output. Like JSP, this can be in the form either of expressions whose value is output or of statements that are used for computation and flow of control. In keeping with the syntax introduced in the previous section, we'll introduce the two new constructs.

 # ⟨java-expression⟩ #
 # java-statements #

The *java-expression* uses parentheses to identify it as a Java expression that is evaluated and the result of which will be output. Java statements are identified with at least one whitespace character after the initial sharp character. Example 12–9 shows both constructs.

Example 12–9: Example Use of Java-Expressions and Java-Statements

```
# String[] names = { "Jack", "Jill" };

  for (int j=0; j<names.length; ++j) {

#

        Button button#(names[j])# = new Button("#(names[j])#");
# } #
```

To complete the design of Java escapes, we need to describe the environment where the expressions and statements are executed. The program generator derived from the template will have the same rough structure that JSP uses (Table 12–2). In particular, a `ProgramWriter` object called `out` will be available. `ProgramWriter` extends `PrintWriter`. The current `XPathContext` will be available in a variable called `context`. This variable provides access to the XML document, the current context node, position, size, and variables. A class instance variable is also provided to store properties. From the main method, the command-line arguments are stored as properties under the names, `arg1`, `arg2`, etc.

Table 12–2: Accessible Variables from a Template

Type and Name	*Description*
`ProgramWriter out;`	The output stream.
`XPathContext context;`	The XPath context including document, context node, position, size, and variables.
`Properties properties;`	Instance variable for storing command-line arguments and other options.

Example 12–10 shows how these variables could be used in a program. The first part shows how to use the out variable to output something in a Java code escape (compare this with Example 12–9). The middle part shows how to access the first command-line argument, typically the specification input file name. The last part shows how to obtain the current context node. In this case, the method getNode-Name will return the element type name of the node, which is part of the standard DOM API.

Example 12–10: Example Use of Accessible Variables in a Template

```
# String[] names = { "Jack", "Jill" };
  for (int j=0; j<names.length; ++j) {
    out.print("Button button"+names[j]+ ";\n");
  }
#

// Specification file: #(properties.getProperty("arg1"))#

// Elements appearing as children under title nodes (if any)
#for j "//title/*"
// #(j.getNodeName())#
#end#
```

12.2.4   *Java Integration*

In addition to the escapes to Java expressions and statements of the previous section, there will also be a need to support imports, declarations, renaming, and implementation options. We'll discuss each of these in turn.

It is not necessary to use the import statement in order to use other Java packages, since fully qualified names can always be used. However, the convenience of using the short names justifies including a mechanism to allow one to specify import statements. JSP uses a general page directive construct, such as:

```
<%@ page import="com.craigc.progen" %>
```

To provide this facility as well as others yet to be mentioned, we'll add the following construct.

```
#declare declarations #
```

Declarations will include import statements and other attributes in a manner similar to JSP (see Chapter 10). Thus, the previous import statement will be rewritten as:

```
#declare import="com.craigc.progen" #
```

Other declarations that one might make include extending a different base class for the program generator, the implements clause, and renaming the program-generator class.

```
#declare extends="MyProgramGeneratorBase" #
#declare implements="MyInterface" #
#declare classname="MyGenerator" #
```

It will also be useful to add class variables and methods to the generated code. This will also be provided with the declarations section, as shown below.

```
#declarations
Java declarations and methods
#
```

Example 12–11 shows the use of the declarations section, where an instance variable, count, is used to count the number of unique variable names needed by the program generator. The method getUniqueVariable increments count and returns an identifier which includes count.

Example 12–11: Example Use of Declarations Section

```
#declarations

// create unique variable names

int count = 0;

String getUniqueVariable() {
    return "var"+(count++);
}
#
```

12.2.5   *Access to DOM*

The new template language assumes that the XML specification input is available through the XPath feature. In addition, the XPathContext assumes that the XML specification is available using the DOM API. Would it have been better to avoid a dependency on the DOM API? As discussed in previous chapters, it is reasonable for program generators to use a DOM-oriented approach rather than SAX. If you really want to avoid depending on the DOM API, this can be done with some slight modifications to the XPathContext class by replacing Document with some other class that represents the XML specification.

The DOM API may be useful for some kinds of processing. Some of the processing might be easier to accomplish by using DOM rather XPath. One reason to use DOM is to get information that might be awkward or impossible to determine with XPath. An example is determining the type of the context node. Using the DOM API, the method get-NodeType provides the answer, but there is no equivalent test in XPath.

Semantic checks are sometimes easier to accomplish using XPath and sometimes easier using the DOM API. An example of a semantic check using XPath is the following expression.

```
//script[not(@goto=//scene/@name)]
```

The above expression returns all scripts whose goto attribute does not match the name of a scene. Although the expression can be difficult to interpret properly, particularly for novices at XPath, it is succinct. The corresponding code using the DOM API would be verbose, clumsy, and also difficult to read without appropriate comments. XPath won't always be the right way to do semantic checks, however. For some semantic checks and analysis you'll simply have to use the DOM API. A finite state machine analysis of the Play domain that includes detection of isolated sets of scenes, sinks (scenes or sets of scenes for which there is no path to other scenes), would be impossible in XPath.[3]

---

[3] This isn't quite true, since the Function Library could be extended to provide either the primitive functions necessary to do this, or simply a function call that will do the entire job. In general, the core function library is insufficient to do all possible semantic checks or analysis.

Sometimes transformations and normalization can be also accomplished more directly using DOM rather XPath. XPath is intended simply to access XML information and not change it. The DOM API will allow you to modify and create new XML structures.

To demonstrate the use of the DOM API, Example 12–12 shows the "normalizing" of scene names. "Normalization" refers to a process that converts expressions to a standard or canonical form. In our example, normalize will mean to simply translate upper-case letters to lower-case. So, in this simple example, we are simply changing the string value of certain attribute nodes. In other situations, normalization may require significant changes or restructuring of the XML tree.

Example 12–12: Normalizing Scene Names

```
#for j "(//scene/@name)|(//script/@goto)|(play/@start)"#

#   j.setValue(j.getValue().toLowerCase());   #
#end#
```

Example 12–12 shows the elegance that can be achieved by using both XPath and DOM. You can't use XPath by itself, because it can't change the tree, and using DOM exclusively would result in many lines of code.

12.2.6   *Whitespace Processing*

Should the generated program be nicely formatted? It has been argued in the past that generated programs need not look pretty, and in fact should look awful to avoid even the temptation of modifying the output. The domain engineer will decide this question. As designers of the new template language, it's our job to provide assistance to those who do wish to carefully control how the generated program is formatted. This is largely a matter of controlling whitespace characters.

The whitespace problem is largely a result of the desire to simultaneously format the generated program along with the program generator in the same file. What we need are some simple rules that will work the way we would expect in most cases, and a simple mechanism to make a change for the few cases where we don't want the default. We'd also like this mechanism to be as nonobstructive as possible so that it doesn't obscure the important text that is being generated.

Both JSP and XSLT have their own mechanisms for controlling whitespace which we will quickly review and critique; then we'll describe the rules for the new template language, giving some examples.

JSP preserves all whitespace characters outside the brackets <% and %>. This very simple rule is easy to remember, but it makes it difficult to format the generated output. Of course, if you are generating HTML then the additional whitespace doesn't make any difference. For other types of output such as Java programs, however, you might like to have some control. Consider Example 12–13, which generates a declaration, and where we wish to put the whole declaration on a single line.

Example 12–13: Desired One Line Output

```
int[] v = { 3, 4, 5, };
```

The JSP to generate this line might be as shown in Example 12–4.

Example 12–14: Simple One Line JSP Solution

```
int[] v = { <% for (int j=0; j<x.length; ++j) { %><%=x[j]%>, <% } %>};
```

If this line gets much longer, it will be difficult to read in the JSP file, but if you break up the line where you think you should, as in Example 12–15, then you will get the declaration spread across multiple lines.

Example 12–15: Spreading the JSP Solution across Multiple Lines

```
int[] v = {
    <% for (int j=0; j<x.length; ++j) { %>
        <%=x[j]%>,
    <% } %>};
```

The generated declaration will now appear as shown in Example 12–16.

Example 12–16: Generated Output from Multiline JSP Solution

```
int[] v = {

    3,

    4,

    5,
  };
```

If we use line breaks in the middle of the `<%` and `%>` constructs, then we can rewrite the JSP file as in Example 12–17.

Example 12–17: Spreading the JSP Solution across Multiple Lines to Generate One Line of Output

```
int[] v = { <%
    for (int j=0; j<x.length; ++j) {
      %><%=x[j]%>, <%
    } %>};
```

The above JSP segment will now generate a single-line declaration, but this is clearly harder to read and maintain.

XSLT is better. The rule is that any text node that is just whitespace is removed. All other whitespace is retained. In addition, one can list a set of elements that preserve whitespace. Text nodes containing only whitespace characters whose parent element preserves whitespace will not be removed. Also, the attribute `xml:space="preserve"`, can be used to preserve whitespace of all descendant text nodes and reversed for the attribute `xml:space="default"`. By default, the only whitespace-preserving element is `xsl:text`. To generate the single-line declaration above with a reasonable template formatting, one can write the XSLT in Example 12–18.

Example 12–18: An XSLT Solution to Generate a Single-Line Declaration

```
int[] v = { <xsl:for-each select="x">
    <xsl:value-of select="x[j]"/>, </xsl:for>};
```

Note that the space and new-line character preceding the `xsl:value-of` element will be stripped by the XSLT whitespace rules. XSLT also provides more whitespace rules for stripping whitespace characters from the XML input file using XSLT top-level elements called `xsl:strip-space` and `xsl:preserve-space`.

Formulation of the rules for the new template language will be guided by the following logic. When a template writer places a character in the template, and there is whitespace preceding that character, what is the intent: to format that character for the template document or for the output document? The rule we use is that if the character will be placed in the output, then the intent is usually to format the output. If the character is part of some template command, then the intent is usually to format the template document. One exception is the expression constructs that evaluate an expression and write the value to the output. These constructs are typically placed to format the output rather than the template document.

In addition, to these rules, we need some way of reversing the rule for the nontypical cases. Since formatting is usually a lower priority goal of template writers, the whitespace processing should not get in the way of understanding the logic of the template. We need some subtle way of controlling whitespace processing that is noticed only when someone is actually trying to figure out formatting issues and in other cases is simply ignored. The way to do this for the new template language is to insert the very subtle period character just after the initial delimiter to reverse the whitespace rule. One more construct is introduced, an empty construct, which is used to remove whitespace preceding normal text. The whitespace rules for the new template language are summarized in Table 12–3.

Table 12–3: Whitespace Rules for the New Template Language

Preserve preceding whitespace	Strip preceding whitespace
normal text	*#.# normal text*
#"xpath expression"#	*#."xpath expression"#*
#(java expression)#	*#.(java expression)#*
#.all other constructs#	*#all other constructs#*

The output occasionally requires some control over indentation. For example, to properly indent recursive structures requires keeping track of nesting levels and having a means of prepending blanks for each output line. The `ProgramWriter` (which extends `Print-Writer`) class provides an autoindentation feature. Two new methods are provided to set and get the current indent String. This String is automatically output after each new-line character.

```
public void setIndent(String s);
public String getIndent();
```

12.2.7 *Character Escapes*

A drawback of using XSLT or the XML version of JSP is the use of character entities. The new template language uses other delimiters that are not normally in a Java program, thus greatly reducing this annoyance. However, the delimiters must still be expressible in the language. We could simply use the Unicode escape sequence, "\uxxx", for representing the sharp character. Alternatively, we can provide a new construct, such as "##", for representing a sharp character (Example 12–19). Since the new template language only uses this single character for all constructs, all other characters can be used as they would normally be used in a Java program.

Example 12–19: The Sharp Character Is Represented in TL as Two Sharp Characters

```
// check ## character
      if (c=='##') {
```

12.2.8 *Command-Line Processing and Subtemplates*

The program generator created with the new template language should be accessible from a shell command line, but also from other Java programs. In particular, templates should be accessible from other templates. Each program generator class created by the new template therefore provides a static main method that processes the command-line parameters. It will also provide a way of accessing the program generator directly from other objects without the need for processing command-line parameters.

The most important command-line parameters for a program generator are the input and output files. The input file is the XML specification and the output file is where the generated program will go. The output file can be optional. If it is missing, the output will go to standard output. Other command-line parameters might be provided to specify other options. An example of using the XYZ program generator with input file spec.xml, output file MyProgram.java, and a third command-line parameter specifying an XYZ-specific parameter is shown below.

```
java XYZ spec.xml MyProgram.java encrypt
```

The main method of XYZ is generated by TL. It will open an output file and copy command-line parameters to the properties instance variable of the generator. The code used for the main method is quite simple and is shown in Example 12–20.

Example 12–20: The Main Method of a Program Generator Named XYZ

```java
public static void main(String[] args) {
    try {
        ProgramWriter out = args.length>=2
            ?new ProgramWriter(new FileOutputStream(args[1]))
            :new ProgramWriter(System.out);
        XYZ pg = new XYZ();
        for (int j=1; j<=args.length; ++j) {
            pg.properties.put("arg"+j, args[j-1]);
        }
        pg.generate(new XPathContext(args[0]), out);
        out.close();
    } catch (Exception e) {
        e.printStackTrace();
    }
}
```

Complex program generators can be organized by creating multiple templates. The master template can call the other templates, much like subroutines. For that reason, we'll sometimes call these templates *subtemplates*. Recursive structures are naturally implemented with subtemplates. The use of subtemplates is easily provided, since the command-line processing will be limited to the static main method. Each program-generator class will have a `generate` method that is used to generate the program to a `ProgramWriter` object. The `generate` method is declared as follows.

```
public boolean generate(XPathContext context, ProgramWriter out) { ... }
```

Parameterized templates can also be created by adding new parameterized methods to the declarations section, or by using the properties variable. Two examples are provided. The first one uses the properties variable for passing parameters, while the second shows how to declare and use additional generate methods.

The first example, `ArrayCode.template`, shows a simple template for generating an array declaration (Example 12–21). The name and the type of the array are passed as explicit parameters to a new generate method. The `generate` method assigns these parameters to instance variables and calls the standard generate method. An example call to this subtemplate is shown in Example 12–23.

Example 12–21: ArrayCode.template

```
#declarations

String type, name;

public void generate(XPathContext context, ProgramWriter out,
            String n, String t) {
    type = t;
    name = n;
    generate(context, out); // call template
}
#
private #(type)#[] #(name)# = {
#for "/value"# #"."#, #.end# };
```

The second example, `CreatePanel.template`, shows a simple recursive template for generating a hierarchy of panels and buttons (Example 12–22). The name of the container object is passed in the properties variable. An example call to this subtemplate is shown in Example 12–23.

Example 12–22: CreatePanel.template: a Recursive Template

```
#for "button"#
#(properties.get("panelName"))#.add(new Button(#"/label"#));
#end#


#for p "panel"#
Panel #"@name"# = new Panel();
#   CreatePanel cp = new CreatePanel();
    cp.properties.put("panelName", context.evalString("@name"));
    cp.generate(context, out);
#
#(properties.get("panelName"))#.add(#"@name"#);

#end#
```

Finally, the next example shows how one template might call the previous two templates. The name of the program generator is derived from the filename (unless you declare it otherwise using a `#declaration classname=...`). Thus, TL will create an ArrayCode.java file from the ArrayCode.template file.

Example 12–23: A Template Calling Two Subtemplates

```
#for j "//array"#
# new ArrayCode().generate(context, out,
                            context.evalString("@name"), "int");
#
#end#


    Frame f = new Frame();
# CreatePanel cp = new CreatePanel();
  cp.properties.set("panelName", "f");
  cp.generate(context, out);
#
```

12.2.9 *Multiple Inputs and Outputs*

In some cases, it is logical to break a complex specification into various parts, with each part in a separate file. Some pieces of a specification also might be reused in other specifications. Sometimes you might organize a specification library, and new specifications might be largely selecting and composing other specifications. To permit this variety of program generators, the new template language should allow multiple XML inputs. Multiple XPathContext objects can be created for handling multiple XML files. The context can be changed dynamically to other files, or the context can be smoothly changed when calling subtemplates.

Alternatively, one can patch together multiple XML trees using the DOM API. Example 12–24 shows how one can organize a library of props, each accessible by the name of the prop. Assume that the XML specification has an element type named include with an attribute named prop that specifies the name of the XML file where that prop is specified, such as:

```
<include prop="proplib/bucketProp.xml">
```

The template segment in Example 12–24 reads each prop specification and generates the code relevant for that prop.

Example 12–24: Multiple Specification Files

```
#for j "//include/@prop"#
# // get specification from prop library
  XPathContext save = context;
  context = new XPathContext(j.getNodeValue()); // gets attribute value
#
  template for prop code
# context = save; #
#end#
```

The new template language will also allow multiple output files using techniques similar to those for allowing multiple specification files. The out variable can be changed to divert subsequent output to a new file. Let's extend the preceding example by saying that we want to generate a public prop class for each prop in a separate file. First, we will put the template for the prop code in a separate subtemplate file called `GenerateProp`. Next, we compute the necessary context and out parameters before calling the `generate` method of `GenerateProp` (Example 12–25).

Example 12–25: Multiple Specification Files and Java Output Files

```
#for j "//include/@prop"#
# // get specification from prop library
  XPathContext pcontext = new XPathContext(j.getNodeValue());
  String pname = pcontext.evalString("/prop/@name");
  ProgramWriter pout = new ProgramWriter(new FileOutputStream(pname));
  new GenerateProp().generate(pcontext, pout);
  pout.close();
#
#end#
```

12.2.10 *Dual Forms: Simple and XML*

The new template language can be simpler without XML syntax, but the advantages to using XML are significant. A way to have your cake and eat it, too, is to provide both a simple template language and a two-way conversion to and from an XML version. Let's see how it works.

First, as with JSP, we need to specify exactly how each TL construct maps to an XML element type. Special characters must also be taken into account. Table 12–4 specifies a few of these translation rules. A complete list of translation rules can be found in the next section of this chapter. Each expression, statement, and path in the second column must also translate character entities. For example, the expression,

```
#"position()<5"#
```

must be translated to

```
<xpath select="position()&lt;5"/>.
```

Table 12–4: Some Translation Rules

Simple Form	XML Form
#"*path*"#	`<value path="`*path*`" />`
#(*expression*)#	`<expr>`*expression*`</expr>`
# *statement* #	`<java>`*statement*`</java>`
#for *var* "*path*"# ... #end#	`<for var="`*var*`" path="`*path*`">` ... `</for>`
#if "*path*"# ... #fi#	`<if path="`*path*`">` ... `</if>`
#declare *attribute*#	`<declare` *attribute*`/>`
<	`&lt;`
##	#
#.*anything*#	`<... whitespace="reverse">` ...
#.#	`<empty whitespace="reverse"/>`

Writing the translators between these two forms is easy. To go from the simple to XML form, you will need a handcrafted program, but to go from XML to the simple form, you can use a fairly simple XSLT document (Figure 12–1). These translators are available at http://craigc.com/.

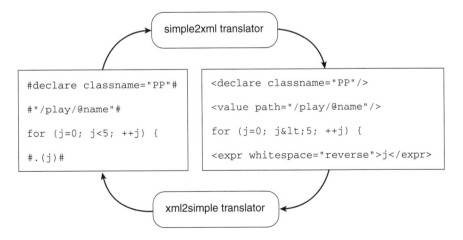

Figure 12–1   Translating between simple and XML forms

Once these translators are established, then tools can be written for either form, depending on circumstance. Editors and browsers can also be based on either form. The simple form would logically be used with text editors, while the XML form could be used with either text editors or sophisticated XML-based browsers and editors.

12.2.11 *Compilation and Interpretation*

Should the new template language be interpreted or compiled? If it is interpreted, the major drawback is the inability to use Java code to control the flow of control. Escapes to the Java language could be allowed as method calls to dynamically loaded objects. Thus, the Java-expressions could be implemented in an interpreter but not Java-statements. Although other Java escapes would be possible in an interpreter, they would be awkward, which would still require compilation and dynamic loading.

The new template language has been designed to permit interpretation but at the loss of some features. The obvious advantage of using an interpreter, as the Figure 12–2 shows, is that program generation is a single-step process. The compiler approach requires additional steps and complexity, but is more flexible with respect to escapes and produces possibly (but probably just slightly) faster generators.[4]

An issue for both approaches is the input form. Although the simple input form is simpler, it would require a handcrafted parser. If the XML input form is used, then the XML tools can be used, resulting in a simpler program.

12.2.12 *Other Features*

Other features that have been found useful in previous program-generator generators are listed below.

---

[4]A third approach not discussed here is to translate the template to an XSLT document and then use XSLT as the program generator engine. This approach would not permit any Java escapes unless they were incorporated in a new XSLT function library.

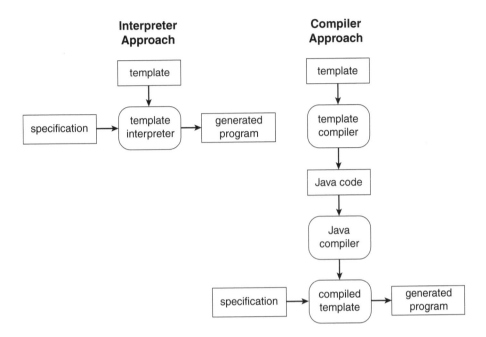

Figure 12–2   Interpreter and compiler approaches to program generators

Tracking current input line number and/or character number: This allows precise error messages and embedding of line information into the generated code to refer back to specific sections of the specification. For example, if the Java compiler emits an error message, it would be very beneficial to relate that error to a specific line of the specification.

Sorting on traversals: A traversal over the XPath tree is normally in document order. Other traversal orders may be useful. XSLT provides a powerful sorting feature to alter the traversal. Such a feature can be useful in TL as well.

Tracking tree information: To improve the efficiency of the program generator it is often useful to cache information associated with the nodes of a parse tree. This information is sometimes referred as *attributes*, not to be confused with XML attribute nodes. However, using the DOM API, new XML attributes can be created for element nodes that can serve this purpose. Alternatively, hash tables can be used to map tree nodes to information attributes.

Language extensions: A feature being considered for JSP 1.1 is a tag extension feature, allowing one to create new custom tags. For some program-generation applications, adding new features to the template language can considerably simplify template pages.

Separators: Often it is necessary to put some separator syntax between the elements of a list. For example, the commas between the elements of an array in most languages won't allow a comma after the last element. In these cases, some additional complexity is added to prevent that last comma from being output. A separator clause could make this common occurrence easier to handle. It might take a form something like:

```
#for j in "//props"# ... #sep#,#end#
```

Utility methods: A variety of useful utility methods could be provided for common needs. These include quotation conventions—for example, converting a string to one with appropriate escapes for newline characters and quotes for Java strings.

12.3 | The Informal TL Specification

The issues and rationale for the new template language have been discussed, and the resulting language is summarized in the accompanying table. Each item in the table has two forms: simple and XML. A template must use one form exclusively, but can be translated to the other form.

Characters

Simple Form:

```
&
<
>
##
char (all other characters)
```

XML Form:

```
&amp;
&lt;
&gt;
#
char
```

Description:

Characters are sent directly to the output. Some characters must be escaped depending on the form. Some whitespace characters will be removed according to the whitespace control rules.

Translation to the Java Language:

```
out.print("&");
out.print("<");
out.print(">");
out.print("#");
out.print("char");
```

XPath Expressions

Simple Form:

```
#"path"#
```

XML Form:

```
<value path="path"/>
```

Description:

The XPath expression, "*path*", is evaluated as a String expression and sent to the output.

Translation to the Java Language:

```
out.print(context.evalString("path"));
```

Java Expressions

Simple Form:

```
#(expression)#
```

XML Form:

```
<expr>expression</expr>
```

Description:

The Java expression, "*expression*", is evaluated and sent to the output.

Translation to the Java language:

```
out.print(expression);
```

Java Statements

Simple Form:

```
# java-code #
```

XML Form:

```
<java>java-code</java>
```

Description:

The Java code is executed as is. The Java code need not be complete statements and may be broken up across the template to allow flow-of-control constructs that include template fragments. A blank (or a period and a blank) must follow the initial delimiter character.

Translation to the Java Language:

java-code

Iteration Over Node Sets

Simple Form:

```
#for  var  "path"#  template  #end#
```

XML Form:

```
<for var="var" path="path">  template  </for>
```

Description:

For each node in "*path*", evaluate the "*template*". The loop variable, "*var*", is optional, and if used becomes both an XPath variable and the Java loop variable.

Translation to the Java Language:

```
NodeList x = context.evalNodeSet("path");
for (int j=0; j< x.getLength(); ++ j) {
    Node var = (Node) x.item(j);
    context.push(var, j+1, x.getLength());
    template
    context.pop();
}
```

Conditional

Simple Forms:

```
#if "path"# template #fi#
#if "path"# template #else# template2 #fi#
```

XML Forms:

```
<if path="path"> template </if>
<if path="path"> template
            <else> template2 </else></if>
```

Description:

The XPath expression, *path*, is evaluated. If true, then *template* is evaluated, otherwise if an else clause is present, then *template2* is evaluated.

Translation to the Java Language:

```
if (context.evalBoolean("path") {
    template
}
if (context.evalBoolean("path") {
    template
} else {
    template2
}
```

Declarations

Simple Form:

```
#declarations java-declarations #
```

XML Form:

```
<declarations> java-declarations<declarations/>
```

Description:

Declarations of instance variables, methods, and other class-level declarations are used to provide control over the class.

Translation to the Java Language:

java-declarations (inserted at the class level, rather than the generate method).

Declare options

Simple Form:

```
#declare attribute(s) #
```

XML Form:

```
<declare attribute(s)/>
```

Description:

The declare attributes define various program-generator options, including classname, extends, implements, and imports.

Translation to the Java Language:

Dependent on the particular declare option (see Section 12.4).

Whitespace Control

Simple Form:

```
#.anything #
#.#
```

XML Form:

```
<anything whitespace="reverse"> ...
<empty whitespace="reverse"/>
```

Description:

An optional period following the initial delimiter controls whether the whitespace preceding the construct is stripped or not. By default, whitespace is stripped for all constructs except characters, XPath expressions and Java expressions. To reverse the default, simply place a period after the initial delimiter character.

Translation to the Java Language:

Whitespace preceding the construct is sent to the output according to the rules expressed in the description.

12.3.1   *The Play Domain Using TL*

The Play program generator expressed in TL is given in Example 12–26. You might like to compare this template with the JSP template (Example 10–13) and the XSLT template (Example 11–18).

Example 12–26: PlayPG.template (Simple Form)

```
import java.awt.*;
import java.awt.event.*;

# String name = context.evalString("//play/@name"); #
class #(name)#Play2 extends Frame {
    /* The Props for #(name)# ***********/
#for "//play/prop"#
    Button #"@name"#Prop
            = new Button("#"trait"#");
#end#

    /* The Events in the #(name)# ********/

    class PropEvent implements ActionListener {
        public void actionPerformed(ActionEvent evt) {
            Object prop = evt.getSource();
#for "//play/prop"#
  # if "position()!=1"#
            } else
  #fi# if (prop.equals(#"@name"#Prop)) {
    #for "trait"#
```

```
                    #(getPropName(context))#Prop.setLabel("#"."#")
    #end#
  #if "./script/@goto"#
                    enterNewScene("#"script/@goto"#");
  #fi#
#end#
              } else {
                  System.out.println("Invalid prop");
              }
          }
      }

      /* Creating and starting up the #(name)# ****/

      String currentScene;

      public #(name)#Play2() {
# String title = context.evalString("//play/title");
  if (title.equals("")) title = "No Title";
#
          super("#(title)#");
          setSize(#"//play/@width"#, #"//play/@height"#);
          setLayout(new FlowLayout());

          // initialize props
          PropEvent a = new PropEvent();
#for "//play/prop"#
          #"@name"#Prop.addActionListener(a);
#end#
          // start scene
          enterNewScene("#"//play/@start"#");
      }

      public void enterNewScene(String scene) {
          removeAll();  // remove previous scene
          currentScene = scene;
#for "//play/scene"#
  #if "position()!=1"#
          } else
  #fi# if (scene.equals("#"@name"#")) {
  #for a "addprop"#
                  add(#"@name"#Prop);
  #end#
                  setBackground(Color.decode("#"@color"#"));
#end#
          } else {
```

```
                System.out.println("Invalid scene: "+scene);
            }
            show();
        }

    public static void main(String[] args) {
        new #(name)#Play2();
    }
}

#declarations
/** gets appropriate prop name for a trait */
String getPropName(XPathContext c) throws Exception {
    String n = c.evalString("@prop");
    if (!n.equals("")) {
        return n;
    }
    return c.evalString(
        "ancestor::addprop/@name | ancestor::prop/@name");
}
#
```

12.4 | Translating TL to the Java Language

An implementation of TL requires creating the following tools. In addition to the two translators between the simple and XML forms, TL requires a translator from one of the forms to a Java program. Part of this translation is defined in the previous two sections.

The first and perhaps most important observation to make about the translator from TL to the Java language is that it is simply a program generator itself. It is a unique kind of program generator in that the programs it produces are other program generators. For this reason you might like to think of the translator as a program-generator generator, or PGG for short. However, this can be a confusing term, so we'll just call this translator TL2Java.

As with any program generator, we'll need to determine what approach to use to build TL2Java. If we were building an interpreter-based TL2Java, then we'd use the techniques described in Chapter 6. In this section we'll look at implementing the whole language, which mandates a compiler-based TL2Java. Choosing the XML form as input to the translator will allow us to use the XML parser rather than handcrafting one. Chapters 9, 10, and 11 provide several different approaches for implementing TL2Java. Any of these approaches will work, but they are rather boring compared to what is described in this chapter. Let's use TL to implement TL. This means writing TL2Java using TL. A template, called suitably enough TL2Java.template, is written. You take this template with you in your time machine, move forward one day, and use TL2Java to translate TL2Java.template to TL2Java.java (Figure 12–3). The next step is to bring the Java program back to the present and compile it, and now you have the translator. This process is called *bootstrapping*, since you are pulling yourself up by your own bootstraps.

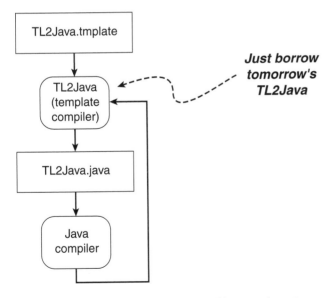

Figure 12–3   Bootstrapping TL2Java with a time machine

If you don't have a time machine, don't sweat it, or rather sweat it out by hand-translating TL2Java.template to TL2Java.java. For a complex language, you can avoid some of the hand translation work by defining a minimal subset of the language that is sufficient to build your translator. This minimal translator is good enough to translate the whole language. In general, like any other kind of software or language, template languages evolve over time. So, the bootstrapping process will continue as long as the language evolves and changes. Once bootstrapping has started, you only maintain the template file, not the generated Java file. A more accurate description of this bootstrapping process is shown in Figure 12–4.

TL2Java will actually require two templates rather than just one, as implied by the figure. A master template translates everything except the body of the `generate` method. A subtemplate is used to generate the code for the `generate` method. This subtemplate is needed because the nested structures such as the iteration and conditional constructs are recursive. However, the subtemplate is almost entirely Java code, so instead of creating a separate template and class, we include it in the declarations section of the master template as a method called `generate2`. The master template, called TL2Java.template, is given in Example 12–27.

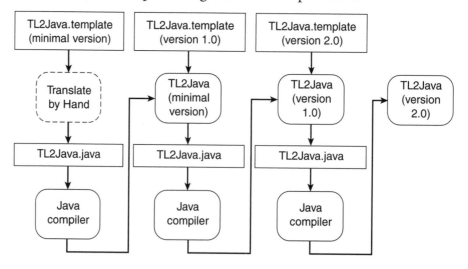

Figure 12–4   Bootstrapping TL2Java without a time machine

To help keep track of versioning history, a little extra information is stored in the `history` instance variable that tracks the dates, input, and output filenames of the sequence of translations shown in Figure 12–4.

Example 12–27: TL2Java.template (Except generate2 Method—Example 12–28)

```
<?xml version="1.0"?>
<tl>
package com.craigc.progen;

import org.w3c.dom.*;
import java.io.*;
import java.util.*;
<for path="//declare/@import">
import <value path="."/>;
</for>

<java>
String className = getClassName(context.evalString
    ("//declare/@classname"));
</java>

public class <expr>className</expr> {
    Properties properties = new Properties();

<for path="//declarations">
<value path="."/>
</for>

    public boolean generate(XPathContext context, ProgramWriter out) {
        try {
<java>generate2(context, out); </java>
        } catch (Exception e) {
            System.out.println("Exception: "+e.getMessage());
            e.printStackTrace();
            return false;
        }
        return true;
    }

    public static void main(String[] args) {
        try {
            ProgramWriter out = args.length>=2
                ?new ProgramWriter(new FileOutputStream(args[1]))
```

```
                        :new ProgramWriter(System.out);
              <expr>className</expr> pg = new <expr>className</expr>();
              for (int j=1; j&lt;=args.length; ++j) {
                  pg.properties.put("arg"+j, args[j-1]);
              }
              pg.generate(new XPathContext(args[0]), out);
              out.close();
          } catch (Exception e) {
              e.printStackTrace();
          }
      }


    String[][] history = {
        { "<expr>new Date()</expr>", // date this file was generated
            <expr>quoteString(properties.getProperty("arg1"))</expr>,
            <expr>quoteString(properties.getProperty("arg2"))</expr> },
<java whitespace="reverse">
          for (int j=0; j&lt;history.length; ++j) {
              out.print("            ");
              for (int k=0; k&lt;history[j].length; ++k) {
                  out.print(quoteString(history[j][k])+", ");
              }
              out.println("}, ");
          }
</java>
      };


  }


<declarations>
String ind = "      ";
int uid = 0;

public boolean generate2(XPathContext context, ProgramWriter out) {
```

   See Example 12–28

```
}

public String quoteString(String t) {
```

  add quotes and convert new lines, tabs quotes

```
}

public String strip(String t) {
```

remove trailing white space characters

```
}

public String getClassName(String className) {
```

if className is an empty string, get class name from properties.get("arg2")

```
}
</declarations>

</tl>
```

Example 12–28: The generate2 Method

```java
public boolean generate2(XPathContext context, ProgramWriter out) {
    out.setIndent(out.getIndent()+ind);
    out.print(ind);
    try {
        NodeList x = context.evalNodeSet("*|text()");
        for (int j=0; j<x.getLength(); ++j) {
            Node n = (Node) x.item(j);
            boolean strip = true;
            if (j<x.getLength()-1) {
                Node n2 = (Node) x.item(j+1);
                int t2 = n2.getNodeType();
                if (t2==Node.TEXT_NODE) {
                    strip = false;
                } else if (t2==Node.ELEMENT_NODE) {
                    String ename = n2.getNodeName();
                    if (ename.equals("value") || ename.equals("expr")) {
                        strip = false;
                    }
                    context.push(n2, 1, 1);
                    String reverse = context.evalString("@whitespace");
                    if (reverse.equals("reverse")) {
                        strip = !strip;
                    }
                }
            }
            context.push(n, j+1, x.getLength());
            switch (n.getNodeType()) {
            case Node.ELEMENT_NODE:
                String ename = n.getNodeName();
                if (ename.equals("value")) {
                    out.println("out.print(context.evalString(\""
```

```java
                            +context.evalString("@path")+"\"));");
        } else if (ename.equals("for")) {
            ++uid;
            String var = context.evalString("@var");
            if (var.equals("")) {
                var = "loopvar"+uid;
            }
            out.println("NodeList x"+uid
                +" = context.evalNodeSet(\""
                +context.evalString("@path")+"\");");
        out.println("for (int j"+uid+"=0; j"+uid+"lt;x"+uid
                +".getLength(); ++j"+uid+") {");
            out.println(ind+"Node "+var+" = (Node) x"+uid
                +".item(j"+uid+");");
            out.println(ind+"context.push("+var+", j"+uid
                +"+1, x"+uid+".getLength());");
            generate2(context, out);
            out.println("context.pop();");
            out.println("}");
        } else if (ename.equals("if")) {
            out.println("if (context.evalBoolean("
              +quoteString(context.evalString("@path"))+")) {");
            generate2(context, out);
            out.println("\n}");
        } else if (ename.equals("else")) {
            out.setIndent(out.getIndent()+ind);
            out.println("} else {");
            generate2(context, out);
            out.setIndent(out.getIndent().substring(
                                    ind.length()));
        } else if (ename.equals("expr")) {
            out.println("out.print("+
                context.evalString(".")+");");
        } else if (ename.equals("java")) {
            out.println(context.evalString("."));
        } else if (ename.equals("empty")) {
        } else if (ename.equals("declare")) {
        } else if (ename.equals("declarations")) {
        } else {
            out.println("//Unknown Element: "+n.getNodeName());
        }
        break;
    case Node.TEXT_NODE:
```

```
        String t = context.evalString("."); // n.toString();
        if (strip) {
            t = strip(t);
        }
        if (!t.equals("")) {
            out.println("out.print("+quoteString(t)+");");
        }
        break;
    }
    context.pop();
    }
} catch (Exception e) {
    System.out.println("Exception in generate2: "+e.getMessage());
    e.printStackTrace();
    return false;
} finally {
    out.setIndent(out.getIndent().substring(ind.length()));
}
return true;
}
```

12.5 | Summary

In this chapter we designed a new template language. It was designed to be concise and simple, using XPath for tree navigation and the Java language for expressions. The language has two forms: a simple textual easy-to-read language and an XML form. A program easily converts between the two, thus allowing simple textual tools and XML tools. Whitespace is managed through nonobtrusive controls.

The template language designed in this chapter is available at http://craigc.com. The rationale for its design can also be easily adapted to other situations. The cost of building such a template language is small.

Further Reading

The ideas of templates and bootstrapping have a long and honorable tradition. Bootstrapping has been used in many languages, both compilers and interpreters. An early UNIX tool, called *yacc* ("Yet Another Compiler Compiler"), succinctly honors this tradition. Yacc is a parser generator. It reads a description of the grammar of the language and outputs a C program that will parse that language. Another UNIX tool, called *Stage* and later renamed *MetaTool*, provides a more complete solution to building program generators. Its input includes a grammatical description (which is used to generate a lex file, a yacc file, and parse tree construction and navigation code) and *product-description* files, which are templates of the desired output of the program generator.

J. Craig Cleaveland and Chandra Kintala, "Tools for Building Application Generators," *AT&T Technical Journal*, Vol. 67, No. 4, 1988.

J. Craig Cleaveland, "Building Application Generators," *IEEE Software*, July 1988; also reprinted in *Domain Analysis and Software System Modeling* by Prieto-Diaz and Arango, 1991.

J. Craig Cleaveland and Thomas T. Wetmore IV, "The Next Generation of Specification-Driven Tools," *Proceedings of the AT&T Conference on Specification Driven Tools*, October 1989.

Composition of Components

- Components, interfaces, and connectors
- JavaBeans as components
- Dependencies between components
- IDLs: Interface Description Languages
- MILs: Module Interconnection Languages
- The Bean Markup Language
- Crafting your own MIL

U p to now, this book has referred to program generators. In practice, most generators actually create components that are integrated with other components to create a software system. Components and their composition into software systems is sometimes referred to as component-oriented programming. The three major constituents of component-oriented programming are components, interfaces, and connectors. Sections 13.1 and 13.2 discuss components. Sections 13.3 and 13.4 discuss interfaces and connectors, respectively.

Program generators support efforts in component-oriented programming in several different areas. One problem with component-oriented programming is finding just the right component to fit into your software system. If component libraries used program generators to provide component families rather than individual components, you would be more likely to find just the right component. Program generators are also used as some of the tools for generating the code for composing systems: the glue that holds a system together.

13.1 | Components and JavaBeans

A software component is a unit of software with a well-defined interface that is designed to be composed with other components. One commonly accepted definition is:

> *A software component is a unit of composition with contractually specified interfaces and explicit context only. A software component can be deployed independently and is subject to composition by third parties.*[1]

The definitions and distinctions between objects and components are an ongoing source of debate and discussion. Generally, we will avoid these debates by focusing our attention on JavaBeans architecture. According to Sun, JavaBeans architecture is a software component architecture that enables creation, assembly, and use of dynamic Java software components. Each bean is a reusable software object that can be manipulated by a visual development tool. The visual development tool provides the environment where a bean is composed with other beans by so-called third parties.

A bean has three kinds of features:

Properties—a bean property is some attribute or characteristic of the bean. Properties have a name and a value of some Java type. Properties include such things as fonts, colors, and labels.

Events—a bean may emit events using the Java event handling mechanism. Events include such things as button pushes and state changes.

Methods—a bean may have methods for publicly accessing other services provided by the bean.

---

[1] Cointe, P. (Ed.). (1996, July). ECOOP '96: Object-oriented programming. Workshop held at the 10th European Conference, Linz, Austria.

JavaBeans are designed so that any Java class can be construed as a bean through a process called introspection. The Java class is loaded into memory and, by examining the public methods of the class, one can infer the set of properties, events, and methods.[2] A property with name "xyz" and type "Abc" is inferred if one or both of the following methods are present:

```
public Abc getXyz();
public void setXyz(Abc x);
```

Similarly, an event of type "XyzEvent" is inferred if the bean has methods:

```
public void addXyzListener(XyzListener x);
public void removeXyzListener(XyzListener x);
```

Finally, all remaining public methods of the Java class are considered methods of the bean. Note that JavaBeans do not consider public instance variables as part of the component model. Such public instance variables, if any, should be ignored.

In this chapter a new domain will be used (Figure 13–1). A shopping cart is a place to store items that you want to buy. It might be a physical shopping cart in a store, a telephone order, or a Web-based shopping cart. In all cases, you can add or remove items from the shopping cart. Given a price list, you can compute the cost of the items in the shopping cart. To compute the total cost you may also need to take into account sales tax, shipping costs, and discount coupons. Both the sales tax and shipping rates may be dependent on the customer's zip code.

Most JavaBeans are GUI components, but we'll show an example of a shopping cart JavaBean that is not a GUI component (Example 13–1). This bean has properties for the customer, tables for taxes and shipping, and a price catalog. It has methods for adding and removing items, and finally a method for calculating the total purchase price. The bean also has one event, which is triggered whenever the items are changed. Sorry, but there won't be any coupons or discounts for this bean.

---

[2]**JavaBeans** also provides a way of explicitly listing properties, events, and methods using what is called a bean info, an object that describes each feature in detail.

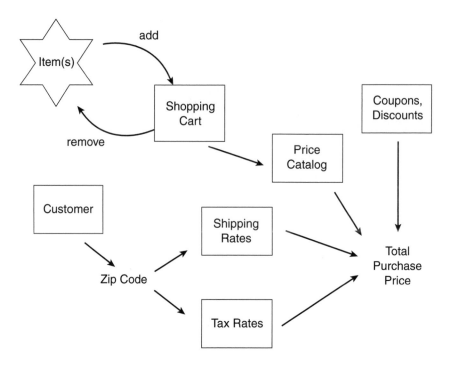

Figure 13–1 The Shopping Cart domain

Example 13–1: The ShoppingCart JavaBean

```
public class ShoppingCart implements Basket {
    public Customer getCustomer() { ... };
    public void setCustomer(Customer c) { ... };
    public PriceList getPriceList() { ... };
    public void setPriceList(PriceList p) { ... };
    public TaxDatabase getTaxDatabase() { ... };
    public void setTaxDatabase(TaxDatabase t) { ... };
    public ShippingDatabase getShippingDatabase() { ... };
    public void setShippingDatabase(ShippingDatabase t) { ... };
    public void addItem(Item i) { ... };
    public void removeItem(Item i) { ... };
    public Enumeration getItems() { ... };
    public int getTotalCost() { ... };
    public void addBasketChangeListener(BasketChangeListener l) { ... };
    public void removeBasketChangeListener(BasketChangeListener l) {
        ... };
}
```

The set of properties of a bean is sometimes mistakenly assumed to constitute the state of the bean. The "state" of the bean is all of the information that will determine its visual display and behavior. Some state information may not be accessible as a property. The JavaBeans component model does not require that the entire state of a bean be made available as properties. For example, the shopping cart bean does not represent the items in the cart as a property, but instead provides other methods: addItem, removeItem, and getItems.

What sets beans apart from ordinary Java classes and objects is a new binding time for configuring beans, called *design time*.[3] Design time occurs after compile time but before run time (Figure 13–2). At

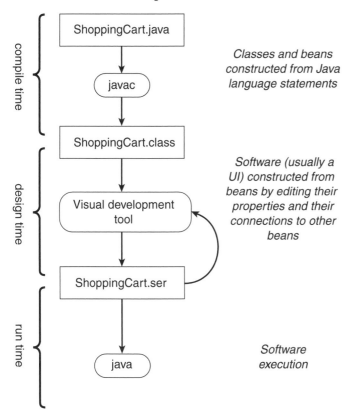

Figure 13–2 Design time lies between compile time and run time

[3]It's unfortunate that the term "design time" is used since nearly all binding times can be considered design times. A more precise name such as "bean configuration time" would have been better.

design time, a designer uses a visual development tool to create, modify, and lay out a design (usually a user interface). The tool will read in beans (by loading either a class or a previously saved bean) and make them available to the designer. When a designer creates a new component from a bean, a new object is created (by either instantiation or cloning). Design time and visual development tools provide a new development layer that allows one to *configure* and *compose* components into larger structures. Although this new layer is often used in conjunction with traditional programming tools, it is a separate and distinctly different type of design activity.

The bean's properties are available in a property sheet, allowing the designer to alter property values. Each type of property may have its own specialized property editor. For example, a `String` property may have a simple text-field editor, and a `Color` property may have a color editor that allows one to mix new colors visually. Upon completion, the bean is saved using serialized IO. The Java language's serialized IO feature provides a way to write objects to a byte stream. The entire state of the object (including any objects that it references) is written to the byte stream. The byte stream can be written to a file, and later read back in to recreate the objects (or rather a clone of the original object). Serialized IO is used to provide data persistence or object transport (see Section 3.4). Serialized IO is a critical feature in the JavaBeans model, since it allows objects to be created, modified, and saved at design time, and later restored at run time.

Some properties are primarily for the benefit of the tool builder rather than the end user, so such properties normally do not change at run time (for example, the font of a typical label). In the shopping cart domain, the tax table and shipping table properties might be determined at design time. Others may be run-time-only properties (for example, a counter that counts the number of times a button was clicked). In the shopping cart domain, the customer property is set at run time. Other properties might be determined at design time or run time depending on the situation. For example the label of a button, while typically fixed at design time, might also be set at run time to reflect the state of the bean. In the shopping cart domain, the price table may typically be fixed at design time, but the price table might be dynamically determined at run time. This might occur, for example, if there are different prices for different kinds of customers.

The JavaBean model does not distinguish between design-time and run-time properties.[4] Any property is potentially usable at either time. In domain engineering terms, the set of bean properties (and events) constitute a mixed set of design-time and run-time variabilities. A bean developer may consider some properties as design-time and others as run-time. Table 13–1 gives the list of properties and events for the shopping cart bean along with the preferred binding times.

Table 13–1: Shopping Cart Variabilities Implemented as Properties or Events

Decision	Property or Event	Preferred Binding Time
What is the sales tax rate?	`taxDatabase`	design time
How do you compute shipping costs?	`shippingDatabase`	design time
Who is the customer?	`customer`	run time
What are the item prices?	`priceList`	design time or run time
What system components need to know when the list of items changes?	`BasketChangeEvent`	design time

13.2 | Components and Dependencies

Component-oriented programming is a style or model of programming. The major entities of this model are components, interfaces, and connectors. The JavaBeans model as described in the previous sec-

---

[4]The distinction between design time and run time can be coded into the methods by using the method Beans.isDesignTime()

tion is one example of a component-oriented programming model. Components and objects have much in common, and typically objects are used as a basis for components, just as Java objects are used for JavaBeans. Objects that have been designed as independent units with well-defined interfaces are components, and by this criterion most of the standard Java classes can be classified as components.

Not all classes can be called good components. A class with public instance variables makes for a poor component. The interface between the class and the rest of the world is not clearly defined with respect to accessing or changing that public instance variable from outside the class. This can be fixed by making the instance variable nonpublic, and if needed a pair of "set" and "get" methods can be added to the interface to provide controlled access or changes to that variable. For the same reasons, static variables (global variables) are counter to good component design.

Information hiding is described in Chapter 4 as one of the key abstraction principles. Information hiding is also a crucial principle in component design. In designing objects (as opposed to components), information hiding helps keep private implementation decisions restricted to the object. This makes it easier to use the object without depending on its implementation. In component design, information hiding is also used in the other direction (Figure 13–3). External details about the environment should be hidden from the component. A component should minimize the assumptions made about the environment and the resources or objects it provides. Such assumptions are called *dependencies*, because the component depends on their existence. In the days before platform independent languages such as the

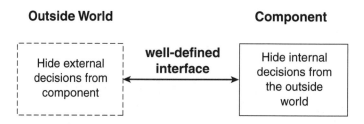

Figure 13–3   Information hiding goes in both directions

Java language, machine and operating system dependencies seriously hampered the development of components. With the Java language, dependencies are now primarily due to poor software designs.

Components will always have some dependencies. For example, the component interface will use certain types, so the component will work only in environments that provide those types. Components are often designed in the context of a specific component model such as JavaBeans or a specific component framework that uses certain interfaces. The dependencies of a component will largely determine the range of systems in which the component can be used. Fewer dependencies mean a wider range of systems that can use the component. The concern about dependencies is a chief difference between designing components and designing objects for a specific software system.

Let's look at some example dependencies. In each case, we'll examine a particular kind of dependency and make suggestions for reducing the dependency.

13.2.1   *Global Variables and Resources*

One of the most popular global variables is `System.out`, which is a public static `PrintStream` object. Since it is a standard object in a standard class, it would appear that using it in a component shouldn't be much of a dependency, since most Java environments should have it. However, the `System.out` might be used for some other specific purpose, and one wouldn't expect that integrating a component into a system would conflict with that purpose.

Some components need a log file to output messages about its operation. Assuming that `System.out` is an appropriate log file would be a bad assumption for any component. So, what is a component to do? One alternative is to create a new log file, but this would also be inappropriate, because it assumes an environment in which you can create and write to files (applets can't). Another alternative is to make the log file a parameter of the component. It could be an optional parameter in a constructor, or it could be set by a method (perhaps called `setLogFile`).

Global variables are often used as a quick and easy way to access resources. For example, it might be tempting to access a global database object directly from an object rather than passing it as a parameter among a lot of method calls. While such direct access simplifies the method calls, it prevents that object from ever maturing to a component. Such an object can only be used in systems that provide that global variable.

To avoid the global variable, the resource object must be passed as an explicit parameter to the object. It can be passed in just the methods that require the resource, or it can be passed in a constructor method or a set method and assigned to an instance variable. Then any method can refer to the instance variable to get access to the resource. Many software systems are designed this way, with each object containing instance variables that refer to other objects of the system. Such a design often leads to a complex web of interconnected objects. Such interconnected objects are difficult to turn into independent components. Attempting to reuse any one object of such a system may require using the whole system.

Oftentimes a variety of such resources are gathered into a single object, sometimes called a "context" object. Then just this one context object is passed around in method calls. This also leads to overly interconnected systems, since every object has access to all resources regardless of whether they are needed or not.

Access to the appropriate resources such as log files, databases, and other objects is a difficult problem when designing components. In designing an object for a particular system, one is tempted to provide more than is necessary. For example, a database object might be passed, rather than the data that is needed from the database object. Thus, the object becomes dependent on the database, rather than a specific data item. In such a case, a better component design would be to replace the database parameter with the specific data needed by the component. Now the component can fit into systems where the data isn't stored in a database. The examples in the next section will demonstrate this problem.

13.2.2 *Types*

A component will depend on a set of types, called the dependent-type-set. A type might be a class definition, a primitive type, or a Java `interface` type. For a component to run the dependent-type-set must be provided by the environment. The dependent-type-set for a component c is defined recursively as follows:

1. The type of c is a member of the dependent-type-set.

2. If t is in the dependent-type-set, then so are all the superclasses of t.

3. If t is in the dependent-type-set, then so are all types referenced in the source code of t, including the types of parameter values, instance variables, local variables, and each expression.

Using this definition, the dependent-type-set for an object designed for a specific system is often most if not all of the types of the specific system. To transform such an object to a component is often an exercise in minimizing the dependent-type-set. Otherwise, trying to use such an object in a different system may amount to embedding the entire original system, which is certainly not in the spirit of component-oriented programming.

In object-oriented design, inheritance plays a major role. In component-oriented design, inheritance is often a hindrance, because the design of the component is distributed across all of its superclasses. Some of those superclasses may reference types that have no role in the subclass. These extraneous types are unnecessary dependencies.

Internal type dependencies are types in the dependent-type-set that are not referenced directly or indirectly in any of the component's interfaces.[5] Internal types are types that are used strictly for implementation purposes and might not be visible outside the component. Internal type dependencies are used merely to support the component, and they might change over time without affecting the component's interface. The component designer has a lot of freedom and flexibility in choosing the internal type dependencies, generally limiting them to primitive types and standard classes. In more complex cases, a set of components may be designed to work with each other, and these would normally be used together, probably as an independent Java package.

External type dependencies are those that the outside world uses to interact with the component. These are determined by the types of the parameters and return values of all the public methods. The component designer has little or no freedom in choosing this set. The component interface designer makes those decisions. In some cases, external interfaces may be determined by an application framework or other predefined interfaces. Once the interface is fixed, the component designer can only determine the internal type dependencies.

Most of the troublesome type dependencies come from external type dependencies that are not primitive or standard library types. To minimize dependencies, Java `interface` types are ideal. A Java `interface` type should not be confused with the generic term "interface." An interface is a way in which two pieces of software interact, typically determined by a set of methods. A Java `interface` type is a Java type that defines a set of methods that might be implemented by a Java class. Java `interfaces` can significantly reduce type dependencies. The extended example below will show how this works.

To show some of the ideas with respect to types, consider the process of converting an old shopping cart class to the bean class

---

[5]To avoid under-the-table interactions, one must be careful about the use of static variables. For example, a class which uses a static variable to track all instances of the class to mediate some kind of interaction between them should be considered an external type dependency rather than an internal type dependency.

shown in the previous section. In Example 13–2, we'll focus on just that part that calculates the tax on the total cost. To determine the tax rate the `getTotalCost` method performs a query using a database object called `MyTaxDatabase`.

Example 13–2: The Old ShoppingCart Class Directly Accessing a Tax Table

```
...
import java.sql.*;

...

public class ShoppingCart {
    ...
    public int getTotalCost() {
        double taxRate = 0;
        Connection c = MyTaxDatabase.connection;
        Statement s = c.createStatement();
        String zc = customer.getZipcode();
        String cmd = "SELECT RATE FROM TAXTAB WHERE ZIPCODE='"+zc+"'";
        ResultSet rs = s.executeQuery(cmd);
        if (rs.hasMoreResults()) {
            taxRate = rs.getDouble("RATE");
        }
        ...
    }
}
```

The `ShoppingCart` class in this example has the glaring reference to the global variable `MyTaxDatabase.connection`.[6] We can reduce this problem by explicitly passing in the global variable. This can be done with either a constructor or a set method. In our example, we'll choose a set method so that it can be a JavaBean. At the same time, let's recognize that the explicit SQL code and connection should probably be confined to the `MyTaxDatabase` object rather than scattered around the program. So let's put the SQL code in the `MyTax-Database` class and call it `getTaxRate` (Example 13–3).

---

[6]This problem does not go away if you replace the static instance variable with a static method that simply returns the global variable.

Example 13–3: The ShoppingCart Class without a Global Variable or Explicit SQL Code

```
...

public class ShoppingCart {
    MyTaxDatabase taxDatabase;
    ...

    public getTaxDatabase() {
        return taxDatabase();
    }

    public setTaxDatabase(MyTaxDatabase td) {
        taxDatabase = td;
    }

    public int getTotalCost() {
        double taxRate = 0;
        if (taxDatabase!=null) {
            taxRate = taxDatabase.getTaxRate(customer.getZipcode());
        }
        ...
    }
}
```

Although this considerably improves the situation, the ShoppingCart class still depends on the MyTaxDatabase class. Wherever ShoppingCart is deployed, then so must be MyTaxDatabase. To remove this dependency we create a Java interface type called TaxDatabase with a single method (Example 13–4).

Example 13–4: The TaxDatabase Interface

```
public interface TaxDatabase {
    public double getTaxRate(String zipcode);
}
```

The MyTaxDatabase class is amended to implement the TaxDatabase interface type (Example 13–5).

Example 13–5: MyTaxDatabase Class Implements TaxDatabase

```
...
public class MyTaxDatabase implements TaxDatabase {
    ...
    public double getTaxRate(String zipcode) {
        ...
    }
}
```

And now the `ShoppingCart` class can use `TaxDatabase` instead of `MyTaxDatabase`, a considerable reduction in the dependent-type-set. This now makes it possible to use the `ShoppingCart` class by passing *any* object that implements `TaxDatabase`, not just `MyTaxDatabase`.

The `ShoppingCart` JavaBean in Example 13–1 has properties for a `ShippingDatabase`, and `PriceList`, in addition to the `TaxDatabase`. Also, there are references to `Item` and `Customer`, which may reference other classes such as a `CustomerDatabase` and an `ItemCatalog`. If all of these types were Java classes rather than Java `interface` types, then the `ShoppingCart` class would be largely useless as a component, since it is so tied to this one particular system. In Figure 13–4 each Java class has been renamed with the prefix `My` to indicate a system specific class.

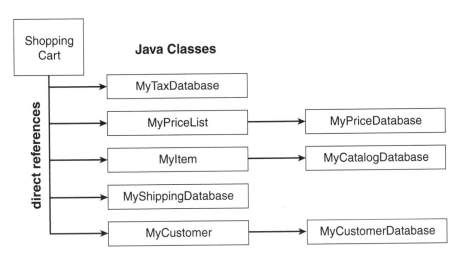

Figure 13–4 `ShoppingCart` with many class dependencies

By using Java `interface` types instead of classes (Figure 13–5), the `ShoppingCart` class limits its dependencies to just the Java `interface` types rather than system specific classes. A Java `interface` type may include one or more import interfaces. In the shopping cart bean each Java `interface` type maps to one import interface (Examples 13–6 and 13–7).

Example 13–6: The Customer Interface

```
public interface Customer {
    public String getZipcode();
}
```

Example 13–7: The PriceList Interface

```
public interface PriceList {
    public double getPrice(Item i);
}
```

Other systems that the `ShoppingCart` component might be used in may have very different ways of handling these interfaces. One system might use a simple formula instead of a database to compute shipping rates. Another system might have a single database object

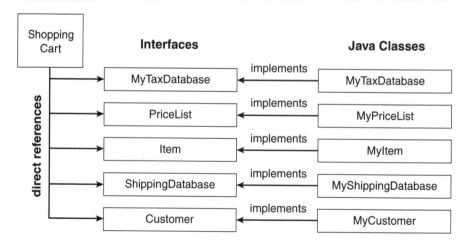

Figure 13–5   `ShoppingCart` using interfaces rather than classes

that handles all the shipping, tax, and price tables, so one Java database class implements multiple Java `interface` types (Figure 13–6).

To complete the job, the shopping cart component itself should also be defined with an interface, which we will call a *basket*. This will allow systems to incorporate baskets such as `ShoppingCart` without explicit dependencies on those components. The basket interface is shown in Example 13–8.

Example 13–8: The Basket Interface

```
...
public interface Basket {
    public void addItem(Item x);
    public void removeItem(Item x);
    public Enumeration getItems();
    public int getTotalCost();
    public void addBasketChangeListener(BasketChangeListener l);
    public void removeBasketChangeListener(BasketChangeListener l);
}
```

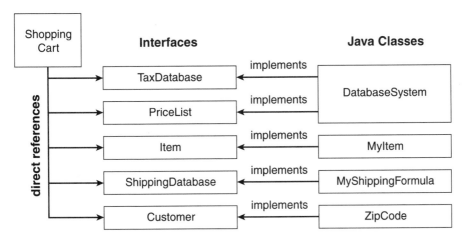

Figure 13–6 `ShoppingCart` **component configured for another system**

13.2.3 *Communication Mechanisms*

One other area of dependencies worth mentioning is that of communication mechanisms. A communication mechanism is the means by which components communicate with other software objects. The examples above assume that communication uses the normal Java method invocations. A distributed software system will also employ other communication mechanisms in order to communicate across process boundaries. These communication mechanisms may be hand-crafted using TCP/IP, or they may use one of a variety of standard communication protocols such as RMI and CORBA.

Ideally, a component is designed to avoid depending on a communication mechanism. However, there is no standard technique for doing so in the Java language. These issues will be discussed in more detail in the rest of this chapter.

13.3 | Interfaces and IDLs

An interface is an interaction between a component and other software elements. Java interfaces are normally limited to the public methods of an object. Other types of interfaces such as global variables are generally removed before calling an object a component. The syntax of an interface is the name of the method, the parameter types, and the type of the return value. The semantics of an interface describes the run-time behavior of the component. An interface description language (IDL) describes the interfaces of a component at the syntactic level. Rarely does the description include semantics.[7]

One of the major uses for an IDL is to provide the information necessary to implement remote procedure call (RPC). Remote procedure call is a communication mechanism that allows a software object to

---

[7] Semantics is sometimes described with pre and post conditions.

call a procedure located in a possibly different process or machine. When expressed in an object-oriented language, remote procedure call becomes remote method invocation. The difference is that one must identify a specific remote object in order to invoke a method.

Common Object Request Broker Architecture (CORBA) is a standard method for communication among distributed objects. Its strength is a language-independent IDL and a set of standards and protocols for supporting communications between distributed objects. RMI (Remote Method Invocation) is a Java API for supporting distributed Java objects. CORBA and RMI have a similar communications infrastructure. Unlike CORBA, RMI is intended for use with only Java objects.

13.3.1 *ShoppingCart Using RMI*

Let's consider the TaxRate example from the previous section and see what would be needed to make TaxDatabase a remote object. To use Java's RMI, you must use an interface that extends `Remote`. Example 13–9 redefines the `TaxDatabase` interface as a remote object. All remote methods potentially throw a `RemoteException` in case of a communications error.

Example 13–9: The TaxDatabase Remote Interface

```
import java.rmi.*;

public interface RemoteTaxDatabase extends Remote {
    public double getTaxRate(String zipcode) throws RemoteException;
}
```

`MyTaxDatabase` is an implementation of `TaxDatabase`. In addition to implementing `TaxDatabase`, the `MyTaxDatabase` object must also "export" itself so that it will be known as a remote object by an RMI registry. The RMI registry is a simple name server that associates a name with a remote object. Clients connect to an RMI registry and request a reference to the remote object using the name of the object (Figure 13–7).

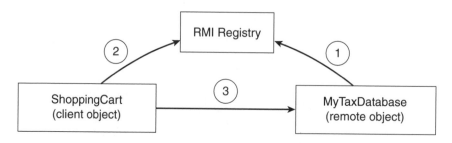

1. Binding a name to a MyTaxDatabase remote object

2. ShoppingCart requests a reference to the TaxDatabase remote object

3. ShoppingCart can now invoke the getTaxRate method on TaxDatabase

Figure 13–7 Getting initial references to remote objects

Once a client has a reference to a remote object, it can act as if the remote object were a local object, calling methods whenever needed. Once one remote object is accessible, other remote objects may also become accessible as the result of parameters and return values.

Underneath remote method invocations, there is considerable complexity. On the client side, we must have an object that will act as if it were the remote object. This object is called a *stub* (sometimes also called a proxy object). Like `MyTaxDatabase` the stub will also implement the `TaxDatabase` interface. The stub will implement each method by converting the parameters into a byte stream, using Java's serialized IO and packaging it with other information about the method to call and send this as a message to the remote system. On the remote side a corresponding object, called a *skeleton*, will receive the message, parse it, reconstruct the parameters, and call the appropriate method on the remote object. After the true method returns, the skeleton will package the return value and send the response back to the stub. One additional layer is needed for the actual communication mechanisms. The process is shown in Figure 13–8, and the detailed steps are as follows:

1. The client object, `ShoppingCart`, makes what appears to be a normal method call, `getTaxRate(zipcode)`.

2. The call is made to a `MyTaxDatabase_Stub` object whose interface mimics the remote object's interface. The stub object converts the parameters into a byte stream and calls a send method of the underlying communication mechanism.

3. The byte stream message is sent over the communication channel, typically an Internet protocol.

4. The byte stream message is received at the other end and passed to a `MyTaxDatabase_Skel` object. This object will parse the byte stream and reconstruct the parameters.

5. The method is called on the true remote object.

6. The method returns a value to the skeleton object, which converts the value to a byte stream.

7. The byte stream is passed to a send method of the underlying communication mechanism.

8. The byte stream message is sent over the communication channel.

9. The byte stream is received and passed on to the stub object.

10. The stub object converts the byte stream to an object and returns the value to the original client object.

Both stubs and skeletons will differ for each type of remote object. The communication infrastructure objects are common and remain the same. Stub and skeleton source code is generated by a program generator called *rmic* (rmi compiler) (Figure 13–9). Rmic reads a TaxRate implementation such as TaxDatabase. From this file, it determines the

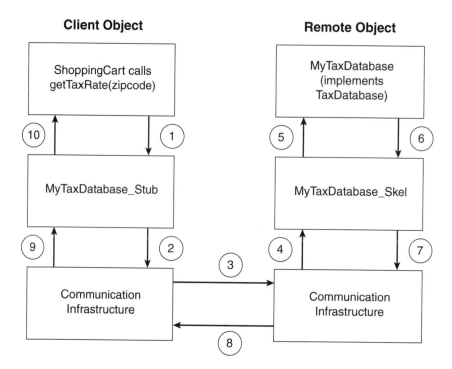

Figure 13–8   Remote method invocation mechanics

remote interface and generates the stub class that implements the remote interface. The stub class has a method for each method in the remote interface. Each such method converts the parameters into a serialized object stream. Rmic also generates the skeleton class. For each method of the remote interface, the skeleton also has a method, which converts the byte stream to parameters and calls the actual method on the remote object. Skeleton and stub classes must also handle the return value in the opposite direction.

13.3.2   *Exports and Imports*

Interfaces are generally divided into *exports* and *imports*, sometimes called *provisions* and *requirements*.[8] Exports (provisions) are the services

---

[8] Also sometimes called "*defines*" and "*uses*."

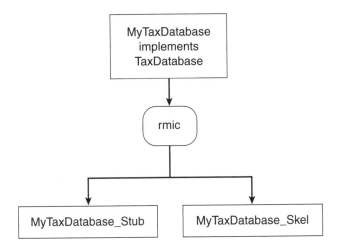

Figure 13–9   The program generator rmic

or methods provided by the component. They are called by other software elements. For example, adding and removing items from the shopping cart component is a service *provided* by the ShoppingCart component. Imports (requirements) are services *required* by the component. Imports are generally implemented as methods that are called by the component to other software elements. The shopping cart component requires the services provided by various databases—for example, the getTaxRate method.

Some people like to think of software components as if they were hardware components and will draw pictures of components like hardware chips. Each import and export is a represented by a "port." In some diagrams, imports and exports may be distinguishable by using different icons, but in this book we'll just use little squares with arrows leading in to mean exports and arrows leading out to mean imports (Figure 13–10).[9] In this hardwarelike model, composition is merely wiring up the imports and exports of various components. However, before exploring connections further, we need to examine how exports and imports are described in the Java language.

---

[9]It may seem counter-intuitive that arrows going into a component identify exports. The arrow represents a request for the service so it is drawn towards the component rather than away. It is the service that is being exported, not the request.

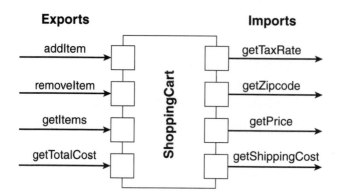

Figure 13-10 Hardwarelike diagram of the ShoppingCart component (ignoring properties and events)

Import interfaces are method calls made by the component to other software elements of the system. This is typically accomplished in the Java language by passing an object with the appropriate methods to the component. The Java event handling mechanism is a good example. A listener object is passed to an object using an addXListener method, and when an event occurs, a method of the listener object is called. In other languages these are also sometimes called callback procedures. To reduce the dependencies, a Java interface type is used to explicitly list which methods might be used. The typical Java import interface includes three things:

1. A Java interface that describes the import interface (for example, the TaxDatabase interface in Example 13–4). The interface has one or more methods.

2. An object which implements the interface. This object will provide the service to the component (for example, MyTaxDatabase in Example 13–5).

3. Method(s) to identify what object will provide the service. Using the JavaBean convention, a property is used with a pair of set and get methods (for example, setTaxDatabase and getTaxDatabase in Example 13–3).

Export interfaces are straightforward compared to imports. They are just methods provided by the component. Import interfaces are more difficult to identify, because they are usually implied by the types of certain parameters of the component's methods. In the ShoppingCart component, each import is identified with a property. For example, the `taxDatabase` property indicates that `getTaxRate` is an import. In general, every property implies an import. A property is something required from the environment. Even primitive-type properties embody an implicit "getValue" method call to some software entity.[10] Such properties imply the need for some information from the outside world about how the component should behave. Using the hardware metaphor, such a port is wired to a constant value rather than to another object (Figure 13–24 shows examples).

JavaBean events also imply imports. Each event implies the need to call some method on some external software object. An "addEventListener" method is equivalent in nature to a "setProperty" method. The only difference is that events will create event objects.

The remaining public methods of a JavaBean are generally the export interfaces. Some of these remaining methods may have "hidden" imports. For example, we might consider removing the `taxDatabase` property and modify the `getTotalCost` method by adding a `TaxDatabase` parameter.

```
public int getTotalCost(TaxDatabase t);
```

This method is still an export interface, since it is providing a service. However, the `getTotalCost` method will still include a call to the `getTaxRate` method. Therefore, `getTaxRate` is still an import interface, even though it is not an explicit property. It is implied by a parameter of an export interface. The only way to remove this import interface from the component is to replace `TaxDatabase` parameter with a tax rate parameter, so that the tax rate is computed *outside* of the shopping cart component.

```
public int getTotalCost(double taxRate);
```

---

[10] This becomes easier to imagine if you replace int properties with Integer and use the intValue method on the property.

Section 13.2.3 introduced the notion of communication mechanism dependencies. We'll finish this section by noting how RMI can be used only if both the remote component and client component are coded to use RMI. Each method of a remote interface must be declared that it throws `RemoteException`. The `Tax-Database interface` (Example 13–4) is used for local method invocation, whereas `RemoteTaxDatabase interface` (Example 13–9) is used for RMI. Software that uses a remote method must check for `RemoteException` either with a try clause or using a method that throws `RemoteException`. The implementation of a remote component must also declare "`throws RemoteException`" even if the component's software doesn't throw one. So we can't directly use `MyTaxDatabase` class but must instead create a nearly identical class, `MyRemoteTaxDatabase`, where the only difference is that each method is declared as throwing `RemoteException`.

While it is reasonable to demand that these exceptions be handled, it makes it difficult to design components without incorporating communication mechanism dependencies. The difficulties go beyond syntax. Local objects are passed by copy using RMI, whereas a local method call will pass an object by reference. The difference in semantics for passing objects in the two communication mechanisms means you can't just arbitrarily substitute one for the other. Multiple copies of class static variables may also prevent objects from being distributed. Local method invocation and RMI are just two communication mechanisms. There are others, such as CORBA. Is it possible to design components that do not depend on a specific communication mechanism?

13.4 | Module Interconnection Languages

A module interconnection language (MIL) is an IDL that also describes the interconnection among a set of components. The connection between two components is sometimes called a *connector*. While an IDL describes components and interfaces, a MIL describes components, interfaces, and connectors. MILs have been used as early as the late 1970s for what was called programming-in-the-large, a forerunner of today's component-oriented programming. Programming-in-the-small refers to the design, coding, and testing of individual components. Programming-in-the-large refers to the composition of components into larger software systems. IDLs have evolved and become parts of widely used standards such as CORBA.

Many JavaBean visual development environments combine both programming-in-the-small and programming-in-the-large. Typical source-code development tools are used for the creation of individual JavaBeans (programming-in-the-small). A visual editor tool allows the designer to combine JavaBeans and connect them together to form a larger component or software system. Although most of these tools are oriented around a GUI, they need not result in user interfaces. A visual editor allows a designer to do the following kinds of things:

1. Add new beans (drag-and-drop operation)

2. Configure beans (change the bean properties)

3. Connect beans (bind events to other beans or scripts)

The next few sections explore a few MIL concepts as they may apply to the Java language and JavaBeans. These include connectors, adapters, asynchronous connections, push and pull connections, composite components, and connection binding times.

13.4.1 *Connectors*

A connector connects the import of one component to the export of another component. Some languages and systems allow each import to be individually connected to any other compatible export at design time. Because the JavaBeans model does not directly model imports (other than events), there is no explicit way to clearly model connections. These are modeled indirectly through properties. A bean property whose type is a Java interface (or class) usually signifies one or more imports. Thus, such connections are implicit when the property is set. A typical JavaBean visual design tool will not explicitly show imports or how they are connected to other objects. Other MIL-like tools will show such connections. Figure 13–11 shows how the shopping cart might be connected to a tax database object. In a JavaBean visual design tool one might see only that the `taxDatabase` property happens to be set to `MyTaxDatabase`.

In this kind of system, a connector may connect any import with any compatible export regardless of the name. Compatible connections are those that are type compatible (same number of arguments and parameters with the same types) and possibly meet other restrictions. Each import and export has a name, but they do not need to be the same. For example, the shopping cart object might have an import called "`getTaxRate`" and the corresponding export on Jack's tax database object might be called "`computeTaxRate`". The MIL will allow these two ports to be connected. Java doesn't work quite that way, so other techniques have to be used to permit this kind of connection, which we'll discuss shortly.

Different MIL systems also use or allow different kinds of connectors. Some systems may assume a certain kind of connector such as method invocation, remote method invocation (or RPC), or a stream. There may also be distinctions between synchronous connections and asynchronous

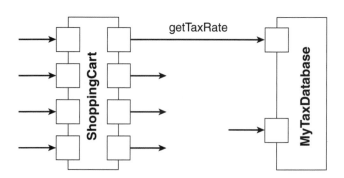

Figure 13–11   A connector between `ShoppingCart` and `MyTaxDatabase`

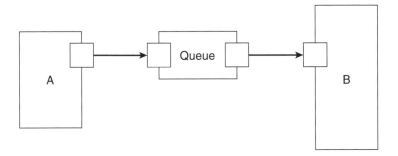

Figure 13–12   Stream connection modeled as a component

connections. Some systems may also support multicast, broadcast, or buslike connections. Some of these more complicated connectors can be considered as other intermediate components. For example, an asynchronous buffered stream between two objects can be modeled as a "normal" method invocation on a Queuing object (Figure 13–12).

Some MILs may also provide techniques for connecting incompatible interfaces by using adapter components. An adapter component converts an interface of one type to another. Adapting interfaces is a very important aspect of reusing components. Unless there is some kind of preplanned application framework with standardized interfaces, it's not likely that a component's interfaces match those of another component. It would be a shame if components that are semantically compatible were unable to communicate due to syntactic differences.

13.4.2   *Interface Adapters*

Let's consider the case of replacing `MyTaxDatabase` with Jack's tax database, called `JacksTaxDatabase`. Jack's tax database has a method called `computeTaxRate`, which accepts a single `int` argument representing a 5-digit zipcode, and it returns a `float` instead of a `double`. To integrate `JacksTaxDatabase` with the shopping cart component will require some additional interface code that will take care of the name change and the conversion of a `String` argument to an `int` argument (Figure 13–13).

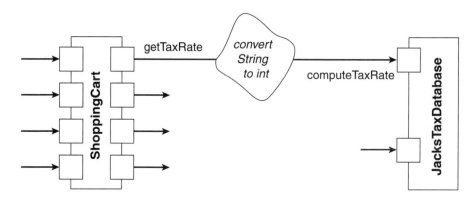

Figure 13–13 Interface adapter is needed

To build the adapter component we will need only the `TaxData-base` interface defined in Example 13–4. There are two ways to build this adapter. The first way is to extend `JacksTaxDatabase` to include the `TaxDatabase` interface (Example 13–10).

Example 13–10: Extending `JacksTaxDatabase` **with the** `TaxDatabase` **Interface**

```
    ...
public class OurTaxDatabase extends JacksTaxDatabase
        implements TaxDatabase {
    public double getTaxRate(String zipcode) {
        return (double) computeTaxRate(Integer.parseInt(zipcode));
    }
}
```

Note that two conversions are needed. Upon entry, the argument is converted from a `String` to an `int`, and upon exit, the return value is converted from a `float` to a `double`.

The second way is to create an independent adapter component (Example 13–11). The adapter implements the interface used by the calling component and directly accesses the appropriate method of the called component. The adapter component requires a property that is set to `JacksTaxDatabase`.

Example 13–11: A Simple Adapter Component

```
...

/** An adapter class to connect JacksTaxDatabase with ShoppingCart */
class SC2Jack implements TaxDatabase {
    private JacksTaxDatabase db;

    public void setJacksTaxDatabase(JacksTaxDatabase p) {
        db = p;
    }

    public JacksTaxDatabase getJacksTaxDatabase() {
        return db;
    }

    public double getTaxRate(String zipcode) {
        return (double) db.computeTaxRate(Integer.parseInt(zipcode));
    }
}
```

We're not done yet. We also need some code to "wire" up the components (Example 13–12). We need to create the adapter component and set up the properties. Assume that `shoppingCart` refers to the `ShoppingCart` object and `jacksTaxDatabase` refers to `JacksTax-Database` object (Figure 13–14).

Example 13–12: Wiring Up the Adapter for `JacksTaxDatabase`

```
{
    ...
    SC2Jack adapter = new SC2Jack();
    adapter.setJacksTaxDatabase(jacksTaxDatabase);
    shoppingCart.setTaxDatabase(adapter);
    ...
}
```

It is understandable to question the value of such an adapter. Isn't it obvious that it would be much simpler to modify either the shopping cart class or Jack's tax database class? For system-specific objects,

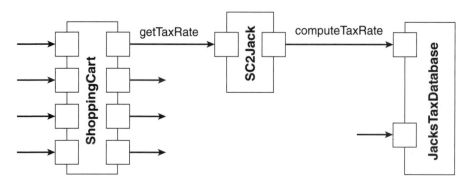

Figure 13–14   An adapter component

that would make sense. Generally, you do not want to modify reusable components. You would lose some of the major benefits of reusing components by modifying them.[11]

Whether you extend classes with new interfaces or create a component adapter, the difficulties of adapting interfaces by hand is not conceptual, but rather tedious and error prone. It also results in a system that is more difficult to understand and modify. Surely, this task should be automated.

Adapting interfaces can become arbitrarily complex. It could involve such things as unit conversions (radians to degrees, grams to pounds) and format conversions (jpeg to gif), optional parameters (default values), matrix inversions, or complex interactions between parameters. Handling diverse interfaces is a major difficulty when integrating disparate components. A MIL language with interface adapters can handle a variety of such needs (Example 13–13). Describing interface adaptations can be succinctly expressed as part of a connection as shown in Figure 13–13.

---

[11]This technique, sometimes derisively called copy and hack, leads to multiple copies of code. It is difficult to maintain multiple copies and difficult to upgrade to newer versions of those components. Touching a reusable component is tantamount to owning it, and thereby incurring the maintenance cost of such a component.

Example 13–13: Examples of Interface Adaptations in a MIL

```
Component ShoppingCart sc;
Component JacksTaxDatabase jdb;
Connect sc.getTaxRate(zc) to (double) jdb.(Integer.parseInt(zc));
Connect box.setCoord(x, y) to panel.setPoint(new Point(x, y));
Connect p.rotate(angle) to q.rotate(Math.PI * angle / 180);
...
```

In some situations, one may need to connect an import to more than a single object. For example, the Java event handling mechanism allows any number of listeners to be notified when an event occurs. We may also want to provide a means to connect an arbitrary import to any number of exports. This capability is easily added to interface adapters. The MIL can allow multiple connections from the same import (Figure 13–15). It only needs to identify which of the connections should be used for a return value. Example 13–14 shows how the `getPrice` import can be used to not only get a price from a component but also deliver the information to a log file.

Example 13–14: Multiple Connections from a Single Import

```
Component ShoppingCart sc;
Component TodaysSpecialPriceList pl;
Connect sc.getPrice(i) to pl.getPrice(i);
Connect sc.getPrice(i) to Log.println(i.getCatalogNumber());
...
```

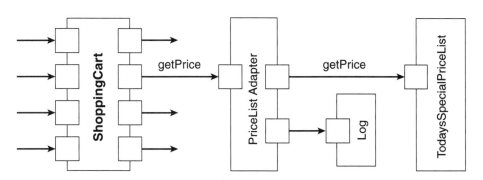

Figure 13–15   Multiple connections from a single import

13.4.3 *Asynchronous Connections*

Let's now look at another adapter example. A synchronous connection, such as method calls, will wait until the called system returns. An asynchronous connection is one that will initiate the connection but will not wait for completion. Therefore, an asynchronous connection will not have a return value. Such connections just send a message. You can think of them as one-way connections. It's sometimes easier to design systems based on asynchronous messages because you don't have to worry about the delays involved when the connections are to remote objects. Every asynchronous connection returns immediately. In such systems, a normal two-way connection becomes a pair of one-way connections. The first one-way connection sends the request. Later, the response comes back using a different connection.

The shopping cart example does not lend itself to this kind of system, but let's pretend we wanted to do this for the getTaxRate connection. We would replace the single two-way getTaxRate connection with a pair of one-way connections that we will call requestTaxRate and taxRateResponse (Figure 13–16). Unfortunately, we can't put both of these methods in the same Java interface type, because one method goes in one direction and the other method goes in the opposite direction. Another complication is that the AsynchTaxDatabase must know where to send the result. Since AsynchTaxDatabase is likely to be serving multiple shopping carts, it won't be a property, but rather an additional parameter of requestTaxRate. The interface definitions are shown in Example 13–15.

Example 13–15: Declarations for Two One-Way Connections to Tax Database

```
...
interface TaxRateRequestor {
    public void taxRateResponse(double taxRate);
}

interface TaxRateRequest {
    public void requestTaxRate(Item i, TaxRateRequestor requestor);
}
...
```

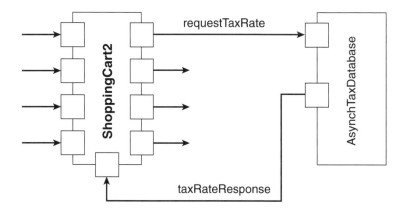

Figure 13–16   An asynchronous interface to `TaxDatabase`

A method invocation is inherently synchronous, so to properly implement an asynchronous connection will require a separate thread of control. Although this thread could be implemented in either of the components, it is more logical to use an interface adapter in order to keep both components clean and independent of such communication mechanisms. This will also solve the problem of interfacing synchronous connections with asynchronous ones. Two such situations arise: integrating `ShoppingCart` with `AsynchTaxDatabase` and integrating `ShoppingCart2` with `MyTaxDatabase`.

In the first case, the shopping cart component uses `getTaxRate` and the tax database uses the `requestTaxRate` and `taxRate-Response` methods. An interface adapter can handle this situation. The shopping cart component will see the connection as a normal single synchronous method invocation, and the tax database will see it as two separate connections, as illustrated in Figure 13–17. The `getTaxRate` method in `TaxDatabaseAdapter` would first call `requestTaxRate` and then wait until the `AsynchTaxDatabase` calls `taxRateResponse` before returning the tax rate value for the `getTaxRate` method.

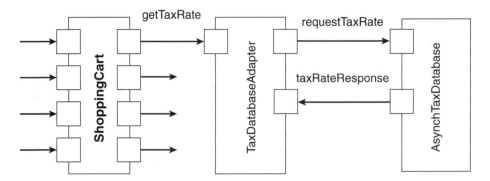

Figure 13–17 Adapter between a single two-way connection and two one-way connections

In the second case, the shopping cart component uses the two connections, requestTaxRate and taxRateResponse, and the tax database just uses getTaxRate. This can also be handled by an adapter, as shown in Figure 13–18. The requestTaxRate method of TaxDatabaseAdapter2 returns immediately after starting a new thread. The new thread performs the getTaxRate method on MyTaxDatabase. When getTaxRate returns a value, the value is passed to ShoppingCart2 using the taxRateResponse method.

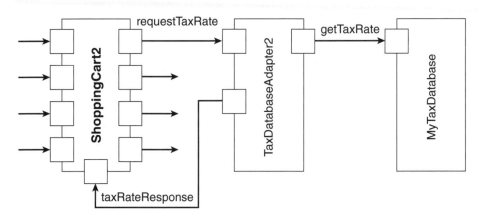

Figure 13–18 Adapter converting two one-way connections to a single two-way connection

13.4.4 *Push and Pull Connections*

Does it make sense to connect two exports? How about connecting two imports? It doesn't make sense to connect them directly, since the connection would have no meaning in Java. However, there are times that you may need to do so. Consider a component, which we'll call Cashier, with an export, setTotalCost, which expects to be called with the total cost of a purchase. ShoppingCart provides an export, called getTotalCost, which will return the total cost. The situation is that Cashier expects an object to call the setTotalCost method, whereas ShoppingCart expects an object to call the getTotalCost method. This situation is summarized in Example 13–16 and Figure 13–19.

Example 13–16: Methods setTotalCost and getTotalCost

```
...
interface Basket {
    ...
    public int getTotalCost();
}

...

interface CheckOut {
    public void setTotalCost(int totalCost);
    ...
}

...

class ShoppingCart implements Basket { ... };
class Cashier implements CheckOut { ... };

...
```

Unfortunately, this incompatibility occurs more frequently than one would like. The first thing to note is that the data flow is from the shopping cart to the cashier. The data is the total cost; the shopping cart is always the source of the data; the cashier is always the data receiver. The cashier assumes it will be notified when the information

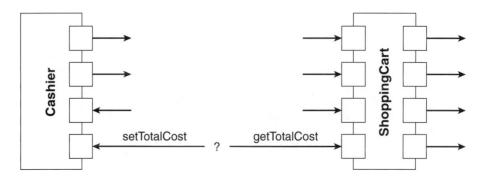

Figure 13–19   Connecting two exports together?

is available. This is called a *push*-oriented connection, because the cashier assumes the shopping cart (the data source) is the "driver" and pushes the data to the receiver when it is available. Push connections occur in event-driven designs. The shopping cart assumes the opposite. This is called a *pull*-oriented connection, because the shopping cart assumes the cashier (data receiver) is the "driver" and will request (*pull*) the data when it is needed. We can connect components together if they are both pull-oriented or push-oriented. But what can we do if one (shopping cart) is pull-oriented and the other (cashier) is push-oriented?

An adapter component can mediate this connection. However, before we can create or generate the adapter component, we need additional information about the nature of the connection. The data passing from one component to another can represent a single value that may change over time (such as a bank balance) or it may represent a sequence of values (such as deposits and withdrawals). The total cost could fall in either category; it could be the current total cost of the items in the shopping cart, or it could be the final total cost of the purchase. From the shopping cart perspective, the data is the current total cost. Without further information, we can't tell what the cashier is expecting. In order to generate the adapter component, we'll need some criteria to tell us *when* to invoke the set-TotalCost method.

Let's examine what to do if we use the simple criteria that the adapter component calls `setTotalCost` whenever the total cost changes. Fortunately for us, the ShoppingCart component creates events whenever the contents is changed, which we'll assume is the only time that the total cost will change. Therefore, we can create or generate an adapter component that listens for basket events, and when they occur, calls the `setTotalCost` method (see Example 13–17 and Figure 13–20).

Example 13–17: PushPullAdapter Component Based on Events

```
...
class PushPullAdapter implements BasketListener {
    Basket basket = null;
    CheckOut checkout = null;

    public void setBasket(Basket b) {
        if (basket!=null) {
            basket.removeBasketListener(this);
        }
        basket = b;
        if (basket!=null) {
            basket.addBasketListener(this);
        }
        notifyCheckOut();
    }

    public Basket getBasket() {
        return basket;
    }

    public void setCheckOut(CheckOut c) { ... };
    public CheckOut getCheckOut() { ... };

    public void basketChanged(BasketEvent event) {
        notifyCheckOut();
    }

    void notifyCheckOut() {
        if (checkout!=null && basket!=null) {
            checkout.setTotalCost(basket.getTotalCost());
        }
    }
}

...
```

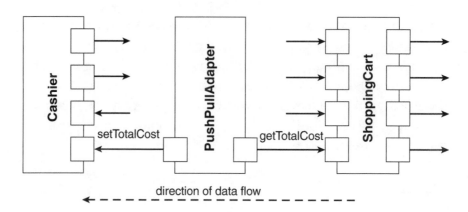

Figure 13–20 A push-pull adapter

If we were not so fortunate as to have a handy event that tells us when the total cost changes, we would have to create a more complex component. The adapter component would need a thread that periodically calls `getTotalCost` to determine if there are any changes. Such an adapter uses a technique called polling, a somewhat more clumsy and inefficient alternative to event-driven design.

Let's now consider the situation of two imports rather than two exports (Figure 13–21). Let `setTotalCost` be an import of `ShoppingCart` and `getTotalCost` an import of `Cashier`. Thus the shopping cart is now using a push connection and the cashier a pull connection. These imports require two new interfaces, which we'll just call `Basket2` and `CheckOut2`.

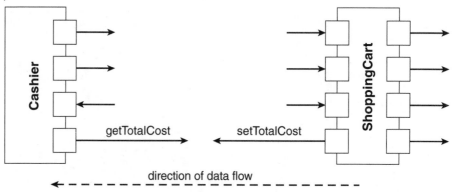

Figure 13–21 Connecting two imports together?

This situation can also be solved with an adapter component. The adapter component keeps track of the total cost. It is updated when the ShoppingCart's setTotalCost method is invoked, and it is returned when the Cashier's getTotalCost method is invoked (Example 13–18). Note the resemblance to a JavaBean property.

Example 13–18: PullPushAdapter Component Based on Events

```
...
interface Basket2 {
    public void setTotalCost(int tc);
}

interface CheckOut2 {
    public int getTotalCost();
}

class PullPushAdapter implements Basket2, CheckOut2 {
    private int totalCost;

    public void setTotalCost(int tc) {
        total = tc;
    }

    public int getTotalCost() {
        return totalCost;
    }
}
```

As before, we need additional information about the data flow. The above adapter component assumes that there is just one current value changing over time. This is implied by the method names, so let's consider an alternative set of methods. The method itemCost is called by the shopping cart component whenever a new item is added or removed from the basket. The method nextCost is called by the cashier component when it needs to know the cost of the next item. This situation requires the adapter component to keep track of a queue of costs, rather than a single current value (Figure 13–22).

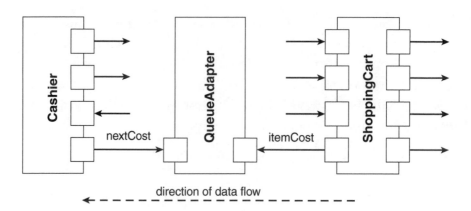

Figure 13–22   Queue adapter connecting two imports

To work properly the queue adapter requires some additional work. Additional methods or parameters are required to determine when the end of the queue is reached. If `nextCost` is called and there is nothing in the queue, then it can wait until something arrives (called blocking), or it might return an empty-queue response (called nonblocking).

The queue adapter represents a large class of common connections between software elements. Java's `InputStreams` and `Output-Streams` are used in TCP/IP connections, piped connections between threads, and even connections between software programs separated by time and space by using files. Streams are sequences of values that might be as simple as characters or as complex as objects (serialized IO). Output streams have write operations (putting something into the queue) and input streams have read operations (taking something out of the queue). Streams are typically JavaBean properties or passed to objects as constructor parameters (for example, creating layered stream objects such as buffered streams and filtered streams).

A classic example of the architectural difference between using streams and layers is a compiler's architecture. The lexer component reads a character stream and produces a sequence of tokens. The parser constructs a parse tree from the sequence of tokens. The interface between the lexer and parser might be layered, in which case the lexer has an export (`getNextToken`) that the parser calls. Or the interface might be a stream, in which case the lexer has an import (`writeToken`) and the parser has an import (`readToken`), both of which are methods of a `TokenStream`.

13.4.5 *Communication Mechanisms*

Some MILs may also take into account different underlying communication mechanisms, making it easier to create distributed systems. Such differences can also be handled by appropriate adapters, although they can become complicated. An RMI interface adapter must take exceptions into account. One way that the `RemoteException` can be adapted to methods not throwing an exception is to convert such exceptions to `RuntimeExceptions`, which the Java language does not require to be caught. Other communication mechanisms, such as TCP/IP, use streams discussed in the previous section. Such a MIL expresses both the connections between components, and the communication mechanisms for those connections. Such a system can remove many communication mechanism dependencies from components.[12]

Some MILs come with program generators that will generate the necessary code, adapters, and other interface needs. A MIL program generator reads a description of the system. It will generate adapter components, interfaces to communication mechanisms, and a system initialization component that will "wire" up the system as described (Figure 13–23).

---

[12] Not all communication mechanism dependencies can be removed this way. For example, timing issues due to communication delays must still be considered. Other features may also constrain the use of communication mechanisms, such as the pass by copy mechanism used in RMI.

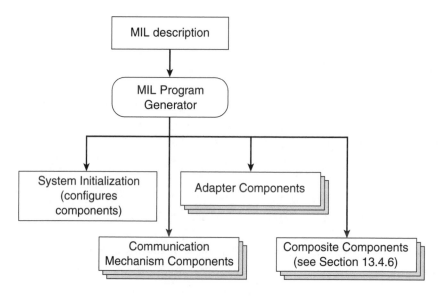

Figure 13–23   MIL program generator

13.4.6   *Composite Components*

Most MILs support hierarchical construction of components. Components can be combined to create new larger components. Designing a system from components and designing a new component from subcomponents is really the same process. The only difference is that the design of a new component must have some way of specifying the ports of the new component. In the simplest case, a port of any subcomponent can serve as a port of the new component. In addition to wiring up the subcomponents, there may also be a need to specify some of their properties. In most cases, specifying a property can be represented by "wiring" a constant to an export.

To illustrate this, we'll create a super shopping cart that is integrated with a particular tax database and shipping database (Figure 13–24). The super shopping cart will still provide the same exports and imports minus those used in the tax and shipping databases. Example 13–19 shows what a MIL might use to describe such a super component.

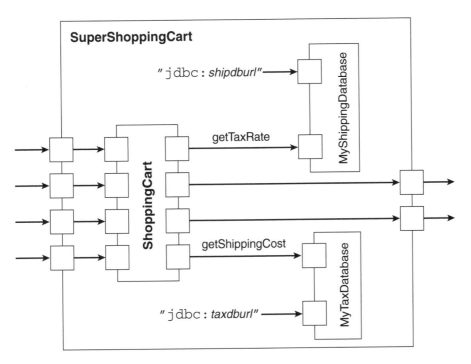

Figure 13–24 SuperShoppingCart component composed of three subcomponents

Example 13–19: MIL Description of the SuperShoppingCart Component

```
Component SuperShoppingCart {
    Subcomponent ShoppingCart sc;
    static Subcomponent MyTaxDatabase tdb;
    static Subcomponent MyShippingDatabase sdb;
    Export sc.addItem(x) as addItem(x);
    Export sc.removeItem(x) as removeItem(x);
    Export sc.getItems() as getItems();
    Export sc.getTotalCost() as getTotalCost();
    Import sc.getZipcode(c) as getZipcode(c);
    Import sc.getPrice(i) as getPrice(i);
    Connect sc.getTaxRate(zc) to tdb.getTaxRate(zc);
    Connect sc.getShippingCost(zc) to sdb.getShippingCost(zc);
    tdb.setDatabaseURL("jdbc:taxdburl");
    sdb.setDatabaseURL("jdbc:shipdburl");
}
```

The `SuperShoppingCart` component source code can be directly generated from this description. Before giving an example of such generated code, we need to address one issue. The subcomponents `tbd` and `sdb` provide the database connections. To create these components with new connections to the database for each new shopping cart is inefficient. A persistent database connection may be desirable and in some cases may be essential for performance reasons. Fortunately, there is a simple solution. Declaring and treating these two subcomponents as static variables rather than instance variables will give us a persistent shared database connection.

The generated code for `SuperShoppingCart` is straightforward. Each subcomponent is a static or instance variable. Static connections and configuration are placed in a static initialization block. The constructor method adds dynamic connections and configuration information. Each export is implemented as a public method. Each import is associated with a Java `interface` type, which is implemented as a property (Example 13–20).

Example 13–20: SuperShoppingCart Component Generated Code Sample

```
public class SuperShoppingCart {
    private ShoppingCart sc = new ShoppingCart();
    private static MyTaxDatabase tbd = new MyTaxDatabase();
    private static MyShippingDatabase sdb = new MyShippingDatabase();

    // static connections and configuration
    { tbd.setDatabaseURL("jdbc:taxdburl");
      sdb.setDatabaseURL("jdbc:shipdburl");
    }

    public SuperShoppingCart() {
        sc.setTaxDatabase(tbd);
        sc.setShippingDatabase(sdb);
    }

    // exports
    public void addItem(Item x) {
        sc.addItem(x);
    }

    ...
```

```
// zipcode import
public void setCustomer(Customer c) {
    sc.setCustomer(c);
}

public Customer getCustomer() {
    return sc.getCustomer(c);
}

    ...
}
```

13.4.7   *Static and Dynamic Connections*

The last feature we'll look at is the binding times for connectors. In the SuperShoppingCart example, two of the three subcomponents were declared static. Having static components simply means that one component is created for the life of the class. Dynamic components, such as ShoppingCart, may be created and destroyed many times. Static connections are established once and remain unchanged for the life of the components. Dynamic connections come and go during run time. MILs do a good job describing static connections but are inadequate for describing dynamic connections.

The shopping cart database connections are typically static connections like those described in the SuperShoppingCart example. The tax database and shipping database connections are established once and for all. The price database may fall into several different categories. There may be a single price list that is used for all customers, in which case a static connection is sufficient and could be implemented in a manner similar to the tax database. Alternatively, there may be several price lists, and at the time of creating a shopping cart one of the price lists is chosen. An extreme example is if the price list is dependent on where the item is picked up (for example, different Web pages or store locations or catalogs may have different prices quoted). This means that the getPrice import may be connected to

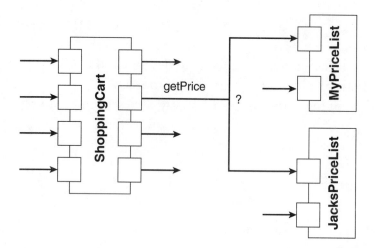

Figure 13–25   Dynamic connection representation problem

one of several different `priceDatabase` objects. How would you represent this kind of dynamic connection in a MIL diagram? It could be represented as a multiheaded connection, where each head represents a *potential* connection (Figure 13–25). There isn't a satisfactory solution to this problem, so dynamic connections are typically expressed only in the underlying implementation language.

Static components and static connections are best described at design time where MIL diagrams make a lot of sense. Dynamic components and connections are run-time decisions that are best left to explicit coding.

13.5 | Bean Markup Language

The Bean Markup Language (BML) is described by its creators as "an XML-based component configuration or wiring language customized for the JavaBean component model."[13] This certainly sounds like a MIL,

---

[13] *Bean Markup Language User's Guide,* by Sanjiva Weerawarana and Matthew J. Duftler, http://www.alphaWorks.ibm.com/formula/bml

but BML goes further than most MILs while at the same time missing some of the essence of a MIL. Nevertheless, BML is worth examining in some detail. BML does not explicitly define interfaces, because it loads the bean classes and examines them directly to determine the properties, events, and methods just like other bean design tools.

Consider the shopping cart domain. One way of describing a configuration similar to the super shopping cart is given in Example 13–21.

Example 13–21: BML Description of the Super Shopping Cart Component

```
<bean class="MyCart">
  <add>
    <bean class="MyTaxDatabase" id="tdb">
      <property name="setDburl" value="jdbc:taxdburl"/>
    </bean>
  </add>
  <add>
    <bean class="MyShippingDatabase" id="sdb">
      <property name="setDburl" value="jdbc:shipdburl"/>
    </bean>
  </add>
  <add>
    <bean class="ShoppingCart" id="sc">
      <property name="setTaxDatabase">
        <bean source="tdb"/>
      </property>
      <property name="setShippingDatabase">
        <bean source="sdb"/>
      </property>
    </bean>
  </add>
</bean>
```

Each `bean` element type with a `class` attribute creates a bean object. These objects can be given unique names with the `id` attribute. Three beans, namely a shopping cart, tax database, and shipping database, are created and added to a "container" bean, which in this example is called `MyCart`. Properties of beans can be set using the property element types with a `value` attribute. For example, the tax database bean's property `dburl` is set to "jdbc:*taxdburl*" and the shopping cart bean's property `taxDatabase` is set to the tax database bean, identified by the `source` attribute which is set to the unique ID of the tax database bean.

BML does not support the definition of *new* Java classes, thus it cannot be used to create hierarchical components in the sense described in Section 13.4.6, where we defined the `SuperShopping-Cart` component. BML does support "container" components with the "`add`" element types. This was designed to make it easy to create GUI hierarchies, based on `java.awt.Container` classes such as `Panel`. BML extends this notion to non-GUI situations by using an "`AdderRegistry`" that defines the semantics of an `add` operation on new kinds of containers. This is needed for the class `MyCart`, which is a poor substitute for `SuperShoppingCart`.

The complete list of BML element types is given in Table 13–2. Several of these element types have been added so that BML can be used on any Java object rather than just beans. For example, the `args` element type is used to create objects with constructors that have arguments. The `field` element type is used to access or change the values of instance variables. Neither of these element types is needed for a purely JavaBean implementation.

The `event-binding` element type adds event listeners. Alternatively the event-binding can be bound to a `script` element type instead of a JavaBean. BML will execute the script when the event occurs. A script is a sequence of statements that includes method calls (using the `method-call` element type), changes to properties of arbitrary beans (using the property element type with a `target` and `value` attribute). The `cast` element type is used to convert values from one type to another. A `TypeConverterRegistry` provides a registration and lookup service for type converters. The combination of type conversions and scripts makes it possible to implement many of the adapter interfaces discussed in Section 13.4. Unfortunately these can be applied only to events and not to other import interfaces.

Table 13–2: BML Element Types

Element Type	Description
bean	Create a new bean or look one up
args	Specify constructor arguments
string	Create a new string bean or look one up
property	Set or get a bean property
field	Set or get a bean field
event-binding	Bind an event from one bean to another
call-method	Call a bean method
cast	Type-convert a bean to be of another type
add	Create a hierarchy of beans by adding one to a bean container
script	Define a script to be executed

BML comes with two implementations called the *player* and the *compiler*. The player is an interpreter that reads the BML document and executes it using the Java language's reflection API. The compiler is a program generator that reads the BML document and generates Java source code that implements the configuration described in the BML document (Figure 13–26).

13.6 | Crafting Your Own MIL

If you have read and absorbed this chapter and book, this section should be very predictable. Go ahead, make some predictions and see how many you get right, before reading onward.

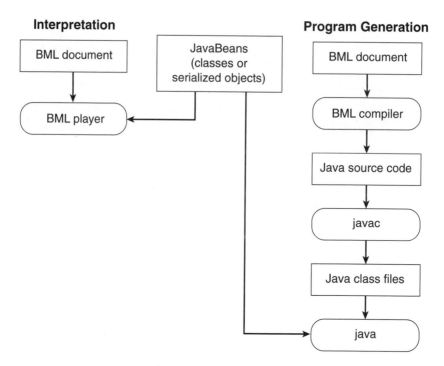

Figure 13–26   The BML player and compiler

There are significant advantages to using XML to represent specifications. BML uses XML to describe bean configurations. Other efforts have also recognized the advantages of using XML as a basis for MILs and MIL-like languages, called Architecture Description Languages (ADL).[14] Using XML does not preclude a more friendly text- or graphical-based language that can be converted to and from an XML representation. An example of this dual-language approach is described at the end of Chapter 12.

---

[14] "The Merit of XML as an Architecture Description Language Meta-Language," by Steve Pruitt, Doug Stuart, T. W. Cook, MCC, October 1998 and "XML Applied to Product Line Software Development" by Charles Goyette, September, 1999. A MIL may not always reveal or describe some of the important architectural features of a software design. For example, in the examples of this chapter, the connections to databases, or TCP/IP connections, are implicit or unseen. An Architecture Description Language (ADL) generalizes the notion of a connector to include connections beyond method invocation. In this view, many of the adapter components in this chapter such as RMI stubs and skeletons, queue adapters, and streams are viewed and described as connectors rather than components. See the Shaw and Garlan reference at the end of the chapter for further information regarding the differences between MILs and ADLs.

The IDL portion of the language—that is, the syntactic descriptions of the methods and parameter types—can be obtained directly from classes. Both RMI and BML take this approach to avoid a potential source of inconsistency, not to mention the extra work involved. There is no reason not to take this approach in crafting your own MIL; however, it would be nice to make this information available. MIL tools to print out the import interfaces, or display them graphically, would aid in the composition of systems.

Import interfaces are not obvious because they are implied by the types of the parameters passed to the component. These parameter types need to be analyzed to determine the set of all import interfaces. However, there is a serious difficulty. The Java language's reflection API will provide all the necessary parameter types, but it won't tell you which ones are specifically used. For example, the `Item interface` might describe a half-dozen methods, but the `ShoppingCart` component might use only one or two of them. This can be determined only by examining the source code.

If the IDL is determined from the classes, then the XML document can focus on connectors, composite components, and adapter interfaces. One reason BML does not support building composite components is that these represent *new* classes. This difficulty can be avoided by not implementing a *player* tool, or by simulating the behavior of new classes, suitably constrained.

13.7 | Summary

Program generators and component-oriented programming go hand in hand. Components and their composition into systems involve some significant problems. Finding just the right component is difficult if software-reuse libraries focus on single components rather than component families. Component families can be developed by taking advantage of design-time and run-time properties. When those are insufficient, generation-time variabilities can be used to design program generators for creating customized components for every occasion.

A second major obstacle to component-oriented programming is configuring and connecting components up to create a software system. Connections between components may require sophisticated interface adapters that can take into account such things as parameter conversions, defaults for optional parameters, synchronous and asynchronous connections, and other communication mechanisms. Writing this interface code is tedious and error prone. It should be left to the expertise of a MIL program generator.

Finally, building such tools and systems is not difficult. It may be difficult to *design* a good language or system, but it is not difficult to build the tools using the techniques described in this book. If you wish to join a community of developers of program generators or tools for component composition, be sure to visit `http://craigc.com`.

Further Reading

C. Atkinson, *Object-Oriented Reuse, Concurrency, and Distribution*, ACM Press/Addison-Wesley, 1991.

J. Craig Cleaveland, Janet A. Fertig, and George W. Newsome, "Dividing the Software Pie," *AT&T Technical Journal*, Vol. 75, No. 2, March 1996, pp. 8–19.

Krzysztof Czarnecki and Ulrich Eisenecker. *Generative Programming: Methods, Tools, and Applications,* Addison-Wesley, 2000.

F. DeRemer and H. Kron, "Programming-in-the-Large Versus Programming-in-the-Small," *IEEE Transactions on Software Engineering*, Vol. SE-2, No. 2, June 1972, pp. 80–86.

M. Shaw and D. Garlan. *Software Architecture: Perspectives on an Emerging Discipline*. Prentice Hall, 1996.

Index

■ T

Y

LICENSE AGREEMENT AND LIMITED WARRANTY

READ THE FOLLOWING TERMS AND CONDITIONS CAREFULLY BEFORE OPENING THIS SOFTWARE MEDIA PACKAGE. THIS LEGAL DOCUMENT IS AN AGREEMENT BETWEEN YOU AND PRENTICE-HALL, INC. (THE "COMPANY"). BY OPENING THIS SEALED SOFTWARE MEDIA PACKAGE, YOU ARE AGREEING TO BE BOUND BY THESE TERMS AND CONDITIONS. IF YOU DO NOT AGREE WITH THESE TERMS AND CONDITIONS, DO NOT OPEN THE SOFTWARE MEDIA PACKAGE. PROMPTLY RETURN THE UNOPENED SOFTWARE MEDIA PACKAGE AND ALL ACCOMPANYING ITEMS TO THE PLACE YOU OBTAINED THEM FOR A FULL REFUND OF ANY SUMS YOU HAVE PAID.

1.　　　**GRANT OF LICENSE:** In consideration of your payment of the license fee, which is part of the price you paid for this product, and your agreement to abide by the terms and conditions of this Agreement, the Company grants to you a nonexclusive right to use and display the copy of the enclosed software program (hereinafter the "SOFTWARE") on a single computer (i.e., with a single CPU) at a single location so long as you comply with the terms of this Agreement. The Company reserves all rights not expressly granted to you under this Agreement.

2.　　　**OWNERSHIP OF SOFTWARE:** You own only the magnetic or physical media (the enclosed software media) on which the SOFTWARE is recorded or fixed, but the Company retains all the rights, title, and ownership to the SOFTWARE recorded on the original software media copy(ies) and all subsequent copies of the SOFTWARE, regardless of the form or media on which the original or other copies may exist. This license is not a sale of the original SOFTWARE or any copy to you.

3.　　　**COPY RESTRICTIONS:** This SOFTWARE and the accompanying printed materials and user manual (the "Documentation") are the subject of copyright. You may not copy the Documentation or the SOFTWARE, except that you may make a single copy of the SOFTWARE for backup or archival purposes only. You may be held legally responsible for any copying or copyright infringement which is caused or encouraged by your failure to abide by the terms of this restriction.

4.　　　**USE RESTRICTIONS:** You may not network the SOFTWARE or otherwise use it on more than one computer or computer terminal at the same time. You may physically transfer the SOFTWARE from one computer to another provided that the SOFTWARE is used on only one computer at a time. You may not distribute copies of the SOFTWARE or Documentation to others. You may not reverse engineer, disassemble, decompile, modify, adapt, translate, or create derivative works based on the SOFTWARE or the Documentation without the prior written consent of the Company.

5.　　　**TRANSFER RESTRICTIONS:** The enclosed SOFTWARE is licensed only to you and may not be transferred to any one else without the prior written consent of the Company. Any unauthorized transfer of the SOFTWARE shall result in the immediate termination of this Agreement.

6.　　　**TERMINATION:** This license is effective until terminated. This license will terminate automatically without notice from the Company and become null and void if you fail to comply with any provisions or limitations of this license. Upon termination, you shall destroy the Documentation and all copies of the SOFTWARE. All provisions of this Agreement as to warranties, limitation of liability, remedies or damages, and our ownership rights shall survive termination.

7.　　　**MISCELLANEOUS:** This Agreement shall be construed in accordance with the laws of the United States of America and the State of New York and shall benefit the Company, its affiliates, and assignees.

8.　　　**LIMITED WARRANTY AND DISCLAIMER OF WARRANTY:** The Company warrants that the SOFTWARE, when properly used in accordance with the Documentation, will operate in substantial conformity with the description of the SOFTWARE set forth in the Documentation. The Company does not warrant that the SOFTWARE will meet your requirements or that the operation of the SOFTWARE will be uninterrupted or error-free. The Company warrants that the media on which the SOFTWARE is delivered shall be free from defects in materials and workmanship under normal use for a period of thirty (30) days from the date of your purchase. Your only remedy and the Company's only obligation under these limited warranties is, at the Company's option, return of the warranted item for a refund of any amounts paid by you or replacement of the item. Any replacement of SOFTWARE or media under the warranties shall not extend the original warranty period. The limited warranty set forth above shall not apply to any SOFTWARE which the Company determines in good faith has been subject to misuse, neglect, improper installation, repair, alteration, or damage by you. EXCEPT FOR THE EXPRESSED WARRANTIES SET FORTH ABOVE, THE COMPANY DISCLAIMS ALL WARRANTIES, EXPRESS OR IMPLIED, INCLUDING WITHOUT LIMITATION, THE IMPLIED WARRANTIES OF MERCHANTABILITY AND FITNESS FOR A PARTICULAR PURPOSE. EXCEPT FOR THE EXPRESS WARRANTY SET FORTH ABOVE, THE COMPANY DOES NOT WARRANT, GUARANTEE, OR MAKE ANY REPRESENTATION REGARDING THE USE OR THE RESULTS OF THE USE OF THE SOFTWARE IN TERMS OF ITS CORRECTNESS, ACCURACY, RELIABILITY, CURRENTNESS, OR OTHERWISE.

IN NO EVENT, SHALL THE COMPANY OR ITS EMPLOYEES, AGENTS, SUPPLIERS, OR CONTRACTORS BE LIABLE FOR ANY INCIDENTAL, INDIRECT, SPECIAL, OR CONSEQUENTIAL DAMAGES ARISING OUT OF OR IN CONNECTION WITH THE LICENSE GRANTED UNDER THIS AGREEMENT, OR FOR LOSS OF USE, LOSS OF DATA, LOSS OF INCOME OR PROFIT, OR OTHER LOSSES, SUSTAINED AS A RESULT OF INJURY TO ANY PERSON, OR LOSS OF OR DAMAGE TO PROPERTY, OR CLAIMS OF THIRD PARTIES, EVEN IF THE COMPANY OR AN AUTHORIZED REPRESENTATIVE OF THE COMPANY HAS BEEN ADVISED OF THE POSSIBILITY OF SUCH DAMAGES. IN NO EVENT SHALL LIABILITY OF THE COMPANY FOR DAMAGES WITH RESPECT TO THE SOFTWARE EXCEED THE AMOUNTS ACTUALLY PAID BY YOU, IF ANY, FOR THE SOFTWARE.

SOME JURISDICTIONS DO NOT ALLOW THE LIMITATION OF IMPLIED WARRANTIES OR LIABILITY FOR INCIDENTAL, INDIRECT, SPECIAL, OR CONSEQUENTIAL DAMAGES, SO THE ABOVE LIMITATIONS MAY NOT ALWAYS APPLY. THE WARRANTIES IN THIS AGREEMENT GIVE YOU SPECIFIC LEGAL RIGHTS AND YOU MAY ALSO HAVE OTHER RIGHTS WHICH VARY IN ACCORDANCE WITH LOCAL LAW.

ACKNOWLEDGMENT

YOU ACKNOWLEDGE THAT YOU HAVE READ THIS AGREEMENT, UNDERSTAND IT, AND AGREE TO BE BOUND BY ITS TERMS AND CONDITIONS. YOU ALSO AGREE THAT THIS AGREEMENT IS THE COMPLETE AND EXCLUSIVE STATEMENT OF THE AGREEMENT BETWEEN YOU AND THE COMPANY AND SUPERSEDES ALL PROPOSALS OR PRIOR AGREEMENTS, ORAL, OR WRITTEN, AND ANY OTHER COMMUNICATIONS BETWEEN YOU AND THE COMPANY OR ANY REPRESENTATIVE OF THE COMPANY RELATING TO THE SUBJECT MATTER OF THIS AGREEMENT.

Should you have any questions concerning this Agreement or if you wish to contact the Company for any reason, please contact in writing at the address below.

Robin Short
Prentice Hall PTR
One Lake Street
Upper Saddle River, New Jersey 07458

About the CD

The CD-ROM included with *Program Generators with XML and Java* contains the following: examples from the book, XML specification, XPath specification, XSLT specification, DOM Level 1 specification, James Clark's xt, and Takuki Kamiya's XPath interface for xt. For a more complete listing, point your browser to index.html.

The CD-ROM can be used on Microsoft® Windows® 95/98/ NT®/2000.

License Agreement

Use of the software accompanying *Program Generators with XML and Java* is subject to the terms of the License Agreement and Limited Warranty, found on the previous two pages.

Technical Support

Prentice Hall does not offer technical support for this software. However, if there is a problem with the media, you may obtain a replacement copy by e-mailing us with your problem at: disc_exchange@pren-hall.com